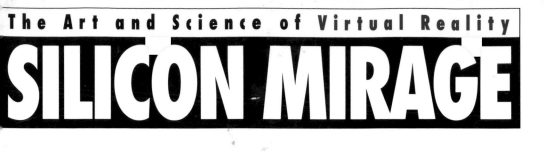

The Art and Science of Virtual Reality

SILICON MIRAGE

teve Aukstakalnis

avid Blatner

oreword by Jaron Lanier

SILICON MIRAGE

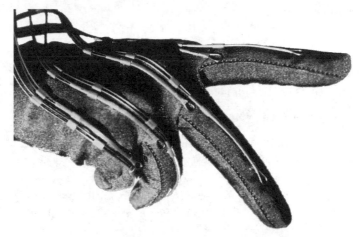

Silicon Mirage

THE ART AND SCIENCE OF VIRTUAL REALITY

by

Steve Aukstakalnis

and

David Blatner

PEACHPIT PRESS

edited by

Stephen F. Roth

AN OPEN HOUSE BOOK

Silicon Mirage
The Art and Science of Virtual Reality
By Steve Aukstakalnis and David Blatner
Edited by Stephen F. Roth

Peachpit Press, Inc., 2414 Sixth St., Berkeley, CA 94710
510/548-4393; fax: 510/548-5991

Library of Congress Cataloging-in-Publication Data
Aukstakalnis, Steve
Silicon mirage : the art and science of virtual reality / by Steve Aukstakalnis and David Blatner.
p. cm.
Includes bibliographical references and index.
ISBN 0-938151-82-7
1. Human-computer interaction. 2 Virtual reality. I. Blatner, David. II. Title.
QA78.9.H85A79   1992
006--dc20   92-29919
                                                                    CIP

ISBN 0-938151-82-7
0 9 8 7 6 5 4 3 2 1

Printed and bound in the United States of America

Permissions

✿   ✿   ✿

The Virtual Office on page xi is by Eli. © Laughing Trout 1991.

Figure 1-1 on page 14 is © 1990 Bill Griffith.

Figures 2-4 and 2-5 on page 35, 3-28 on page 84, 3-31 on page 88, 5-2 on page 145, 8-3 on page 191, 8-4 on page 192, and 10-1 on page 212 are courtesy University of North Carolina at Chapel Hill Department of Computer Science.

Figures 3-2 on page 47, 12-3 on page 234, and Color Plate 3 are courtesy University of Illinois at Urbana/Champagne; National Center for Supercomputing Applications.

Figures 3-4 on page 52, 3-5 on page 54, 3-6 on page 55, 3-7 on page 56, 3-16 on page 68, 4-4 on page 108, 4-5 on page 110, 4-6 on page 111, and 4-7 on page 112 are from *Perception* by Robert Sekmuler and Randolph Blake. © 1985 by Alfred A. Knopf, Inc. Reproduced with permission of McGraw-Hill.

Figures 3-9 on page 60, 3-11 on page 61, and 3-19 on page 74 are from PhotoDisc Volume II. Courtesy PhotoDisc, Inc.

Figure 3-20 on page 75 is from "The Eyegaze Development System: A Tool for Human Factors Applications." Courtesy LC Technologies, Inc.

Figures 3-23 on page 79 and 3-35 on page 91 are reproduced courtesy of LEEP Systems, Inc. Photograph by Urlicli O. Figge.

Figure 3-24 on page 80 is reproduced courtesy LEEP Systems, Inc.

Figures 3-25 on page 81, 3-26 on page 82, and 8-1 on page 186 are courtesy of Dr. Ivan E. Sutherland.

Figures 3-27 on page 83 and 11-2 on page 220 are courtesy NASA.

Figures 3-29 on page 85 and 3-30 on page 87 are from "Exploring Virtual Worlds with Head-Mounted Displays" by James C. Chung et. al. Courtesy University of North Carolina at Chapel Hill Department of Computer Science.

Figure 3-32 on page 89 is courtesy Virtual Research.

Figures 3-33 on page 89, 3-38 on page 97, 6-1 on page 160, and 6-11 on page 174 are courtesy of VPL Research, Inc. © 1992.

Figure 3-34 on page 90 is courtesy CAE Electronics Ltd.

Figure 3-36a on page 94: Permission for reprint, courtesy Society for Information Display.

Figure 3-36b on page 94 is courtesy Reflection Technology.

Figures 3-37 on page 96 and 12-1 on page 230 are courtesy Imaging Technology Branch, NASA Ames Research Center, Wade Sissler.

Figure 4-10 on page 118 is courtesy NASA VIEW.

Figure 5-3 on page 147 is reprinted from *Presence: Teleoperators and Virtual Environments,* Volume 1, Number 1, Winter 1992, Grigore Burdea et. al., "A Portable Dextrous Master with Force Feedback," by permission of The MIT Press, Cambridge, Massachusetts, © 1992.

Creating a New Media

❁   ❁   ❁

Reading this book is a delight for me because it fills a surprisingly long-standing gap in the literature of virtual reality. For the enormous amount of interest and activity that virtual reality has inspired in the last few years, it is absolutely remarkable that I have had no book to recommend to people who come to me with the simple question, "What can I read to understand what this is all about?" I feel that now there is such a book, and you are holding it in your hands.

Silicon Mirage is organized around the human sense organs, and this is entirely appropriate. Virtual reality is distinct from other configurations of computer technology primarily in that it places the human being in the center. When we work with virtual reality systems, we begin with the question, "What, exactly, is a human body, and how might we design a machine that will most comfortably suit the natural modes of perception and action of a person?" So I am delighted to see an exposition that starts with the human body and nervous system and treats the virtual reality equipment as transient attempts to mirror that biological invariant.

Commentary on virtual reality has over-emphasized the bizarre and exaggerated speculations of those on the periphery of the field. I hope the reader will agree with me that the core of the subject is actually more interesting than the rants about electronic drugs or a new form of pornography.

Virtual reality is ultimately a new way for us to study ourselves. Virtual reality also represents an example of how a community can take into its own hands the design of the next generation of media technology. Marshall McLuhan pointed out the vital importance of the structures of media technologies in our lives, and with virtual reality we see a community struggling to create a new media that will humanely inspire new types of connections between people and new explorations.

Jaron Lanier
Founder and chief scientist
VPL Research, Inc.

Myth and Reality

✿   ✿   ✿

Believe it or not, we actually considered calling this book *Real World Virtual Reality.* That oxymoron encompasses, in four words, our whole vision of the book: an in-depth explanation of what virtual reality really is, how it really works, and what people are really doing with it (and planning to do with it). We wanted to do for virtual reality what Woodward and Bernstein did for Watergate.

The days when people will blithely ask "Virtual *what?"* are clearly numbered. Within the next fifteen years, virtual reality will become an increasingly important technology found in offices, laboratories, schools, and homes around the world. But—as happens with many strange, new technologies—virtual reality has fallen prey to the extraordinary descriptions and claims of both journalists hungry for a story and developers searching for funding. In many cases, the hype has surpassed the reality.

We wrote this book because we wanted to pull apart the myths surrounding virtual reality and offer a concrete exploration of the topic. Because so many people will be affected by virtual reality, it was important to us to write the book in an easy-to-read style that almost anyone could understand. (In fact, our criterion was that the book must be understandable to both our mothers.) On the other hand, we were tired of seeing poorly researched or superficial articles and books that simply skimmed the surface of this technology, never really digging deep into this profoundly rich subject. So we added the kind of depth of information that even a techno-dweeb could appreciate.

We want to make two things clear, right up here in the front of the book. First, the principle focus of this book is fully immersive virtual reality. We'll discuss what that means in Chapter 2, *Virtual Immersion.* So although we do explore some of the fringe applications that have appropriated the name virtual reality, we won't dwell on them longer than to point out their existence.

Second, while this book is intended to provide an easy-to-understand explanation of the technology and a number of its real-world uses, it is impossible for us to provide a complete listing of products and projects, along with the developers behind them. This is both because of the space limitations in this book, and the fact that the technology is in a state of constant change. If you are looking for such a comprehensive list, we recommend the virtual reality industry study that Steve compiled, published by Matrix Information Service in Lathrup Village, Michigan. It's expensive, but it contains the most comprehensive list of information regarding this industry that we've seen.

✿   ✿   ✿

About This Book

The first section of the book is an introduction to virtual reality. It covers the basics: what virtual reality is and why it's such an important technology. This introduction includes everything from what

The virtual office

virtual reality can really do to visions of what it will do in the future. The rest of the book is then broken into three sections, covering the tools of virtual reality, applications in virtual reality, and issues in virtual reality.

The Tools of Virtual Reality. We believe that in order to understand virtual reality, it's important to first understand how we perceive the everyday reality around us (we'll explain why we think this way later in the book). So the four chapters in this section relate to real-life sensations: seeing, hearing, feeling, and recognition. And each of the first three chapters focuses first on human perception and then on how virtual reality lets us manipulate these senses into believing we're in another world. Next, each chapter discusses the state of the art in virtual reality technology—both commercially available tools and those that are still hidden in laboratories around the world. The goal of these chapters is to provide you with a solid understanding of the infrastructure beneath the shiny surface of virtual reality.

Applications in Virtual Reality. Chapters seven through fourteen cover the real-world applications of virtual reality technology. From architecture and design to education and entertainment, virtual reality is just beginning to be used in interesting, entertaining, useful—and profitable—ways. We also discuss the amazing but probable applications that the future has in store for us, including virtual surgical simulations for doctors and three-dimensional models of molecules and galaxies that scientists can "fly" through. Many of the examples in these chapters are being used today by corporations and research labs on the cutting edge of the field.

Issues in Virtual Reality. The final section of this book, *Issues in Virtual Reality,* focuses on how virtual reality can affect us physically (Chapter 15, *Human Factors*) and socially (Chapter 16, *Social Considerations*). In these two chapters, we discuss the physiological and psychological impact of virtual reality and how researchers are solving the present-day concerns of critics. Plus, we continue to explore how virtual reality will be applied in the future, including the arts, psychology, and the military. The final chapter covers the future of this exciting technology, including the possibilities of retinal imaging and direct neural input. We also take the opportunity to examine two of the major virtual reality myths that have emerged: virtual sex and intelligence augmentation.

❁   ❁   ❁

Acknowledgements

Writing a book about virtual reality has proven to be an exciting challenge because the topic is simultaneously vast and yet quite narrow. It is vast in being such an inclusive technology. That is, virtual reality includes elements of computer science, electrical engineering, psychology, and interface design. Plus, its applications are so enormous that every profession—from doctors to pilots, from teachers to scientists, from soldiers to clergy—may someday have cause to use it in one form or another. Nonetheless, it is a narrow topic in that the number of people, companies, and universities currently developing virtual reality tools is still small.

This book could not have been successfully completed without the generous help of many individuals. We'd like to thank a few of those people directly.

First of all, our thanks to the many people who helped us compile accurate information for the book, including Jaron Lanier, Michael Evans, and Dave Edwards of VPL Research, Creon Levit, Steve Bryson, Dov Adelstein, and Rick Jacoby at NASA's Ames Research Center, Mark Bolas of Fake Space Labs, Eric Howlett of LEEP Systems, Linda Houseman at the University of North Carolina, Steve Venema and Blake Hannaford of the University of Washington, Walter Greenleaf of Greenleaf Medical Systems, William Chapin and Scott Fisher of Telepresence Research, Scott Foster of Crystal River Engineering, Mitch Barker of the Federal Aviation Administration, Chris Currell of Virtual Audio Systems, and the coordinators of SIGGRAPH.

Our thanks, too, to the folks at Espresso Roma, Hot Lips Pizza, Pankos, Harvard Espresso, and Schultzy's Sausage in Seattle for the superb fluids and munchables that kept us motivated to the end.

The People Who Made This Book

We especially want to thank some of the people who helped in the creation of this book. Our editor, Steve Roth, for holding the rudder steady throughout the process. Our publisher, Ted Nace, for taking a chance on a new book and being so supportive in its creation. To Gaen "Luddite" Murphree, for her amazing sense of language. To book designer extraordinaire Olav Martin Kvern, and to production man Jeffrey "Loose" Cannon, a guy with a history of ideas. The folks at Peachpit Press have always been very helpful, including Keasley, Gregor, Cary, Paula, Susanne, Paul, April, and John.

We'd also like to thank a few people individually.

Steve: "I would like to extend my sincere thanks and gratitude to my family and, in particular, my mother and father, who, as parents, friends, mentors, and business partners, served as the essential catalysts for this project. Next, thanks to Lisa von Trotha for your never-ending love and patience. The impact you have had on me is impossible to express in such a small place. Fingha Powa!

"Additional thanks go out to Sandra Helsel, Timothy 'King Tito' Moore, William Shortt, and my coauthor David 'uhhh…okay' Blatner, who patiently taught me how to reduce the geek factor in my writing.

"And finally, my deep appreciation goes out to Sue Twigg, who offered her friendship and home in the mountains near Aspen, Colorado, during the closing stages of this project. Your kindness and patience were key to the successful completion of this book."

David: "First of all, thanks go to my friends and family who put up with me for a year and a half of kvetching: Debbie Carlson, Barbara Blatner, Richard Fikes, Alisa Blatner, Adam and Allee Blatner, Don Sellers, Susie Hammond, Leslie Simons, Doug and Hiromi Peltonen, Don Munsil, Sarah Stone, Baby Jesse, and Ragnar. Also, thanks to the many people who patiently explained specific elements of virtual reality, including Doug Schuler, Dave Anders, the Brickens, and of course my coauthor, Steve, without whom this book would never have happened."

Steve Aukstakalnis
David Blatner

Contents

✿　　✿　　✿

PART I

Introduction to Virtual Reality

CHAPTER 1

The Silicon Mirage

✣   ✣   ✣

At over 600 miles per hour, O'Neill passed over the length of a football field every time he blinked. Not that he could see much below him. In the pitch black of night, his jet fighter-bomber soared over the invisible landscape on its way to the coast. To reach a safe military base, he had to evade detection over eight hundred miles of enemy territory, and he was confident that the high-tech equipment that surrounded him would enable him to succeed.

Pushing a button near his right hand, O'Neill activated the aircraft's voice command system. A soothing voice responded quickly in his ears, "Computer ready."

O'Neill paused momentarily, then proceeded: "Terrain enhancement on." Banking to the left, the jet's on-board computer showed him that what had looked like a black void was now revealed as a long range of mountains. The aircraft's computer quickly converted data from the Defense Mapping Agency's world topographic database into a spider's web of thin green lines that clearly outlined the mountain's peaks and valleys. This webbed image of lights, projected from a bundle of fiber-optic cables directly onto the inside of his helmet's visor, appeared as an overlay to the outside world.

Off in the distance he could see a bright yellow circle. He stared at it and told his computer, "Identify." Information immediately poured out of the fiber-optic bundle and appeared next to the yellow circle: City: Masonville. Population: 1,200. Elevation: 2,300. SAM Threat: low.

O'Neill flew close to the ground. Suddenly, as he crested the ridge of a hill, O'Neill's enhanced view of the world lit up like a Christmas tree. The voice buzzed in his ear: "Warning: radar alert." In an instant, the computer started drawing light blue domes that appeared to float over the landscape. O'Neill knew that these were regions of airspace actively being searched by ground-based radar and that by carefully maneuvering his jet between these computer-generated domes, his presence was almost sure to be concealed.

❀   ❀   ❀

When Dr. Hiroshi Miyakawa opened the door to the white, sterile operating room, he couldn't help feeling nervous. Like an actor walking onstage wondering if he would still remember his lines, Miyakawa took a deep breath and walked toward the operating table.

A nurse approached. "The patient is ready, doctor."

But this was no ordinary patient. In fact, although the room was complete with measurement and monitoring equipment, no person lay on the table. Instead, the doctor slipped his hands into gloves surrounded by wires and metal joints and placed a pair of lightweight goggles over his eyes. The patient, absent from the real world, was now seen clearly by Miyakawa in the goggles' tiny image displays This extraordinary patient was entirely computer generated, from the elasticity of the skin to a wound in the chest.

In fact, although the scene Miyakawa watched was still somewhat crude, the effect was so eerie that it was difficult to remember that this was just a practice surgery, and no human life was at stake.

Reaching out, Dr. Miyakawa could feel the virtual scalpel in his gloved hand, and when he cut the skin, tiny computer-controlled motors silently whirred, creating a resistance that could only be described as lifelike. Retraction of the skin, blood flow, internal anatomy, and potential problems were all carefully programmed into the computer and displayed to the surgeon as he progressed.

Two hours later, after practicing the virtual surgery twice more, Dr. Hiroshi Miyakawa removed the wired clothing and walked down the hall to his living patient, calm and prepared to perform the delicate procedure.

❋ ❋ ❋

In the three hours that the fire had burned, it gutted most of the central offices in the chemical factory and had begun to spread into the laboratories. The fire department knew that the fire had to be stopped soon or else cannisters of deadly chlorine gas would certainly be ruptured. But the risk involved with entering the building was extremely high, and it was probable that several members of the crew would be killed if they attempted to do so.

As Maria Juarez slipped into the telepresence suit, carefully fitting her arms into lightweight metal sleeves and placing display goggles and headphones over her eyes and ears, she thought about the job ahead of her. It was dark and silent inside her apparatus, as no signal was being passed from the mobile computer workstation in the emergency response truck. Twenty feet away, specialists prepared the six-foot-high, fireproof robot that would enter the building and smother the fire.

"Display on!" shouted one of the technicians.

Juarez's field of view suddenly lit up. She could see the scientists, hear their voices…but why were they loo**k** g at her? The discon–gruity of being instantly transported **er** place passed quickly, and she reminded herself that aw were fed from cameras in the robot's eyes. The me from microphones deep in the robot's hea nding on firm ground away from the robot e robot itself.

As Juarez moved the small joystick co hand, the robot rolled past the scientists, toward the burning building. Connected to the remote workstation with a high-frequency radio link, the robot—or was it Maria?—moved into the building, turning, rolling, searching. Juarez turned her head left and right, scanning the lobby area, listening to the roaring fire coming through the walls. She saw the button that would open a sliding door into the storeroom, and as she reached out with her hand, the robot's arm followed with incredible precision. The shielding armor of the robot felt no pain as the flames burned around it. Then, expertly maneuvering through the area, Juarez sprayed the fire with smothering foam from tanks within the robot.

Later that day, when the chlorine tanks were safely removed and the fire was under control, Juarez removed her equipment and chuckled at the thought of the old joke about "coming back to your senses." Her eyes were once again hers, her arms controlled only her arms, and although she didn't mind being a powerful robot for a time, she was glad to be back.

These three scenarios are not science fiction. They're not Hollywood movie scripts. And they're not far-fetched visions of military technology. Most aspects of these scenarios exist now. Voice recognition, head-mounted displays, and position tracking are all elements of a technology so new that its inventors are still arguing over what to call it. But even now, in its infancy, the technology shows promise of drastically changing our society, the way we live, and how we interact with complex machines.

The names for this technology vary from the academic (*high fidelity simulation*) to the obscure (*digital interactive environments*). But the phrase that has stuck—perhaps not surprisingly—is the sexiest and most marketable name of the lot: *virtual reality*. The expression *virtual reality* is like *artificial intelligence* or *chaos theory*. The first time we heard these words we said, "Hey, what's this all about? We want to know more about it." These technologies have something else in common: the response from the media—hype, exaggeration, and reporters' imaginations run amok. If you believe everything you hear, it's the second coming.

But what exactly *is* virtual reality? Why is it so important? How close to reality is it? Is it all media hype with little grounding? What could it be used for? And what applications can we expect in the future? These are the questions that this book is designed to answer, in clear terms, without the hype.

✿ ✿ ✿

What Is Virtual Reality?

Virtual reality is a way for humans to visualize, manipulate, and interact with computers and extremely complex data. It's as simple as that. Methods for human-computer interaction are called computer interfaces, and virtual reality is just the newest in a long line of interfaces. So what's so special about that? Why are magazines, newspapers, television, and Hollywood films paying so much attention to something as dull as a new interface? And why devote an entire book to explaining it?

Virtual reality represents a major leap in creating ways to interact with computers and to visualize information. Instead of using screens and keyboards, people can put displays over their eyes, gloves on their hands, and headphones on their ears. A computer controls what they sense; and they, in turn, can control the computer. But we're getting ahead of ourselves. Let's look first at human interfaces and why virtual reality makes sense, and then take a look at various people's visions of the technology.

Interacting with Machines

The concept of creating better, more intuitive interfaces certainly didn't begin with computers. Every tool we use has a human interface, and the interface depends greatly on both the skill of the designer and the complexity of the job the tool must do. For example, a hammer has a simple human interface, and it's a very limited tool. On the other hand, if you've ever stood in front of a photocopier with fifty different buttons, you know what it's like to use a complex tool with a poor interface. "I know what I want, but how do I get this machine to do it?"

The more complex the tool, the harder it is to design a good interface. Given that computers are thousands of times more complex than photocopiers and millions of times more complex than hammers, it's no wonder that so many people are either scared of computers or just generally try to avoid them. But it doesn't have to be like this.

Human-Computer Interfaces

Let's face it: computers can be really difficult to work with. First off, they're incredibly stupid; they only do what you tell them to do. Second, they only understand obscure languages. Third, although they are great at processing information, available methods of human-computer interaction are extremely limited.

Early computers were difficult to communicate with because information had to be passed between computers and humans by flicking switches and punching holes in paper. Later, computers were designed with better interfaces that enabled text-based communication. For example, if you wanted the computer to perform a calculation, you could type in a program that told the computer how to do it. When the program finished running, the computer could type back the answer. The problem with text-based systems, however, is that they generally require you to remember a plethora of bizarre text codes and syntax.

In the 1970s the graphical user interface (GUI) was developed in order to make communication between humans and computers easier. Using a GUI system such as the Apple Macintosh or Microsoft Windows, you can tell the computer what to do by using a pen or a mouse to click on pictures or drag items around a screen. Information can be passed back to you in the form of pictures, words, or sounds. Not only is this method easier to work with, but it's also easier to remember how to use (that's why most people call it "user friendly").

Note that all of these interfaces involve putting information into a computer and then receiving information back in some way. It's like carefully filling out a request slip at a library, then having the librarian hand you back a single book. Every time you want a book, you have to fill out a slip. Wouldn't it be nice, researchers asked, if we could simply stroll through the library ourselves, pulling books off the shelf when we wanted?

The result was a major paradigm shift in the development of computer interfaces: virtual reality. In a virtual reality system, you are no longer looking at data on a computer screen; rather, you are seemingly immersed within the data itself. You can use virtual reality technology to fly through three-dimensional environments that represent extremely complex data, reach out and manipulate these representations with your hand, or experience visiting a world that would be physically impossible in our own reality. The shift of focus from working with alphanumeric data to working in a three-dimensional representation of that data can alter drastically both the manner in which we work with computers and our productivity and enjoyment when working with them.

The Scope of Virtual Reality

Consider a statement made by Ivan Sutherland, one of the fathers of virtual reality, in his 1965 paper "The Ultimate Display": "If the task of the display is to serve as a looking glass into the mathematical wonderland constructed in a computer memory, it should serve as many senses as possible. So far as I know, no one seriously proposes computer displays of smell or taste." The workings of a computer is, indeed, a wonderland full of possibility. But how best to get that world out of the computer and into our heads?

The virtual reality computer interface can address not only sight, but also hearing and touch. It is a fully interactive computer system that envelopes you in a three-dimensional world. For example, in one of the scenarios at the beginning of this chapter, this interactive world was the virtual surgery patient. In the following four chapters, we'll describe the technology, how it works, and what it's used for. For now, however, let's simply concentrate on the ideas behind it.

A computer is programmed to create a model of a three-dimensional object in its memory. Let's say it's an architect's plan of a future building. Although the plans for the building are actually stored in millions of zeros and ones, the computer knows how to display the building through special equipment. You can see the building as you walk around or through it. You can reach out and touch parts of it. For example, you can turn the water on in the kitchen sink. And you can hear within the model, too; you can hear the running water in the sink.

The model is truly three dimensional. When you turn your head, the model remains stable as you turn inside of it, and you can see the other side of the room. The sound of the water burbles from the faucet behind you now.

But the world you see is virtual; it exists only in the computer and in the equipment you're wearing. Someone watching you would only see a person in funny-looking headgear looking around a room with computers in it. As Howard Rheingold noted in his book *Virtual Reality*, "You tend to crawl around on the floor when exploring virtual worlds. Like sex, exploring virtual reality seems to require bodily positions that look amusing to others."

We can see the power of this system in many ways. An architect can evaluate how the sun's rays filter into a room. Perhaps the architect notices that light would enter a window in a more pleasing manner if the window were slightly higher on the wall. Reaching out, the architect grabs the window and moves it higher. "Much better," she says, while the computer automatically updates the architectural plans in its memory. What might have taken building complex models of wood and paper—or possibly even building the house—to find out, could now be found in a matter of minutes.

something that humans are extremely good at: observing and understanding spatial information. We do it every day just by living, and now we can use the same mental tools to work with computers.

❀ ❀ ❀

Visions of Virtual Reality

We're fascinated by the love-hate, attraction-repulsion attitude that many people have when it comes to computers. And these reactions appear to be exponentially more extreme around the topic of virtual reality. While some people profoundly embrace the technology, their minds racing to find new and exciting uses for it, other people are moved to proclaim this the latest step in a destructive path towards apocalypse. The idea that any tool could be powerful enough—even if only in people's imaginations—to evoke these responses forces us to take a moment to explore the various visions that people have and have had about virtual reality.

First let's take a closer look at the phrase *virtual reality* and other words commonly associated with this technology. Then we'll look at how virtual reality has appeared in the media.

What's in a Name?

One of the biggest obstacles that researchers in this field bump up against is just what to call it. Whereas some technoids have tried to label the interface *high fidelity simulation,* other people insist that the technology is really *artificial reality* or *virtual environments* rather than *virtual reality.* Some people—especially those who believe that the words *artificial* and *virtual* create oxymorons when combined with *reality*—are more inclined to the term made famous by William Gibson in his 1984 science fiction novel *Neuromancer: cyberspace.*

Nonetheless, as we go to press (late 1992), some general definitions are beginning to fall into place. Let's review them here.

Environment. A "world" that exists entirely within the memory of a computer. A world might be a three-dimensional model of a house, the display of a set of complex data, or any number of other things. You can explore the world using a variety of methods, including virtual reality technologies.

Artificial reality. A computer environment that is responsive to human manipulation. Coined by Myron Kreuger in his book *Artificial Reality,* first published in the mid-1970s, the term *artificial reality* was originally intended to cover all aspects of two-dimensional and three-dimensional viewing technology.

Virtual reality. A computer-generated, interactive, three-dimensional environment in which a person is immersed. Coined by Jaron Lanier, founder of VPL Research, in 1989.

Cyberspace. A computer environment spanning multiple computers, multiple users, and multiple sets of data. Each computer acts as a window into the information that defines the cyberspace. The word *cyberspace* has been used to describe various nonvirtual online computer services that presently exist.

VR in Science Fiction

In retrospect, science fiction authors of the mid-twentieth century often appear to have been uncannily accurate prophets. Stories written about space travel, society and culture, and unborn technology were ridiculed by some and revered by others. In fact, an argument could be made that science fiction writers powerfully altered the course of history (and continue to do so) by introducing concepts and possibilities to a generation of future scientists.

These scientists, who are today creating the technologies that will take us into the twenty-first century, may have read such authors as H. G. Wells and E. E. Doc Smith, who wrote in detail about telepresence and telerobotics as early as the 1930s. And it was not long after that when Robert Heinlein alluded to telepresence, Aldous Huxley wrote about three-dimensional movies called "feelies," and Cordwainer Smith wrote about virtual overlays. Later, Ray Bradbury

THE SILICON MIRAGE   13

and other authors wrote stories that certainly included various virtual reality topics. However, science fiction really met virtual reality in the early 1980s in short stories and novellas published in magazines like *Omni*. And it wasn't until 1984 that the word *cyberspace* found a place in reader's vocabularies through William Gibson's Hugo award–winning book, *Neuromancer.*

Now, in the 1990s, an entire subset of science fiction that relates to virtual reality and cyberspace is deemed "cyberpunk" fiction, and television viewers are treated to Star Trek's hyper-VR system called the Holodeck. Although some published stories are realistic in writing about the technology and what applications may be possible in the future, many others are purely fictional and exploit misunderstandings about virtual reality and what it can do.

For example, in the recent film *The Lawnmower Man,* a person is made smarter through the use of drugs and wild virtual immersion experiences (see Color Plate 2). The scientist in charge twists and turns a three-dimensional image of a brain, affecting the subject's brain waves, fearing that one small slip will create a vicious monster. Although the film is fun to watch (we really enjoyed the computer graphics), the way it portrays virtual reality is problematic, at best. When researchers call computers "brain augmenters," they are referring not to making people smarter but to making people able to obtain and process information more quickly and efficiently through computers.

Nonetheless, now that the science has actually caught up to the fiction, writers are looking even farther towards the future. It will be interesting to see how close some science fiction writers come to predicting how this and other technologies will progress.

VR in the Media

For the past five years, virtual reality has popped up in magazine and newspaper articles, comic strips, books, radio, and television shows. From *Scientific American* to *Newsweek*, from sitcoms like *WKRP in Cincinatti* to BBC's *Horizon* documentaries, from the *New York Times* to *Zippy the Pinhead*, little tidbits of VR information have titillated the public's curiosity (see Figure 1-1). Unfortunately, the reported information has often diverged from the real story.

FIGURE 1-1   VR enters the popular culture

A recent BBC documentary presented a conversation between Electronic Frontier Federation president John Barlow and VPL president Jaron Lanier in which the following interchange concerning people being introduced to virtual reality took place:

John: "The second question is always sex, and the third question is drugs."

Jaron: "What's the first question?"

John: [laughing] "What the hell *is* it?!"

How true. And, in fact, many of the most prominent articles and reports on virtual reality focus on elements that are misleading or wrong entirely. And whereas misinformation in Hollywood movies like *Lawnmower Man* can be laughed off as fiction, we have been troubled by the shallow nature of some nonfiction articles.

For example, the *Wall Street Journal* caused both nervous laughter and outright concern when it published a front-page article in 1990 entitled "Computer Simulations One Day May Provide Surreal Experiences. A Kind of Electronic LSD?" The article, which has become a classic in the virtual reality industry, included Timothy Leary's comment that virtual reality is "getting closer and closer to the psychedelic experience."

Some people have suggested that the future of virtual reality is dubious because of its potential use as a psychedelic drug. In fact, this assumption couldn't be further from the truth. As we noted earlier, the technology is simply a tool. The tool can be used to create fantastical environments, even those that appear hallucinatory, but to say that experiencing these environments is druglike simply ignores both free will and common sense. For one thing, you can always unplug the system or remove the equipment at will.

A similar focus on virtual reality technologies as able to create virtual sex is similarly untrue. As a popular computer-magazine writer recently noted, "Where would you go to get fitted [for the equipment]?" Nonetheless, sex sells, and virtual sex (sex with a computer or sex over long distance, commonly called *teledildonics*) seems to sell even better. We'll look more at the concepts of virtual reality as a drug in Chapter 16, *Social Considerations,* and of teledildonics in Chapter 17, *The Future of Virtual Reality.*

The media can only be blamed so far for the propagation of these myths. To some degree, virtual reality researchers themselves are involved with telling wild stories of future applications. There is no doubt that we are in for seeing some amazing applications of virtual reality in our lifetimes, but it's important to keep a critical eye when exploring what virtual reality is and what it can do.

❊   ❊   ❊

What Virtual Reality Can Do

In his 1965 book, *Understanding Media,* Marshall McLuhan wrote, "The hybrid or meeting of two media is a moment of truth and revelation of which new form is born…The crossings of media release great force." Television was the synthesis of radio and film. Each alone had its strong points, but when brought together, they resulted in an extremely powerful crossbreed.

In many ways, this sort of bringing together is exactly what researchers have done with virtual reality. The technologies of computer graphics, data communications, and computer programming have been loosely melded with the technologies of the telephone, the television, and the video game. The result is a single, ever-changing technology, immensely superior to each of its predecessors.

Let's use the example we began earlier—of the architect using virtual reality to see a building before it's built—to explore the four basic uses of virtual reality: modeling, communication, control, and arts and entertainment.

Modeling. People build models in order to understand something. We're not talking about the little plastic models of B-52s that you may have glued together in fifth grade. Rather, the models that we all build daily may be internal, mental models of our environment, such as a model for how a company is organized or a three-dimensional understanding of where we are in a room. A model may also be an external, physical explanation of events, objects, or information. For example, an architect's blueprint is a model that embodies a great deal of information describing a building.

It's a good thing that we're proficient at creating models, because they're extremely important to our understanding of the world. Virtual reality lets us experience even more complex and sophisticated models, more quickly and easily than ever before. For example, architects can create ten different three-dimensional models for a single potential building, then walk through them and evaluate the designs in a way that would be impossible with complex, two-dimensional drawings. In designing a house, an architect can listen to how loud the hi-fi system in the kid's bedroom sounds through the walls. At a single command, she can change the type of wall material to see how the sound changes.

Understanding the complex three-dimensional structure of molecules is extremely difficult because we can't compare it to anything at a level that we can see. However, a chemist or a student can use virtual reality to visualize a model that reflects what molecules look like and how they act and by manipulating that model more quickly reach a higher level of understanding.

The key is this: it's difficult to form and work with complex three-dimensional models in your head. It is as if you tried to plan the building of a new home entirely in your head, from clearing the lot to the final landscaping work. When used properly, a computer can act as a "brain augmenter" to help with these complex tasks.

Communication. While you may or may not believe in the biblical story of the Tower of Babel, there is little doubt that people around the world have a lot of difficulty communicating with each other. In fact, we often have difficulty communicating with members of our own family, much less those who speak a different language. However, the task of communicating between people, and between computers and people, is essential to our lives today.

The plans that our hypothetical architect draws up are only effective as far as they can be communicated. That is, when another architect looks at them, the two architects can say, "Hmmm...yes. I see what you mean." But if we, the clients, looked at the plans, we wouldn't know what was going on.

This is a problem because architects aren't usually the people who are going to own or use the buildings they design. If an American firm designs a building for a bank in Thailand, the bankers are going to want to see and understand what the building is going to look and feel like before they throw several million *bhat* at it. Virtual reality technology moves beyond language and educational barriers by creating models that anyone can understand. Hopefully, many mistakes and miscommunications can be avoided in the new process.

Note that virtual reality systems can be networked together, allowing multiple users to enter into a three-dimensional model at the same time. These people may be across the room from one another or across the world.

While sharing virtual environments is not a refined, daily practice at this time, the potential applications are staggering. For example, when the architect in San Francisco wants to have a conference with another architect in Bangkok, they could use virtual reality technology as they might use a video-telephone. The virtual environment might be a conference room with a large table in the center. On the table is a blueprint. The two architects can see computerized images of each other, look at the blueprint together, and point at areas on the blueprint while talking. They can then switch to looking at a three-dimensional model of the building to see the blueprint data displayed as a finished structure, and then walk through the building, discussing it, gesturing, changing the position of walls, and so on.

Control. If you ever write a book about something like virtual reality, you'll find yourself, like us, explaining the topic about a hundred times to friends, relatives, and your publisher. One friend, after a particularly long explanation, recently retorted, "Well, if it's all inside computers, how can it affect the outside world?"

Computers are increasingly in control of the world around us. Physicists rely on computers to control the operation of nuclear reactors, telephone companies use computers to control telephone systems, and manufacturers use computers to control factory lines. Banks are now just as concerned about magnetic computer tapes as they are about the cash or gold they have on hand. And money can be transferred across the world in a blink of the eye. As John Barlow said, "Cyberspace is where your money is."

With billions of pieces of data traveling around the world's computer networks every day, we are nearly incapable of making sense of it. There's too much information, and it all moves too fast. In the future, virtual reality could be the tool to help us harness this information, make sense of it, and control it. For example, financial markets are extremely complex, but if the millions of numbers and variables are translated into three-dimensional graphic images that we can manipulate with our hands, we can much more easily understand and control what is going on with all that money. We'll discuss financial markets in more detail, including the exciting applications that are beginning to be used, in Chapter 13, *Information Control.*

Robots, too, are controlled by computers. And today's robots build cars, enter spaces that are unsafe for humans, and perform tasks at a precision and speed that humans can't match. Virtual reality technology lets us manipulate robots like never before and even get the sense that we are the robot itself. This control is called *telepresence* and is a field much larger than present-day virtual reality (see Chapter 14, *Telepresence*).

Finally, virtual reality technology can put control in the hands of those who previously had little: those with physical disabilities. Take the example of a person constrained to the movement of two fingers on a single hand. Those two fingers, perhaps in conjunction with chin and eye tracking, can manipulate a computer well enough to pull that person into a virtual environment. For example, from the confinements of a wheelchair or a bed, a person could teleoperate robots, push virtual buttons, or move through virtual space to investigate a piece of virtual art.

Arts and entertainment. With all this talk about molecular engineering and computers controlling the world, it's sometimes
difficult to remember that a major element in computers and virtual
reality is entertainment. Video games comprise one of the largest revenue-generating fields in computer technology, and there
are more computers in people's homes for the use of entertainment
than for anything else.

Virtual reality doesn't just open new doors to the entertainment
industry, it opens the windows and the chimney flue, too. Let's take
a look at a few ideas that are popping up now.

- Video games that place you inside the action as a participant.
  You can play against the computer or against someone else.
  The "someone else" might be across the room or across the
  world. And that person who just beat you in a game of virtual
  tennis may be a paraplegic who can't get out of a wheelchair.

- Games that are so interactive that participants can change the
  scenery, change the characters, and even change the rules.
  These games could become like interactive movies or theatre,
  with people participating from around the world. For example,
  virtual reality games based on the popular role-playing game
  Dungeons and Dragons are beginning to appear in which not
  only can more than one person play at the same time, but the
  players must cooperate in order to "win" against the computer.

- Interactive music videos that place you in a concert hall or
  even onstage with a rock and roll band. You command the
  computer to make you the rock star. A virtual guitar appears
  in your hand and a virtual crowd of screaming kids appears
  looking at you.

- Virtual systems for relieving the monotony of using an exercise machine. Use a rowing machine hooked up to a computer that shows a peaceful lake at dawn, or jog on a treadmill
  while seeing a beautiful neighborhood. As you pull the oars or
  turn the treadmill, the scene that you watch in the miniature
  displays changes, giving the effect that you are actually moving across the lake or through the town.

These systems don't have to be restricted to worlds like our own, either. It might be fun to create and explore a world in which physical laws work differently: zero friction, extra gravity, and non-Euclidean geometry would make for an interesting scenario. Just the act of creating these three-dimensional worlds could be fun in itself.

❀   ❀   ❀

What Is Reality?

"Reality: what a concept!" These unforgettable words of comedian Robin Williams may be the closest some of us ever get to a true understanding of reality. Philosophers and artists have tried for millennia to penetrate the mystery of reality, with varying degrees of success. And now Jaron Lanier and a bunch of "hippies with Macintoshes" (as one anonymous critic called VR researchers) are beginning to discuss creating not an alternate reality but *many* realities. And in these discussions, some people are now implying that these so-called realities will someday be indistinguishable from our own, phenomenological reality. Let's take a quick look at this claim and what it implies.

First of all, we know the question is begging to be asked, "Well, what, exactly, is reality?" But as much as we'd like to be definitive about this, we choose instead to take a deft leap to the side, leaving these sorts of arguments to the philosophers and ethicists.

We will say, however, that the reality in which we live is infinitely deep and complex. For example, how we perceive reality determines what our idea of reality is. If we hear a dog in front of us and then *see* a dog in front of us, not only do we tend to think that the dog we see is the dog that made the sound, but also that both the dog and the sound are "real." Neither of these may be true.

Perhaps the key here is that instead of focusing on what reality *is*, we should think more about *what* is reality. That is, if we release ourselves from necessarily emphasizing that there is a reality out there, we are freed to look at what is relevant to us in a reality. And what, then, could be relevant to us in an alternate reality?

Crude Reality

Let's be very clear about this: the majority of virtual realities created to date have been extremely crude. They generally look more like a video game and are much slower to react than you'd expect. The bottleneck is certainly not lack of imagination or design, but rather the limitations of present-day hardware. Computers today just aren't powerful enough to generate anything nearing what we consider to be real life.

Nonetheless, there is something astounding that happens the first time you experience a virtual reality. You are, for possibly the first time in your life, suddenly projected into a totally different environment. You are in two places at once: your body is encumbered with gadgetry, but your mind and much of your *perceived* reality is hovering around somewhere else. Perhaps you're above a rudimentary model of the Seattle Space Needle or enmeshed in a molecule or on a single island of land floating in the midst of a lonely, almost-empty universe. For many people in VR research today, it was this first glimpse into a new world that acted as their "conversion experience"; they saw the potential of virtual reality and knew they wanted to work in that field.

After an early virtual reality session, those elements of reality that we think are as solid as a rock start to blur slightly. Incredible as it may seem, even that crude, low-resolution, limited environment you explored may make enough of an impression that you feel that you were really there. The memory is logged away as a "true" experience. You might later stop and think, "Did I really visit the Space Needle today? No, that was just VR."

Perhaps a parallel can be drawn between virtual reality and one of its predecessors: film. Early in the history of film when people were unfamiliar with the medium, audiences reported feeling that when they saw a train coming at them on the screen, they thought the train was real.

However, as people reached a level of sophistication in watching film, they were able to differentiate between what was real and what was on the screen. We can see that the screen image is not interactive, it's not usually three-dimensional, and it doesn't surround us (we're not immersed in the image); and so we know that it's not "real." However, all of these elements have been addressed in virtual reality, and once again we're at a level of attempting to become sophisticated viewers/participants.

For example, while the visual appearance of the simulation may seem to be nothing more than cartoonish or less than lifelike, actions within the virtual environment can often invoke a physical response. If you put on a head-mounted display, turn around, and immediately see a baseball bat being swung toward your head, you will, without question, duck your head, or at least flinch in expectation of the blow that will never come.

Three Stages of Virtual Reality

Before we continue, we think it's important to comment on what we consider to be the three basic stages of virtual reality: passive, exploratory, and interactive. Each of these offers slightly different features. And each progressive step is that much more difficult to create.

Passive. Today we have many opportunities to participate in passive experiences. That is, when we watch television or a movie, take a ride at an amusement park, read a book, or even listen to the radio, we are generally passive. Other than changing the channel or going to get a bag of popcorn, we don't have much control over the environment we're experiencing. There is a corresponding stage in virtual reality in which we can watch, hear, and perhaps even feel what is happening in the virtual environment around us. The environment might move around us, making it appear that we're moving through it (a "forced fly-through"), but we can't control it.

Exploratory. The second stage in virtual reality is that of being able to explore the space. Moving around the virtual environment, whether by flying, walking, crawling, or whatever, is a major leap in functionality. Instead of just seeing a three-dimensional room with a box in it, you can move around the room and see what's on the other side of the box or find out what's inside the box or leave the room to see what's in the rest of the house. This is the level that many of the basic architectural walk-throughs and virtual art pieces are at right now.

Interactive. The third and most powerful stage in virtual reality is the interactive. At this point, a virtual reality system lets you experience the environment, explore it, and—finally—interact with and change it. You might do this by reaching out at grabbing a virtual book and opening it or moving furniture around a simulation of your apartment to see what looks best. Depending on the software, it might even include changing the environment itself ("I want this room to be smaller...and give me another table in that corner...and put a giant tortoise doing a dance over by that wall").

The Silicon Mirage

So once again we return to the question at hand: Will it be possible to create realities so clear and complex that we won't be able to perceive the difference between our everyday reality and a computer-generated one? That's the Turing test of virtual reality, isn't it? If we can achieve that, we have created the ultimate computer environment.

We're convinced that the answer is no. Although one day we may have the technology to generate photorealistic images in real time, computers will never truly be able to create anything as complex, as detailed, and as organic as our world. Chaos theory is beginning to show us that there is a level of complexity, randomness, and uncertainty in the universe that is impossible to predict or recreate. Meanwhile, researchers in artificial intelligence have, over the past twenty years, found out how difficult it is to simulate even the simplest forms of common sense reasoning we all routinely perform every day.

Ultimately, however, we look toward our experience of reality itself to answer the question. And we find what appears to be a core paradox: the more we search, the more we learn, and the more we discover about reality, the less we seem to know about the whole. The complexity of reality and what can be experienced indicates a mystery so profound and subtle that not only can it not be created by the human mind—it can barely be comprehended. And when, through spirituality, mysticism, or the use of psychedelic drugs, people actually do appear to gain some sense of the boundlessness of reality, they find it numinous and ineffable.

But the worlds that we use computers to create may eventually be so realistic, so enticing, and so interesting that we may intensely want to believe in them, and they will become like mirages in a desert. The synthetic images made of electrons and plastic will appear to be real enough. But in the final analysis they will never be more than a silicon mirage.

CHAPTER 2

Virtual Immersion

✿   ✿   ✿

Perhaps the only reason people don't think about their normal state of immersion in reality is that they can't think of how *not* to be immersed in it. We think about being immersed in water or immersed in work, and each of these we can come out of (we sometimes talk about "coming up for air" from being immersed in a project or a relationship). But each day, as we wake up, we become immersed in the reality around us. One of the key elements of virtual reality is the sensation of being immersed in a computer-generated environment. By immersion we mean the feeling of being actually inside and surrounded by the environment.

For example, when you watch a movie, you get the sense of looking into some strange world where images float around in front of you. If the movie is in a cinema, you generally feel as if you're looking at that world through a giant window. If the movie is on television, the window is more like a small portal. The same is true of watching a computer screen. In a virtual environment, however, you no longer have the sense of looking into a different world, but rather of looking at that very world from within (see Figure 2-1).

In the next four chapters, we're going to explore the technologies involved in creating, experiencing, and manipulating virtual reality. But before we do that, we want to explore three aspects of virtual immersion essential to the technology: three dimensionality, position/orientation tracking, and interactivity. Each of these relates directly to the three levels of virtual reality that we described in the last chapter: passive, exploratory, and interactive.

FIGURE 2-1   Virtual immersion

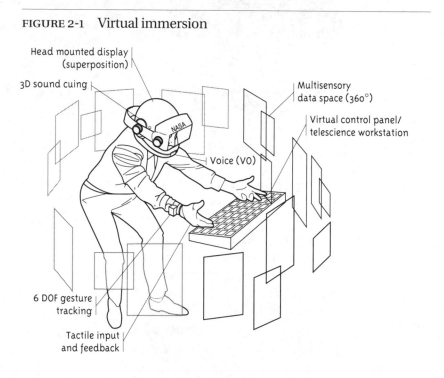

✿ ✿ ✿

Deep Spaces

Being immersed means being surrounded by something; everywhere you look, it's there. No matter where you go, there you are. As we drive to work, do our job, have fun on the weekends, or whatever, we are constantly surrounded by things that we can see, hear, and touch. Being surrounded by stimuli that trigger these sensations enables us to be constantly creating and updating mental models of our environment. If you hear a telephone ring, you may first think it's coming from the office in front of you. On a second ring, if you tilt your head, you might realize it's coming from behind. We build these sorts of dynamic models thousands of times each day, without even thinking about them, in order to understand and function in our world.

To create a sense of immersion in a virtual environment, we must be able to surround ourselves with various stimuli in a manner that makes sense and that follows rules similar to those of the real world. That is, when you turn your head to the left, you see the objects to the left of you. When you walk forward, you get closer to the objects in front of you. These are elementary features of our sense of being immersed in an environment; and when you're in a virtual environment, you expect the same results.

How we experience a three-dimensional world depends on the equipment we use and how the system is programmed. First, a computer must contain a model of a three-dimensional space and "understand" the idea of moving through this sort of world. That's complicated enough. Next, the computer must be programmed to let us experience that environment in various ways. Finally, we must use specialized equipment to enter into these virtual worlds. This equipment has to keep track of where we are and what we're doing, so that the computer can update its internal models and displays accordingly. The equipment must also be able to give us a compelling sensation of being immersed in an environment. As soon as we enter into a new environment, we begin to build dynamic three-dimensional models of that world. Where are the objects, where are the sounds coming from, what do things feel like? We can then use our mental models in a virtual world in the same way as we do in the real world: to increase our understanding and ability to function.

The three ways of sensing a virtual world are seeing, hearing, and feeling.

Seeing. Computer-generated modeling has focused primarily on visual imagery over the past twenty-five years, and for good reason. Sight is the predominant sense for most of us, and the ability to understand patterns in visual displays is one of our strongest points. Every virtual reality system today is designed to create a three-dimensional visual space. Some are more complex than others, but most at least generate basic visual cues such as perspective and shading. We cover the visual aspect of virtual reality in the next chapter, *Seeing*.

Hearing. Our ability to hear sounds in three-dimensional space, called our aural system, has been less heavily examined by researchers but is now becoming recognized as a major factor in virtual reality technology. By subtly changing prerecorded or computer-generated sounds, we can simulate three-dimensional sound fields that encourage the suspension of disbelief while in a virtual environment. For example, if you are getting an aerobic workout while bicycling through a virtual landscape (see Chapter 9, *Entertainment*), it would be significantly easier to feel immersed in that environment if you hear the sounds of the world around you (birds chirping, cars going by, or whatever). Similarly, our sense of hearing can be a great aid in understanding a virtual world. If you are flying a jet plane, it's much more intuitive to hear another airplane behind you than to have to figure it out from a two-dimensional radar map. We discuss three-dimensional sound and how it is used in virtual reality in Chapter 4, *Hearing*.

Feeling. The final method of sensing a three-dimensional virtual world is feeling. Our sense of touch, as we'll see in Chapter 5, *Feeling*, is important for exploring the world around us and maintaining our internal model of where and what is in our environment. Actually being able to touch something in a virtual world is an extraordinary experience; and although the ability is somewhat limited with current technology, it significantly increases the feeling of immersion. It is also a major step in one's ability to function in the free-floating world of virtual reality.

Each of these sensations—seeing, hearing, and feeling—is important to creating a successful sense of immersion in a virtual world. They all rely significantly on the technology of position and orientation tracking.

✿   ✿   ✿

Position/Orientation Tracking

As we noted earlier, it's important for virtual worlds to follow rules similar to our own. If you look down, you want to see what's below you. If you press a virtual button, you want the button to move or somehow react to being pressed. In order for any of this to happen, the computer must know where you are and what you're doing. To achieve those results, the computer must be able to sense where your head and hands are and in which direction they are turned. This is called position/orientation tracking.

With this information, the computer can determine what images to display at any given moment, thus giving the appearance that while you move, the three-dimensional model you're inside of remains stable—just like the real world. When the correlation between how a person moves and what they see breaks down, the sense of virtual immersion is reduced. For example, if you walked forward but saw things move away as if you were walking backward, you would first become disoriented, then less convinced of being immersed in this virtual environment.

If you break down all the directions, you find that there are six basic functions with which you can place your head or hands anywhere in space. First, there are three movement functions: you can move forward/backward, left/right, and up/down (the x, y, and z coordinates). Next, there are three turning, or rotational, functions: you can make your head or hands roll, pitch, or yaw (see Figure 2-2).

These are called the six degrees of freedom. Note that the word *degrees* here is used to describe the ability to move rather than the amount you can move. For example, you can turn your head 90 de-

FIGURE 2-2   Six degrees of freedom

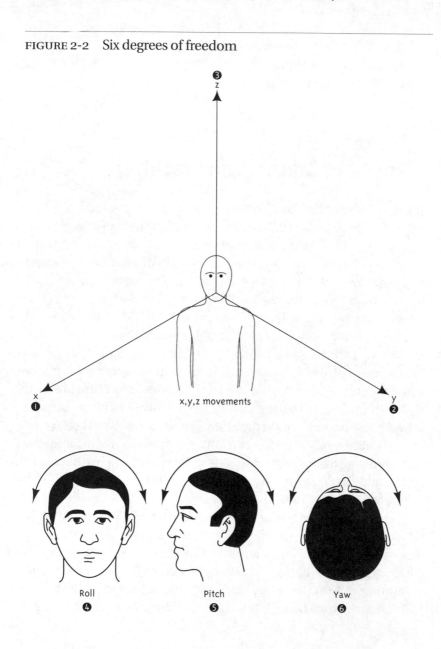

grees to the left, but turning on this axis is only one of the six degrees of freedom.

There are presently five basic position-sensing methods in use: mechanical, ultrasonic, magnetic, optical, and image extraction.

Mechanical. Ivan Sutherland, known by many as "the father of head-mounted displays," designed and implemented two methods of position sensing. The first method makes use of a mechanical armature with one side connected to the top of a helmet and the other end connected to an encoding device on the ceiling. As the user changes head position, movements in the joints of the arm are relayed to the computer and the computer can update the screen display (see Figure 3-25 in the next chapter).

While mechanical position/orientation tracking is the most precise method of tracking, it has the disadvantage of being the most limiting. You can't always move where you want to; the arm only extends so far. In Chapter 3, *Seeing*, we'll see that Fake Space Labs and other researchers are using this arm-based mechanical tracking technique but with the BOOM apparatus rather than a head-mounted display.

Ultrasonic. Sutherland's second method of position tracking uses ultrasonic positioning techniques. A small device that produces inaudible clicking sounds is attached to the top of a helmet, and four small microphones are attached to a frame on the ceiling. Because sound travels at a relatively constant speed, the ultrasonic clicking sounds reach the four microphones at slightly different times. Combining a comparison of the microphone's information and an understanding of mathematics provides fairly accurate position and orientation data.

Ultrasonic position/orientation tracking is relatively flexible, though not exceedingly precise. Also, if there is an obstruction between the source "clickers" and the receiving microphones, or if the clickers are too far away from the microphones, the position tracker's performance is significantly reduced.

Ultrasonic position tracking was used in the Nintendo Power-Glove, the popular toy created by Abrams-Gentile Entertainment, to work with some Nintendo-based games. For example, when someone wearing the glove punched toward the television, the position tracker would relay information (such as the speed and duration of the punch) to the game, and the game would show a character throwing the punch. Although the system was popular with game players, it wasn't very precise (what can you expect from a toy?).

Magnetic. Some environments, such as the cockpit of a jet airplane, are so cramped and noisy that neither mechanical nor ultrasonic position sensing work well. A third method, developed to take these sorts of situations into account, has ended up being the primary position-sensing technique in virtual reality research today: magnetic position sensing.

The underlying concept behind a magnetic positioning system is simple. Electrical current sent through a coil of wire generates a magnetic field oriented along a single axis. Conversely, when a coil of wire is exposed to a magnetic field, an electrical current is generated which is proportional to the field's strength. The closer to the axis of the magnetic field, the greater the electrical charge generated.

If you mount three coils of wire at right angles to each other and feed them electrical current, the coils create magnetic fields along three axes. And if you move a second three-coil set through these magnetic fields, it produces three distinct electrical charges depending on its position and orientation. You can then manipulate these values mathematically to provide position (x, y, and z) and orientation (roll, pitch, and yaw) information about the sensor (see Figure 2-3). This three-coil system was first developed by Polhemus Navigation Sciences, of Colchester, Vermont, and is known as the Polhemus magnitic positioning system (or more simply, a Polhemus tracker).

There are two problems with magnetic position sensing: latency and accuracy. Latency refers to the lag time between when someone wearing a magnetic position tracker moves and when the computer actually receives and processes this information. At the time of this writing, all researchers in the virtual reality industry agree that latency must be reduced significantly for these systems to be effective in the future.

FIGURE 2-3   Magnetic position sensing

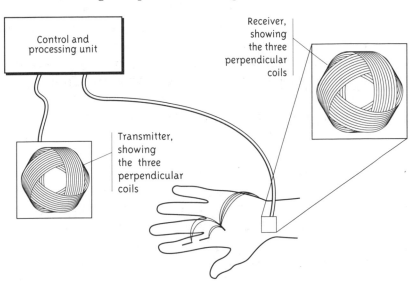

The second problem, measurement accuracy, results from an interesting side effect. The magnetic fields generated by the first three-coil set (the transmitter) are picked up not only by the second three-coil set (the receiver) but also by other large highly conductive metal objects in the area.

Currently most magnetic trackers use alternating current (AC) magnetic fields to measure position and orientation. However, because AC current fluctuates, eddy currents are generated in nearby metal objects. The result is that the metal objects in turn give off their own magnetic fields, significantly reducing measurement accuracy.

There are currently two solutions to this problem. First, the secondary magnetic fields can be mapped out and compensated for in the system software. Second, you can use direct current (DC) position trackers. Ascension Technology took this route and has created several position trackers based on DC technology.

DC systems also generate eddy currents, but only on the rising edge of each electrical pulse. These eddies rapidly drop off when the field achieves a steady state. Therefore, if we measure the receiver's position during the steady-state phase of each pulse, the eddy effect is minimized. If you then subtract the Earth's magnetic field and the transmitter's steady-state magnetic field from the total field registered, you can provide even more accurate measurements.

Magnetic position trackers based on AC technology can also distort images on liquid crystal display (LCD) screens. This is cause for concern as LCD is the principle imaging technology used in commercial head-mounted displays (see "Optics and Hardware," in Chapter 3, *Seeing*).

Optical. The original model for optical tracking was based on placing a light-emitting diode (LED) on a person and using a video camera and image-processing software to track the position of the LED (see "Image extraction," below). However, in 1984 Gary Bishop and Henry Fuchs of the University of North Carolina developed a tracking system that operates exactly opposite to this. In their system, the cameras are mounted on the person's head and the lights are mounted in a stationary position.

In their prototype, the ceiling of a 10-by-12-foot room is composed of 2-foot-square tiles, each containing thirty-two infrared LEDs that flash on and off in a computer-controlled pattern. Next, four small cameras are mounted on a helmet on the user's head (see Figure 2-4). These aren't your garden-variety video cameras, however. At the back of each camera is an image sensor called a lateral-effect photodiode, which is extremely good at tracking and reporting the location of these ceiling-mounted LEDs.

When an LED is turned on, it produces a spot of infrared light. If that spot falls within the viewing area of one of the cameras (see Figure 2-5), the sensor reports the coordinates of that LED to the host system. To calculate the position and orientation of the user's head, the four image sensors must see and report the photocoordinates of at least three LEDs.

As with all position/orientation-tracking systems, this too has its limitations. For example, if one stands close to a wall or leans over too far, the sensor cameras point at a side wall where there are no LEDs. Another factor limiting the system is its weight: carrying ten pounds of camera equipment becomes tiring pretty quickly.

FIGURE 2-4   Head-mounted optical tracker

However, the accuracy of optical-tracking technology makes up for many of these limitations. The system described above is sensitive to head movements of less than .08 inches and angular motions

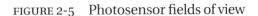

FIGURE 2-5   Photosensor fields of view

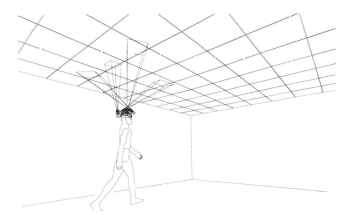

of less than .2 degrees. During normal operation, two to four sensors capture the image of between ten and fifty LEDs. This results in a sample rate of between 20 and 100 cycles per second.

Image extraction. The fifth method of position and orientation sensing is image extraction. Although this technique is the most calculation intensive of the four, it is clearly the most powerful and easy to use (from the user's viewpoint, not the technician's or developer's). When watching a person in a virtual reality system that uses image extraction, it appears as though the computer isn't tracking them at all. However, behind the scenes a video camera or set of video cameras pointed at the participant captures video images describing where the person is and what they're doing.

Although this sort of computer visual processing is extremely difficult, it shows great promise for virtual reality systems because of its relative simplicity of use.

❋   ❋   ❋

Interactivity: Explore and Manipulate

The third element of virtual immersion is interactivity, which means that you can both explore and manipulate a virtual world. This is the fullest form of virtual reality. Some systems only include the ability to explore, but full interactivity includes both.

In the real world, when you want to pick up an apple, you reach out and pick it up. The apple "responds" by moving where your hand takes it. If this seems incredibly simple, it's because that's the way we're used to the world working: every action has an equal and opposite reaction. These interactions between people and things are natural and enable us to manipulate our environment. Similarly, in a virtual world we often want to interact with objects, requiring that we can see them, feel them, and move them. So when you want to pick up a virtual apple, you can simply reach out and pick it up, too.

Both exploration and manipulation are handled through position/orientation tracking along with navigation equipment such as a joystick, the DataGlove, or the Spaceball (see Chapter 6, *Recognition*).

✿ ✿ ✿
Using Virtual Reality

The next four chapters break virtual reality technology into four basic areas: seeing, hearing, feeling, and recognition. The first three relate to what we, as users, experience, and the fourth relates to how we can interact with or modify those experiences. While reading each chapter, keep in mind the basic, everyday sense of how reality looks, sounds, and feels, and how we can interact with it. Re-creating our reality may not be the ultimate goal in virtual reality applications, but it offers a good model for how virtual realities might function.

PART II

The Tools of Virtual Reality

CHAPTER 3

Seeing

Look around you. Unless you're sitting in an empty room, chances are that during a quick glance around, you took in enough information to fill a giant encyclopedia. You probably saw one or two hundred different objects, each one of which has texture, color, size, and shape. All that information is almost instantaneously processed using the two most sophisticated pattern-recognition devices in the world: your eyes and your brain.

In this chapter, we're going to focus on these two parts of the body. First we'll discuss why vision is important to the study of virtual reality. Then we'll get into a detailed discussion of how the eyes and brain work together. And finally we'll get to the heart of the matter: how the enabling technologies of virtual reality work with the eyes and the brain to create their "magic." Although it may be tempting to jump right to the third part of this section, we think you'll appreciate it more if you start with the first two sections.

✿   ✿   ✿

Visual Communication

Watching television, reading a book, and looking at a computer screen all have one thing in common: they're methods of transferring information through the eyes to the brain. When you think about what you know about the world, it's amazing how much of it was learned by using your eyes. It's for this reason that when we try to understand how humans sense the world around them and how to create virtual worlds, we begin with an exploration of visual communication.

In a simplified explanation, the brain has two mechanisms for processing, or understanding, visual information that's passed to it: conscious and preconscious processing. Let's look at the strengths and weaknesses of each.

Conscious Processing

Information processing that requires a concerted mental effort is referred to as conscious processing. For example, when you move your eyes around a photograph, actively seeking out visual details, you are consciously processing visual information. Or, when you're flipping through a telephone directory searching for a name, you're using a conscious visual process. Trying to find the word in Figure 3-1 is another example of conscious processing.

FIGURE 3-1   Conscious visual information processing

In many instances, conscious processing requires some form of learned skill. An example of this is an architect interpreting a floorplan or a blueprint. Without an understanding of what the signs and symbols on a blueprint or on a page of text mean, we cannot fully process the visual information (at least, not past "I don't get it").

Preconscious Processing

Information processing that is beyond voluntary control is referred to as preconscious processing. Preconscious processing includes the basic ability to perceive light, color, form, depth, and movement. For example, we have a basic internal understanding of the colors red and white and the shape of an eight-sided octagon. We may or may not understand that what we are seeing is a stop sign, but our conscious mind is primed with the information.

Although preconscious visual processing is invisible to our conscious awareness, it provides a tremendous amount of information to our conscious mind. Without this preconscious infrastructure, we would either have to laboriously "think" about everything in our visual field or go without much of the information we need to make decisions about our environment.

It is important to remember two things about preconscious processing. First, no conscious processing of visual information is required. Second, and perhaps more importantly, no matter how visual information is presented to the brain, it must pass through the preconscious visual-processing system before reaching any conscious processing. For example, when approaching an intersection, your preconscious mind first registers the red and white octagon on a post by the side of the road before your conscious mind registers that it's a stop sign and you decide to stop your car.

If the information that is passed to the mind is highly coded or symbolic, the preconscious mind can only do so much interpretation before it passes it on to the conscious mind. For example, we might see a mathematical equation on the page of a textbook and effortlessly recognize the symbols and numbers. But actually solving the equation requires conscious actions on the part of the individual.

Note that the words *preconscious* and *subconscious* refer to different things. How the subconscious mind relates to virtual reality could (and should) be the topic of a book by a psychologist. Here, we focus primarily on physiology and the processing of information.

❋   ❋   ❋

Signs and Symbols

Humans have been using images and symbols as a means of communicating with each other for the past ten thousand years. We can find some of the earliest documented examples of using graphical depictions as a means of communication on the walls of a cave in Lascaux in southern France. Using basic inks, the artists expressed the raw excitement and energy of the hunt in a way that we can understand even today.

Since then, humankind's ability to communicate visually (and to some extent our interest in communicating visually) has increased not steadily but exponentially. Art was the primary method of expression for several thousand years and was then replaced by hand-written language, which, in turn, became obsolete after the fifteenth century when Gutenburg produced his first movable-type printing press (though movable type had already been used for hundreds of years in Asia). Over the past one hundred and fifty years, a plethora of new and efficient communication tools have been invented and quickly placed into ubiquitous use. Photography was invented in the mid-1800s, and lithography near the close of the nineteenth century. The twentieth century has brought us motion pictures, teletypewriters, television, video, and finally computers.

Each of these forms of technology is primarily visual in its means of communication. And each uses particular signs and symbols to deliver its messages.

Computers as Communicators

Our inclusion of computers in our list of visual communication tools may surprise you. While it's true that computers have been used primarily as storage devices and giant calculators, we believe that the ultimate use of computers is as a medium for communicating information.

As we noted in the last chapter, it wasn't so long ago when people had to use punch cards, paper tape, or toggle switches to communicate with a computer. Since the 1970s, however, researchers have been developing computer interfaces based on a more graphical approach. These graphical user interfaces developed into systems such as the Macintosh and Microsoft Windows. They let us create, manipulate, and retrieve large quantities of information through tools such as a mouse, a pen, or even a pointing finger. And rather than see this information on reams of computer paper full of numbers and symbols, we can use a number of graphical tools such as a monitor or a head-mounted display.

But we're jumping ahead of ourselves. We need to cover more background information on our visual apparatus and why current graphics-based technology is a significant step in the right direction.

❀   ❀   ❀

Visual Thinking

Working with a mental image of some complex structure or concept can be an extremely difficult task. This is particularly true when the image is three dimensional or when it represents abstract information. There are a number of examples that demonstrate our ability to process information more efficiently by externalizing these complex mental models.

A classic example of the power of visual thinking is the model James D. Watson and Francis Crick constructed of a DNA molecule while investigating the underlying patterns of its basic components. A traditional approach of analyzing reams of data was difficult because of the number of potential combinations of these building blocks, as well as the irregular geometry of the molecule. Instead, the two scientists developed another means through which to visualize their research data: they built a model out of wooden sticks and balls.

By building a model, Watson and Crick were able to use the extensive pattern-recognition powers of their preconscious minds to reveal the double-helix pattern. The key was not just a deep understanding of the enormous quantity of data; it was constructing a three-dimensional model that *showed* them what the data meant.

Computer Graphics

When most people think about computer graphics, they usually think about the special effects in films like *Star Trek, Terminator 2*, or *The Lawnmower Man*. However, the promise of computer graphics is far beyond creating "cool" pictures to look at. When we think of a computer as a communications tool, we see that computer graphics are extremely useful for revealing information hidden in complex data sets. The data sets could be numbers from an accounting balance sheet, scientific findings from aerodynamic studies, or even a constant stream of numbers from a stock exchange. A computer can be the liaison between humans and raw data by creating images that allow us to explore the data more intuitively.

For example, let's look at the problem of monitoring smog. Researchers at the Pittsburgh Supercomputing Center are using computer graphics to study smog density and movement in major metropolitan areas such as the Los Angeles basin and Mexico City. Normally, scientists plot air-quality measurements on 2-D maps of the region (see the graphs in the upper-left corner of Figure 3-2). While this method gives a relatively good "snapshot" picture, it reveals very little information about the complexity of smog move-ment and density over time.

However, scientists have achieved a greater understanding of the mechanics of air movement by displaying air-quality data in a 3-D "movie." This technique incorporates visual cues that are quickly di-gested by our preconscious visual processes and are therefore much easier to understand (see Figure 3-2 and Color Plate 2). For example, rather than bars, lines, and numbers on a 2-D map, the video movie represents specific volumes of air as small colored spheres. When the visualization is in motion, you can closely study the ebb and flow of the smog pockets and the effects of prevailing weather, tidal motion, and other large-scale meteorological phenomena.

Mapping Vast Quantities of Information

Even all the data gathered in the United States census, mapping general smog movements, or the combinations of DNA building

FIGURE 3-2   Mapping air quality in 2-D and 3-D

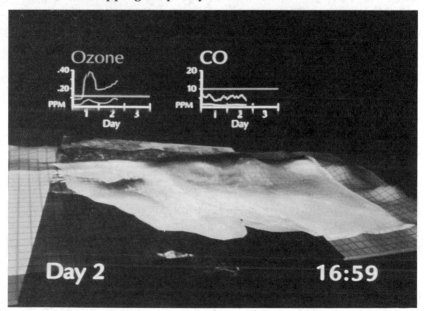

blocks are relatively small when compared to some tasks mathematicians and scientists are now undertaking. For example, calculating the launch trajectory of the space shuttle or visualizing the complex flow patterns of a thunderstorm or hurricane require millions of pieces of information.

Similarly, the process of figuring out how air flows around a complex shape like an airplane takes extraordinary computing power; and when you're finished, all you've got is several billion numbers that describe flow vectors in three-dimensional space. But when you use those numbers to create a three-dimensional graphical representation, all of a sudden the information has meaning and is useful. The numbers are the information that the computer graphic successfully communicates to the scientist.

Multidimensional Modeling

The more variables you want to work with, the more useful it is to model them in three dimensions. Mapping the average daily precipitation over the past ten years requires two variables: the rainfall and the day. With these variables, you can easily draw a graph that shows how the precipitation rises and falls throughout the decade. Adding the average daily wind velocity to the scenario increases the complexity. For each day there are now two variables that need to be taken into account. This information requires a three-dimensional graph (see Figure 3-3).

But what happens to this model when you want to add another variable? We are only accustomed to thinking and seeing in three dimensions, so adding another physical dimension to our graph is quite difficult. Fortunately, there are other methods of displaying variables. For example, we could add average daily temperature by using a color scale. Hotter areas might be more red; cooler areas might be more blue. After working with this color graph for a while, you could recognize the patterns of how these four variables work together and affect each other.

Various researchers have also used movement, clarity, size, and other visual cues to communicate information and facilitate human understanding.

FIGURE 3-3   Two and three variables in a graph

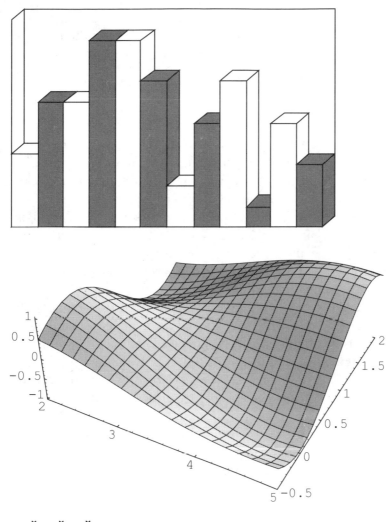

❀ ❀ ❀

The Visual System

Anyone who has ever lost the sense of sight, either temporarily or permanently, can tell you exactly how much most of us take this sense for granted. We rarely think about being able to see and even less frequently think about how the process of seeing works. In this section we're going to take a look at the human visual system, how it works, and why. It's our belief that a greater understanding of this physiology enables a greater ability to manipulate synthetic visual cues and, by doing so, create more effective visual communication and better virtual realities.

Sight

It was a common belief in early Greece that we are able to see be- cause our eyes send out beams of light, which, in turn, carry copies of the objects they strike back to our minds. Although this model is somewhat humorous, the Greeks were not entirely incorrect. Cer- tainly our eyes do not emit light beams, but the eyes do collect light that is reflected off an object's surface. These reflected light pat- terns fall upon the interior of the eye, where they are converted into neural impulses and then sent on to the various visual-information centers of the brain for interpretation.

As we will discover, the human visual system is a remarkable information processor. The exceptional resolving power, ability to perceive depth and to distinguish between even the slightest differ- ences in color, form, and texture together provide the brain with a tremendous amount of data from which to construct our percep- tion of the world. These perceptions are critical to how we interact with the three-dimensional environment that surrounds us.

Not surprisingly, it is now common to refer to the eyes as an actual part of the brain. Both have direct, unimpeded neural connections to the visual cortex. Various components of the eyes are actually made up of the same tissue from which brain matter originates. And of the approximate ten billion neurons in our heads, nearly half are dedi- cated to the processing and evaluation of visual information.

Visual Information Pathways

All data processed by our visual system initially begins as some form of light energy. The surfaces of objects absorb and/or reflect this light, depending on various characteristics. For example, we see a bright color like yellow as "light" because it reflects more wavelengths than a dark color. And we see dark colors as "dark" because they absorb many of the light's wavelengths rather than reflecting them into our eyes. Similarly, shiny surfaces reflect more light than dull surfaces.

The next step in understanding how we see the light that enters our eyes is to explore each part of the eye, from the cornea to the retina, and the retina to the brain.

The cornea. As we look at various objects or scenes of interest, the light that enters the eye first passes through the clear bulge known as the cornea (see Figure 3-4). It is interesting to note that the cornea is actually composed of the same fibrous material as the whites, or sclera, of our eyes. The significant difference in the transparency of the two regions is due, in part, to the manner in which this fibrous material is organized.

The iris. The next stop that light rays take is to fall upon one of the most well-known components of the human eye, a circular membrane known as the iris. While you may be unfamiliar with its name, you're probably familiar with one of its characteristics: color. In fact, we usually refer to the color of someone's eyes by the color of their iris (the word *iris* is Greek for rainbow). It is the combination of blood vessels and pigment that creates the color of the eyes.

The pupil. By their position, the eyelids are the primary determiner of how much light enters the eyes. However, there's a second area at which the light is regulated: the pupil. The pupil, seen as a black circular area in the middle of the iris, is actually an opening lined by two small sets of muscles around the inside edge of the iris. If the eye wants less light, the inner band of muscles—those that run circularly around the edge of the iris—contract, and the pupil decreases in size. If more light is desired, the exterior set of muscles—those that run radially out from the center—contract and the pupil enlarges.

The pupil is similar to the aperture of a camera and has similar uses, too. For example, reducing the size of the pupil increases the range in which distant objects will be in focus, also referred to as depth of field. As we'll see later, the pupil is an important element in eye tracking.

FIGURE 3-4   Cross section of the eye

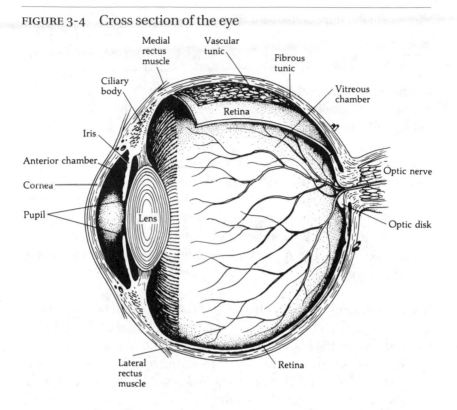

The crystalline lens. Positioned directly behind the pupil is the crystalline lens. Another natural engineering marvel, the muscles around the lens can rapidly alter the lens's shape. This provides us with the ability to shift our focus between objects close and far away. This is referred to as accommodation. Accommodation is one method we use to perceive depth in the three-dimensional world around us (see "Spatial Vision," later in this chapter).

The lens changes over time. In the first month or two of life, an infant is not able to accommodate at all. The lens then becomes more elastic and controllable until approximately the age of sixteen, after which it's a slow downhill battle toward inelasticity and thickness (the lens adds new fibers continuously throughout one's lifetime, resulting in a 400 percent increase in the thickness of the lens by the age of ninety).

Age has another effect on the lens, too. Because the lens is slightly yellow, as light passes through it, some blue light as well as some potentially harmful ultraviolet light is absorbed and thereby prevented from entering the eye. As we get older and the density of the lens increases, more light is absorbed. This is one explanation for why people of different ages may argue over whether a color is green or blue.

The retina. Light entering the eyes finally falls upon the retina, a thin layer of light-sensitive tissue lining the majority of the eye's interior. Under great magnification we can see that this paper-thin tissue, which converts incoming light into electrical impulses, is actually an extremely complex layered structure (see Figure 3-5). It is here that images we see are first processed, so we'll take a moment to make a detailed investigation.

Perhaps the strangest feature of the retina is that it appears to have been installed backwards. Before light can actually come in contact with the mechanisms that convert it to neural impulses, it must travel through the several layers of interconnected cells that collect this neural information.

Registering the Presence of Light

If the light energy has managed to progress through the entire optical pathway of the eye without being absorbed or scattered, it will finally come in contact with vast fields of light-sensing mechanisms known as photoreceptors. There are two distinct types of photoreceptors, and their names are derived from their shapes: rods and cones.

Rods and cones. You can think of each eye as containing two cameras. One camera uses highly sensitive black-and-white film (the rods), and the other uses a less sensitive but extremely high-resolution color film (the cones). Rods convey information about brightness but not color, and cones provide information about color and detail. There are three different types of cones. The first shows a peak sensitivity at a wavelength of 435 nanometers (for sensing blue), the

FIGURE 3-5   Retinal layer of the eye

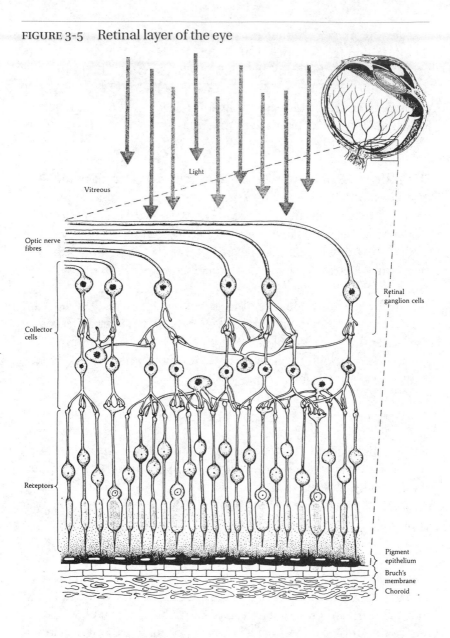

second at 535 nanometers (for sensing green), and the third at 565 nanometers (for sensing red). With an understanding of these basic photoreceptors, we can better understand not only how and why we see things, but also how best to display virtual images to our eyes.

Photoreceptor distribution. Although we talk about rods and cones as though they were something we could hold in our hands, they are actually extremely small. There are approximately 120 million rods and 8 million cones in each human eye. The distribution of rods and cones is not equal throughout the eye, and this has a major effect on how we see the world (or worlds) around us.

When you center your attention on a particular point, the light entering the eye is focused on the rear wall of the retina in an area known as the fovea (from the Latin for *pit*). This region is both the thinnest part of the retina and the part with the highest concentration of cones. As you move away from the center of the fovea, the density of cones drops off drastically and remains distributed in much smaller numbers throughout the remainder of the retina. The geographic distribution of rods is just the opposite. As shown in Figure 3-6, there are almost no rods at the center of the fovea, but rods make up the dominant presence in most other parts of the retina.

It is simple to demonstrate the differences in sensitivity and distribution between the rods and the cones. First, close one eye and focus the other on one word (any word) in the middle of this page. While remaining focused on that word, you'll find it nearly impossible to read the text only two or three lines above. This shows that the rods are very poor at discerning detail. However, they are very sensitive to light, answering a question that has bothered us for years: Why is it that we sometimes can't see stars in the sky when we look directly at them? When we focus a dim light on the fovea, it's

FIGURE 3-6   Distribution of rods and cones

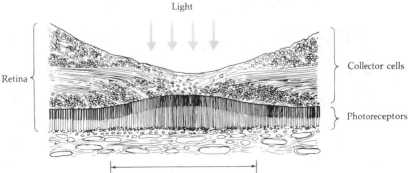

Light

Retina

Collector cells

Photoreceptors

0.2 mm

difficult to see (more cones, fewer light-sensitive rods). But look off to the side, and the dim light is focused on another part of the retina where there are many more rods.

To show that the color-sensitive cones are most densely packed in the foveal region of the retina, try the following experiment. Pick some multicolored object in your vicinity and look directly at it. Note that it is fairly easy to see all the fine details and boundaries between colors. Now turn your head so that the object is to the periphery of either eye. Notice how the closer the object is to the extreme periphery, the more difficult it is to discern detail or color.

The blind spot. While we are not generally aware of the existence of a blind spot in each eye, there is an area near the fovea completely void of any photoreceptors. This small circular region is known as the optic disk. It can be thought of as the collection point for neural impulses on their way to the brain from the retina (see Figure 3-7).

The presence of the blind spot can be easily demonstrated. Holding the book at arms length, close your left eye and stare at the X in Figure 3-8 with your right eye. Both the X and the dot should be visible. Slowly begin to move the book closer to your face while staring at the X. You will notice that the dot will disappear when the book is approximately 8 inches away from your face and reappear as the book is moved closer.

FIGURE 3-7   From the outside looking in

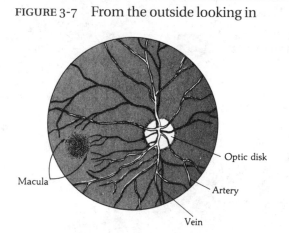

FIGURE 3-8   Your blind spot

Note that the line appears to remain continuous. This is only one example of how our eyes and brain maintain a consistent sense of presence, even when visual information is missing.

Color vision. Although we have only three different types of cones in our retinas, the human visual system is capable of distinguishing about 200 different hues and millions of different shades and tints. How can this be?

We perceive color by "mixing" the information from each type of cone, and the light/dark information provided by the rods. Mixing light is different than mixing paint, though. In painting, the more color you add, the darker the result. However, in mixing light, the more colors you mix, the lighter the result.

As we said earlier, the cones register light best at red, green, and blue wavelengths. If incoming light contains equal amounts of red, green, and blue wavelengths, the image looks white or gray. Any other combination of light waves creates what appears to be a single, separate color. When we look at color displays later in this chapter, we'll see that we can exploit the way the eye sees color to create color images.

This red-green-blue model of color vision is somewhat simplified and doesn't explain some oddities in our perception of color. For example, we should be able to see a red-green color just as well as we see a blue-green one, but we can't. It appears that the brain "postprocesses" the cones' information with a set of rules such that "if both green and red light is detected, only pass on the information for one of the colors" (see "Visual Processing," later in this chapter).

Sending the Message

As light patterns land on the retina and bathe the photoreceptors, an interesting transformation occurs. Contained within each of the rods and cones are light-sensitive molecules known as photo-pigments. When light strikes a photoreceptor, the normally stable photopigment molecule undergoes an alteration of its shape. In this process known as isomerization, the instability of the photopigment molecule causes its two primary components to separate tempo-rarily. At this point, the electrical properties of the photoreceptors are altered and chemicals (known as transmitter substances) are re-leased by the photoreceptor. These changes, which take only one-thousandth of a second to occur, begin a neural impulse that carries detailed visual information from the eye to the brain.

Visual Processing

Although the process of evaluating visual signals begins in the neurons attached to the rods and cones, most visual processing oc-curs in the brain's visual cortex. Researchers are still discovering the intricate ways in which we understand the multitude of information passed to the brain from the eyes, as well as our other senses (as we'll see in later chapters). However, the basic methodology is be-coming clear. It appears as though we process visual information by breaking stimuli down into smaller chunks of data and then passing those chunks of data through a series of filters.

These filters are nothing other than neurons in the brain set to look for particular types of information. For example, a particular neuron may look for a drastic color change between two nearby cones. Whenever information is passed to it that fits this descrip-tion, it fires a stimulus to the next neuron in line. The next neuron may have a slightly more defined criteria, such as if these photore-ceptors are catching this color change. As soon as it sees this kind of trend, it signals that there's an edge happening in this area of your field of view.

The neurons get more and more specialized as you explore far-ther along the neural paths. One set of neurons might only look for horizontal lines, while another might look for 45-degree lines. Other neurons might be programmed to fire only when they recognize all of the essential stimulus of a familiar person's face or the markings of a dog.

✿   ✿   ✿

Spatial Vision

Every second, our brains are fed billions of pieces of visual infor-mation in the form of electrical impulses. Our goal in processing this information is to acquire an understanding of our environment. For example, we might want to know if a car is coming towards us, or how far away a mountain is, or where we should reach to pick up a teapot. To find solutions to these problems, we must have a sense of spatial distance.

It is important to clarify that we use the term *depth perception* in two ways. First, we use it to refer to judging the distance between one's vantage point and some distant object, such as when a quar-terback prepares to throw a pass to a receiver downfield. Second, we use it to refer to judging the distance between two objects or between two points on the same object. This is also known as relative distance.

Once the visual information is processed by the ganglion cells and an image is pieced together in the visual cortex, the brain finds cues, such as edges, that help determine depth perception. The brain uses four basic types of depth-perception cues: static cues, motion cues, physiological cues, and stereoscopic cues. Let's take a look at each of these, how they work, and how we can use them.

Static Depth Cues

The first depth-perception cue we'll look at is static depth. This covers any visual cue that can be seen in a still-frame picture, such as a photograph. Similarly, if you cover one eye and remain still, you can gather some information about the spatial depth of your envi-ronment, even though what you're seeing is being filtered through only one flat, two-dimensional retina.

The six static depth cues that we'll cover here are interposition, shading, brightness, size, linear perspective, and texture gradient. Each of these can be used to give a greater sense of reality to a virtual environment.

Interposition. When two objects are positioned such that one blocks a portion of the other from view, the partially blocked object is perceived to be more distant. This effect, known as interposition, is a powerful depth cue. Even when other cues provide conflicting information about spatial depth, the interposition of the objects usually takes precedence (see Figure 3-9).

Shading. One of the more powerful depth cues we experience is shading. In fact, shading not only provides information regarding depth but also highly useful information regarding an object's physical features (see Figure 3-10). For example, light falling on a curved surface from an angle does not form a defined border as well as light falling on the side of a cube. Also, shadows cast by an object can give the appearance of depth and relation.

Brightness. Because the air around us contains water vapor and other particles, light that travels to our eyes from far-off objects becomes duller and more hazy than light that travels from close objects. Brightness, therefore, becomes a factor in ascertaining depth, especially over larger areas. For example, the farther away mountains are, the more blurry and dull they appear.

Size. An object's size also plays a significant role in depth perception. No matter how large or small an object is, the closer it is to the

FIGURE 3-9   Interposition

FIGURE 3-10   Shading

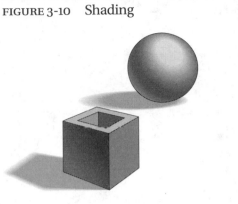

observer's viewpoint, the larger the image projected onto the retina. Conversely, the farther away an object is, the smaller the retinal image.

The most important factor in using size as a depth cue is the viewer's familiarity with the object. Based on size alone, for instance, you might think that the van in Figure 3-11 is a toy.

Linear perspective. Changes in the perceived appearance of an object as it recedes into the distance is known as perspective. The change in brightness is one form of perspective. Another, more commonly recognized form is linear perspective (see Figure 3-12). If we look at a building, we see that the lines formed by the roof and

FIGURE 3-11   Size judgments

FIGURE 3-12   Linear perspective

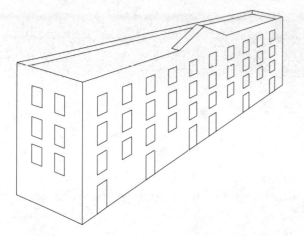

the ground appear to converge. As long as we are certain that the building's height is uniform, we can accurately gauge the depth of the building.

The cause of this perceptual phenomenon is simple: the farther you are away from an object or feature, the smaller the image projected onto the retina. Note that perspective cues can be easily manipulated to alter the perceived depth of an object. The more radical the perspective cue, the deeper the object appears.

Texture gradient. Another perspective cue is texture gradient. If you look up at a sky full of clouds or down at a field of wheat, you can see that the texture of the sky or of the field is coarse (well defined) where close to you and fine (densely packed and less well defined) farther away (see Figure 3-13). Though texture-gradient cues are often subtle, they are nonetheless powerful at generating a sense of depth.

Motion Depth Cues

There's only so much information that we can distill from a two-dimensional view using static depth cues. For example, cover one eye and look at a leafy plant or a tree. While a static depth cue, such as interposition, tells you something about the position of the leaves and branches, much of the plant simply appears a jumble, and you

FIGURE 3-13   Texture gradient

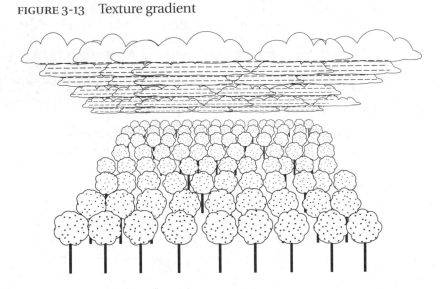

can't discern what's in front of what. However, when you move your head to the side or when the wind ruffles the leaves and branches, the true positions are quickly perceived.

Motion parallax. As you move your head from side to side, objects closer to you appear to move faster than those farther away. This is because the images of closer objects are larger and move across your retina faster than the images of distant objects. If you remain stationary, motion parallax can be created when objects themselves move. For example, a spinning carousel or a turning sign gives an indication of depth because of motion parallax.

Physiological Depth Cues

If static and motion depth cues were our only aids to under-standing the three-dimensional world around us, we would only need one eye, and we'd be forever bobbing our heads back and forth, side to side. Fortunately, most people have the functional use of two eyes. This is, perhaps, the single most important depth cue for short-range viewing (under 20 feet) and is crucial for providing a deep image in a static scene.

The two physiological depth cues are accommodation and convergence. These are oculomotor cues; that is, they're tied directly to how the eye moves.

Accommodation. Earlier in this chapter we noted that we can focus on distant objects by flexing muscles that alter the shape of the crystalline lens, a process known as accommodation. The muscles around the lens are most relaxed when you look at objects farther away than a few meters. When you look at closer objects, the muscles have to work to adjust the lens. The brain monitors the level of accommodation and uses it as a depth cue.

Note that distance judgements based solely on information derived from accommodation are often inaccurate. You can test this by covering or closing one eye and trying to pick up something in front of you. Unless you're careful, you're likely to reach too short or too far.

Convergence. The second oculomotor function is convergence. Convergence is based on measuring how far the eyes must turn inwards to view objects relatively close to the face. As with accommodation, when you look at objects closer than 20 feet or so, the eyes must adjust by turning inward. Past 20 feet, the convergence angle between the eyes reduces to zero. That is, both eyes are looking straight ahead (Figure 3-14). In the absence of other depth cues, convergence can provide reliable depth information, but it is not a very powerful depth cue.

Stereoscopic Cues

Some animals, such as rabbits and deer, see the world very differently than we do, not just because they're looking to eat someone's garden but also because their eyes each point in different directions. Human eyes, on the other hand, both point in the same direction. This gives us an interesting ability: we can distill relevant depth information by comparing the views from the left and right eyes. While both of our eyes view much of the same visual space, each eye views from a slightly different angle (see Figure 3-15). Even with the

FIGURE 3-14   Convergence angles

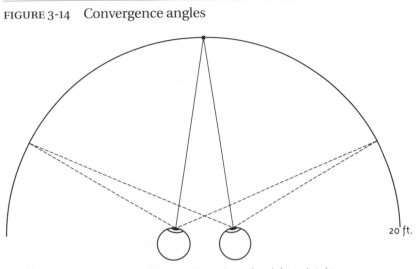

The eyes rotate inward in order to fuse left and right images of close objects. For objects more than 20 feet away, convergence is not useful as a depth cue.

relatively small separation of 64 millimeters (2.52 inches), each eye's view of an object does not appear exactly the same. This is called binocular disparity, or stereopsis.

To demonstrate this phenomenon, place two objects on a table in front of you with one object closer to you than the other. Cover your left eye and look at the two objects, taking note of the distance between them. Now cover your right eye and again look at the two objects. Notice the perceived difference in depth cues between the two objects. Angles vary, interposition may be different, and so on. The differences in lateral separation between the two objects are referred to as retinal disparities or binocular disparities.

How, then, does the brain fuse the two images together? While the process is not fully understood, we do know that there are neurons within the brain that respond to only select types of stimuli (see "Visual Processing" earlier in this chapter), several of which are associated directly with binocular information. For instance, there are specialized neurons that are maximally active when both eyes are viewing matched features. Others respond maximally when features

FIGURE 3-15   Stereopsis

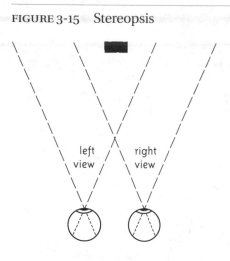

viewed from both eyes appear on the same depth plane as the point of fixation, and still others when features appear on a depth plane different from the point of fixation.

✿ ✿ ✿

Visualization Tools

Now that we have an understanding of our visual system, how we process visual information, and how we build internal models of the world around us, we can take a leap forward and explore creating simulated three-dimensional environments, otherwise known as virtual realities.

Earlier in this chapter, we discussed how humans can use visual thinking to understand complex information and how computers can help us by graphically displaying complex data. If Watson and Crick had had the use of today's computers, understanding the double-helix structure of DNA would have been greatly simplified. And if today's researchers had the use of tomorrow's even more powerful virtual reality systems, they could explore the molecular surface of a virus by walking around it or find the patterns that 100 million stars form, giving new insight into why our universe is structured the way it is.

But how do these systems work to provide us with effective visual information? What sorts of systems are available now? In the remainder of this chapter we will focus on these questions.

Building 3-D Worlds

Humans are three-dimensional creatures. Not only do we have width and height and depth ourselves, but we're used to working in environments that have these components as well.

By mimicking disparities in a pair of images, we can actually trick the visual system into perceiving depth in two-dimensional images. Sets of images that can create this illusion are called stereo pairs, or stereograms, and can be created by special cameras or generated by computers.

Figure 3-16 shows a synthetically created stereo pair. Of course, simply looking at this pair won't create a 3-D image. The trick is to somehow get one image into one eye and the other into the other eye. You could use a stereoscope, the stereogram viewing apparatus—complete with lenses and a partition—invented by Charles Wheatstone in 1838.

You could buy a similarly functioning set of lenses at many stores that specialize in maps (although their customers use them primarily for viewing photographs taken by satellite or high-flying aircraft). Or you can perform this simple, try-it-at-home experiment. Using the images in Figure 3-16, place this book on a flat surface or hold it steadily about a foot away from your eyes. Put your index finger in between the images and focus on it. Then slowly bring your finger toward your nose, focusing on it as long as you can. Remove your finger, but keep your eyes crossed. Now comes the hard part. The stereo pair should look like a stereo threesome at this point. Stare at the center image while keeping your eyes crossed until it comes into focus (you'll still see two out-of-focus images in the periphery). We find that it's helpful to keep our eyes moving around the central image in a figure eight pattern.

FIGURE 3-16   Stereo pair

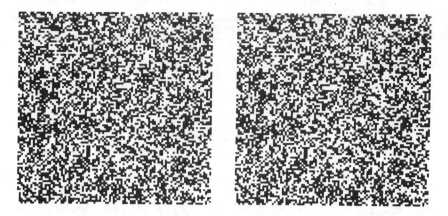

It can easily take five to ten minutes to achieve focus of the center image, especially if you've never done this before. However, once it focuses, you will see it in 3-D. And having successfully combined your first stereo pair, the task becomes easier in the future. Note that when you pull your eyes away from the image, you may feel somewhat disoriented.

The Power of 3-D

The amazing thing about stereo pairs is not just that they work, but that the brain obtains information when viewing them together that it can't obtain when viewing them apart. In the previous figure, the stereo pair looks like a bunch of random dots. When viewed in stereo, however, the image looks like a depressed region under a plane.

While static cues help somewhat with depth perception, we derive most depth information from binocular disparity (stereopsis). For example, Figure 3-17 shows an object that is unintelligible when viewed straight on. The only way to gain a sense of which lines in the graph are above which is to see the object in stereo.

It follows, then, that if you could create two-dimensional stereo pairs that move, you could begin to create a sense of an interactive three-dimensional world. If, for example, you could create a stereo image on a computer screen, you could animate and manipulate

FIGURE 3-17   Unintelligible without a stereo view

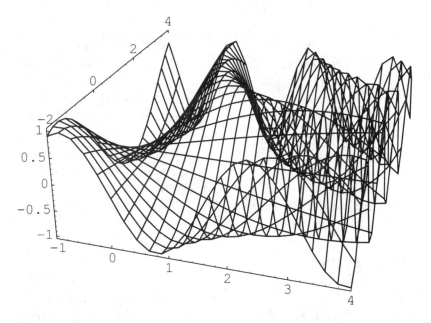

computer data in a truly three-dimensional way. This, then, is the beginning of virtual reality.

The method behind generating stereoscopic images on a flat computer screen is actually very simple. The image for the left eye is shown first, then the image for the right eye, then the left eye, and so on. The computer shows each image very quickly (typically for about one-sixtieth of a second), and the rapid alternating between the two appears like a blurry double-exposure photograph. In order to view the image correctly, you must wear a pair of glasses that contain thin, lightweight liquid crystal displays (LCDs) that alternately block out the unwanted views for each eye. These glasses, commonly called shutter glasses, but originally developed and named CrystalEyes by Lenny Lipton, founder of StereoGraphics Corporation of San Rafael, California, have become a standard feature for stereoscopic computer graphics applications.

The synchronization between the glasses and the alternating screen images is, of course, essential. It's accomplished through infrared signals emitted from a source on the monitor and picked up by a sensor mounted inside the glasses.

Visual Immersion

While perceiving three-dimensional images is an important factor in building and experiencing three-dimensional worlds, even more important is interacting with and experiencing a sense of immersion in that world. In the previous chapter, we discussed such aspects of virtual immersion as position/orientation tracking and interactivity. Also important to a sense of immersion are sensory-specific details. For example, to create a sense of visual immersion, a virtual reality must take three additional factors into account: field of view, frame-refresh rate, and eye tracking. The quality of each of these in a virtual environment can spell the difference between successful immersion or not.

Field of View

The idea behind the OmniMax theatre is to create an enormous screen and then curve it above and around the audience. It's exciting to watch a film in an OmniMax theater. You get the feeling of actually being there within the images because the screen is large enough to effectively fill your entire field of view. Because you have fewer visual references to your true surroundings and can even turn your head to see different parts of the movie, you feel like you're right inside it.

When you're looking straight ahead, each eye is capable of providing visual information as much as 90 degrees off its central axis. Combining the images from both eyes provides a lateral field of view of approximately 180 degrees. Because you can pivot your eyes to the left and right about 45 degrees (and you probably do this more than you're aware of), you can actually perceive an additional 90 degrees, making for a total lateral field of view of approximately 270 degrees (see Figure 3-18)

Note that when we talk about field of view, we're not talking about what you can focus on. We're including any and all perception of motion and objects. For example, you may be able to see a flash of moving light in the far extremes of your periphery, but you probably won't be able to tell what it is or where it's going. While it seems

FIGURE 3-18   Field of view

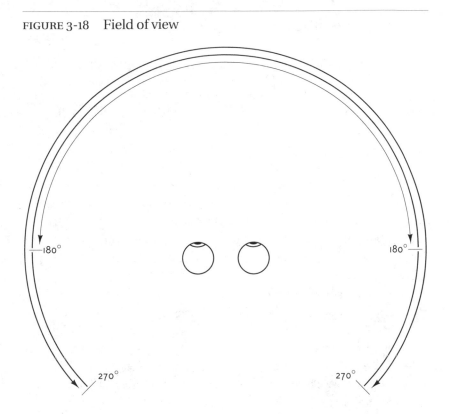

like that level of perception is useless, it turns out that it's extremely helpful in providing a sense of our environment. You can test this for yourself by wearing a pair of glasses with side blinders on them and trying to back your car down a driveway. Without all the peripheral cues, you are forever moving your head around to see where you are.

The trick, then, is to fill as much of this field of view as possible, no matter where your head is turned. Scientists will go to some extreme to achieve this. For example, during the days of the Apollo space program, scientists, unsure of how best to view photographs that had been sent back from the moon, taped them to the inside of a large sphere that had a hole cut out in the bottom. They then took turns sticking their heads up inside the sphere to look at the 3-D imagery. Now special optic lenses and equipment can be used to create a similar effect (see "Optics and Hardware," later in this chapter).

Frame-Refresh Rate

Virtual realities are created by computers that use position and orientation sensing to generate a sequence of images one frame at a time. The sequence is displayed for you in real time (that is, the computer generates the images on the fly rather than in advance like an animated movie) and can be adjusted at any moment by a turn of the head or a signal from the computer.

In the world around us, we perceive no lag time between looking and seeing. If we look down, we immediately see the ground below. However, this is not always the case with virtual realities at this time. Computers still aren't fast enough to process the enormous number of calculations necessary to generate all the images we want in real time. Of course, time heals all wounds, and as time goes by, computers will be made faster.

The number of scenes, or frames, that a computer can generate and display in a given amount of time is called the frame-refresh rate. If the frame-refresh rate is high enough, the eye blends the images together, and we see a continuous scene. For example, movies on video cassettes are recorded at thirty frames per second. At this rate, the eye does not distinguish one frame from the next. Many virtual reality systems presently display between two and fifteen frames per second; the number is dependent upon the complexity of the image. Although a fifteenth of a second may not seem like much time, the lag between when you move and when the image is updated is actually significantly more noticeable than frame-refresh rates of over twenty frames per second. In fact, some researchers believe that frame-refresh rates of forty to sixty frames per second actually increase realism dramatically.

Note that the frame-refresh rate is not the same as the lag time associated with position sensing. For example, a user's position in 3-D space must be measured, passed to the computer, and calculated properly before a scene is generated. Consequently, there is a delay between when someone moves and when the computer reflects those movements in the display. The time required to measure the user's movement is called the latency rate. The time required for the computer to draw the new image is referred to as the frame-refresh rate.

Eye Tracking

Until now, when we've discussed position and orientation tracking, we've assumed that the direction in which the user's head is pointing is the direction in which he or she is looking. Of course, this isn't always the case. Our eyes are able to swivel on an axis regardless of head motion. And, in fact, where we direct our eyes is the best indication of where we direct our attention. The trick, then, is to track not only the position of the head but also the line of sight.

Eye tracking is currently being used in the control of wheelchairs and computers by the severely handicapped, as well as in military research on hands-off interfaces between pilots and aircraft. Eye tracking is also being used extensively in such military and telerobotic applications as targeting of weapons and sensors. Eye tracking can also be a powerful addition to virtual reality systems. For example, if you are sharing a virtual environment with several other users, it's helpful for the computer to know exactly who you're looking at. But there's another, more technical reason why eye tracking is helpful in virtual reality.

The reason is based, in part, on the design of the human eye. As we noted earlier, the greatest amount of visual detail is provided by the foveal region of the retina. This area, directly opposite the crystalline lens at the back of the eye, has the greatest concentration of photoreceptors. So it makes sense that an image would need to be the sharpest wherever the eye was looking, that is, where the image would focus on the fovea. The parts of the image farthest from the eye's point of focus would require less detail. Because the level of detail in computer-generated images has a direct relationship to the computational load required to render that image, a system that tracks the eyes can be more efficient in its image generation.

Most of the head-mounted displays that we discuss later in this chapter provide wide horizontal and vertical fields of view, with a consistent image resolution. However, a "smarter" system would reduce the computational load by providing a high-resolution inset area wherever the eye was looking, and generate a low-resolution background image everywhere else (see Figure 3-19).

Presently, the primary methods of eye tracking involve bathing the eye in a low-intensity infrared light. This light creates a bright

FIGURE 3-19   A high-resolution inset

image of the pupil and a bright spot reflecting off the cornea that can be captured by a video camera focused on the user's eyes. Image-processing software then analyzes the video image, finds the pupil and cornea, and calculates where the eye is looking (see Figure 3-20).

Once the system knows where you're looking, the computer can be controlled through measuring "gaze duration." For example, you could press a button or select a key by staring at it for a specific length of time. Or in a virtual reality, you could navigate by staring in a particular direction.

While eye tracking can be quite effective, a number of funda-mental design and performance issues must be worked out before the technology can enter the mainstream. For example, because no two pairs of eyes are alike, systems must be recalibrated for each user. There is also a problem with involuntary motions such as blinking, competing reflections from the sclera, and the speed at which the eye movement is measured. Also, eye-tracking systems must become significantly smaller before they can be integrated into head-mounted displays. Despite these current obstacles, we

FIGURE 3-20   The Eye-gaze eye-tracking system

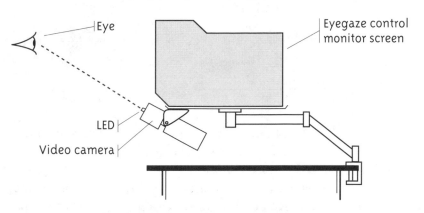

predict that in a few years eye-tracking technology will significantly enhance the effectiveness of virtual reality systems and the sense of immersion.

❀   ❀   ❀

Optics and Hardware

The final frontier of creating a sense of visual immersion in virtual realities is not the ability to create complex three-dimensional models or calculate where a user is located and is looking in three-dimensional space, but rather the simple (and yet excruciatingly hard) task of presenting the eyes with images. In this section, we will take you through the process of displaying images. Then, in the next section, we will consider the display technology presently available and explore where the field is headed.

Imaging Devices

An imaging device creates pictures. Common examples are televisions, computer screens, films, and laser printers. We are less concerned with items like films or laser printers because they generate images that cannot be quickly modified or interacted with. A television screen, on the other hand, can change extremely quickly depending on how it's controlled. Precise control of the images generated on a television screen creates the moving pictures we're familiar with.

Every television and computer screen contains one of two imaging devices: either a cathode ray tube or a liquid crystal display.

Cathode-ray tube. Cathode-ray tubes (CRTs) are perhaps the most common imaging devices. Almost every television and computer screen is built with them. CRTs are self-illuminating, meaning they produce their own light. This is accomplished by directing a narrow electron beam through a vacuum tube onto a phosphor-coated surface (see Figure 3-21). When an electron hits the surface, a phosphor releases energy in the form of light.

In order to form images on the screen, the electron beam is rapidly steered around the phosphor-coated surface at a rate of approximately 650 meters per second. At such speeds, images can be drawn fast enough to avoid flicker and allow images to move around the screen. And because electrons are so small, CRTs can provide extremely high image resolution.

Another benefit of CRTs is that they're much easier to watch than LCD displays. The contrast ratio (the ratio of bright areas to dark areas) is much greater, so blacks are really black and whites are really white. And because there are generally more grays and intermediate

FIGURE 3-21   Basic CRT design

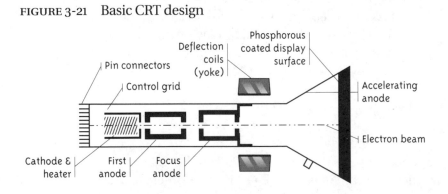

colors available on CRTs, images can have better shading and smoother lines.

Liquid crystal display. The operating principles of a liquid crystal display (LCD) are significantly different than those of a CRT. The most basic difference, though, is that LCDs are light modifiers, or light valves, rather than light producers. That is, they can block light from passing through (see Figure 3-22). LCDs typically consist of two small panes of glass, between which are a vast array of cells (pixels) containing a liquid crystal substance. When no electrical current is sent to an LCD pixel (it's turned off), the crystals are oriented in a particular direction, blocking light from passing through, and the pixel remains dark. However, when a small electrical current is sent to the cell, the crystals' orientation is altered, allowing light to pass.

The most common LCDs are found in digital watches. In normal daylight, ambient light enters the watch's LCD and reflects off the rear wall. Images such as alphanumeric characters are produced by

FIGURE 3-22   LCD operational diagram

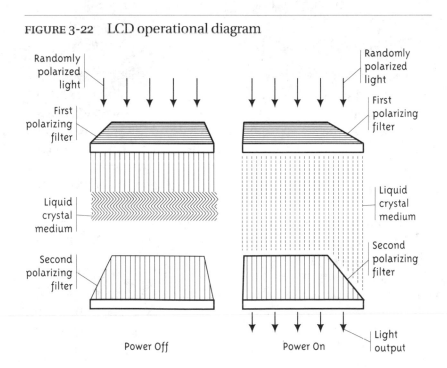

blocking areas of the reflected light. When there's no ambient light, the LCD has no light with which to polarize, resulting in a blank display. So watch manufacturers often add a tiny light bulb to supply artificial light.

The color LCDs used in some televisions and head-mounted displays use the same technology as black-and-white LCDs, but work in conjunction with light filters to present various colors. Light travels first through the LCD layer and next through a layer of red, green, and blue filters. When an LCD pixel is turned off (that is, when light is not allowed through), it remains dark. When an LCD pixel is turned on, light passes through to a colored filter (usually just a piece of colored plastic). The combination of pixels lighting red, green, and blue filters creates the illusion of multiple colors.

LCDs are a relatively inexpensive alternative to miniature CRTs. In addition, they are easier to use and draw less power. One the other hand, LCDs can offer a significantly lower resolution than can CRTs. Virtual reality systems have to take these pros and cons into account when making hardware choices.

Optics

The second hardware element in virtual immersion is optics. Just as you can't create a virtual reality by placing a digital watch close to your eyes, you can't convey a compelling sense of immersion by displaying stereo images on a small, flat CRT or LCD surface. At best, you might see a stereoscopic view of the image. Current literature suggests that a sense of immersion in an image requires a field of view of at least 90 degrees, thus filling the region directly viewable on the optical axis of the eye (see "Field of View," earlier in this chapter). The greater the lateral field of view, up to 270 degrees, the more enhanced the sensation and the more you feel as though you're really in the virtual world.

But how can we create an effective sense of immersion from images generated on such small imaging devices? Although one might initially consider using a wide-angle (or fish-eye) lens to bring the entire image into view the resulting distortion improperly maps the position of objects within the image.

To portray these images without distortion, LEEP Systems/POP-Optix Labs, of Waltham, Massachusetts, developed a unique set of optics known as the LEEP (Large Expanse Extra Perspective) stereo-scopic wide-angle viewing optics (see Figure 3-23). This six-lens (three for each eye), 6.5-power optical set is capable of taking an im-age from 2.7-inch LCDs and spreading it over 120 degrees of the user's horizontal and vertical fields of view. This creates an approxi-mately 90-degree binocular field of view (see Figure 3-24).

To generate such a large field of view, the images displayed on the LCD are first compressed around the edges. When the images pass through the LEEP lenses, the image is uncompressed. When you view a LEEP-compressed image through the proper lenses, it really feels as though you could fall right into the picture.

Since the time of NASA's first LCD-based head-mounted display, the LEEP optical system has become the de facto standard within the virtual reality industry.

FIGURE 3-23   LEEP stereoscopic wide-angle viewing optics

FIGURE 3-24   Field of view provided by the LEEP system

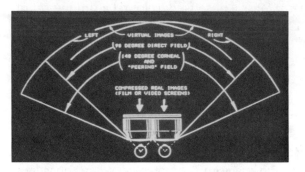

❋ ❋ ❋

Display Hardware

The final step in presenting visual virtual environments is, as Stephen Sondheim would say, putting it together. Position/orientation trackers, imaging devices, and specialized optics must work as a single unit. The resulting display hardware comes in all shapes and sizes, and though they all have roughly the same types of components, they vary widely in usability and configuration. The three basic display methods are stereoscopic head mounted, monocular head mounted, and head coupled. In this last section, we'll look at each of these, what they do, and how their images are presented to our eyes.

Note that many of these products are usually coupled with audio headphones and gesture/voice-recognition devices. We'll cover those technologies in later chapters.

Stereoscopic Head-Mounted Displays

If you were to sit down and try to create a single unit that included position/orientation tracking, imaging devices, and optics, you would probably come up with something that looked like a giant pair of goggles mounted on a helmet. You wouldn't be the first to think of it. These complex helmets are called head-mounted displays, and researchers have been working with them for the past twenty-five years. In this section we'll take a look at the various types that exist as of this writing. While new models will most certainly continue to be developed, those discussed here should offer a general understanding of head-mounted display techniques.

Sutherland's Sword of Damocles. Ivan Sutherland, one of the earliest pioneers in computer graphics, is credited with the development of the first head-mounted display in 1968 while he was a student at Harvard University. This device was affectionately known as the Sword of Damocles because it hung from the ceiling by a large and ominous-looking arm that served as a mechanical position tracker (see Figure 3-25).

FIGURE 3-25 Sutherland's Sword of Damocles

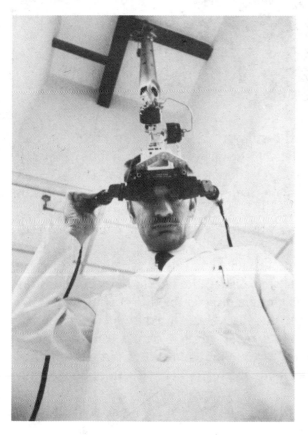

Sutherland used two small CRTs mounted to the sides of the helmet to display basic wire-frame stereo images. These images were reflected off glass lenses and into the eyes by simple optical components. The system was capable of displaying simple wire-frame geometric shapes that appeared overlaid on the user's true physical surroundings (see Figure 3-26).

FIGURE 3-26   Shapes overlaid on reality, as in Sutherland's system

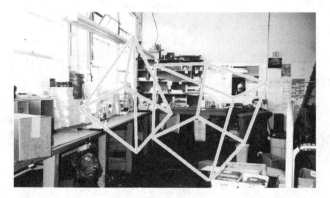

NASA head-mounted displays. In 1984 scientists at NASA's Ames Research Center, in Moffet Field, California, began efforts to develop their own stereoscopic head-mounted displays for research in telerobotics and space station management. With only a small operating budget and a desire to develop systems that were above all practical, the NASA scientists pursued low-cost alternative head-mounted displays.

The initial NASA virtual reality head-mounted display was built from a pair of relatively inexpensive Radio Shack black and white pocket televisions, which were disassembled to acquire their LCDs and their light sources. These LCDs measured 2.7 inches diagonally and had a resolution of 320 by 240 pixels. Not only were these LCDs significantly less expensive than miniature CRTs, but they also had extremely low power requirements, a necessity in building lightweight devices.

The LCD display provides 76,800 pixel elements with which to build an image. Not only is this not enough pixels to create a detailed image, but the operating distance between display and viewer effectively reduces the resolution even further. Most miniature liquid crystal displays are designed to be viewed from about 2 feet away. At that distance, the individual pixels are too small to be seen, so the images appear relatively sharp.

When you look more closely at an LCD, the image detail is reduced because you can actually see the individual pixels of light that make up the image. The same thing happens in magazine photographs. From a normal viewing distance, the image looks clean and sharp. But if you look closely, you can see that the picture is actually created by thousands of tiny colored dots, and the image no longer seems clear.

As LCD technology evolves, these limitations may become less of a problem. Nonetheless, the benefits of LCDs still outweigh the negative factors, and NASA is continuing to use them in its head-mounted displays (see Figure 3-27).

FIGURE 3-27   A recent NASA head-mounted display

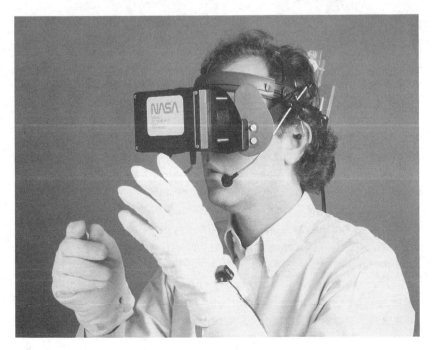

UNC head-mounted displays. Although researchers at the University of North Carolina have been developing head-mounted displays since the early 1980s, they are, perhaps, best known for the one they developed in 1989 with the Air Force Institute of Technology at Wright-Patterson Air Force Base. This innovative head-mounted display is built on and around a bicycling helmet (see Figure 3-28).

FIGURE 3-28   UNC/AFIT head-mounted display

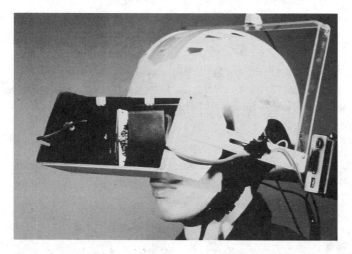

A container that houses two LCDs, fluorescent backlighting fixtures, and specialized optics is positioned on the front of the helmet on small support arms connected to the sides of the helmet. The electronics that control the display are carried in a small box mounted toward the rear of the helmet. Note that it's critical to balance the various elements of a head-mounted display or else it will forever be falling off or shifting on your head.

In designing their head-mounted display with LCDs, the UNC researchers had an obstacle in their way: the nose. If you place a large LCD plate in front of each eye, you have the choice of either dispensing with the nose or moving the LCDs too far away from the eye. The former is, well, uncomfortable, and the latter results in the center of the LCDs not lining up with the eye's optical axis. UNC researchers developed a third solution: angle the LCDs away from the nose (see Figure 3-29). The process sounds easier than it is. When

FIGURE 3-29   UNC/AFIT head-mounted display diagram

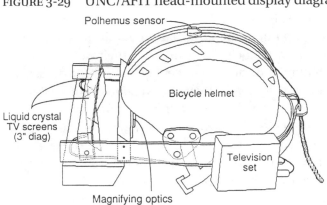

the images are tilted away from the face, they must be optically corrected for, or else the virtual environment will look askew.

The color LCDs used in the UNC system measure 3 inches diagonally. Early versions used only simple magnifying optics, and the user was able to experience a horizontal field of view of approximately 55 degrees. More recently, researchers replaced the original optics with the LEEP optical components described earlier in this chapter, significantly boosting the field of view and offering a significantly better sense of immersion. Position and orientation of the user's head is tracked through the use of a Polhemus magnetic positioning system.

While this display was developed as a laboratory research system—not for commercial sale—it strongly demonstrates the relative ease of constructing such systems from off-the-shelf products and proves that it's possible to piece together an LCD-based head-mounted display for less than half of what the commercially available systems cost.

More UNC head-mounted displays. The NASA and the UNC LCD-based head-mounted displays that we've discussed both operate by placing a light source and LCDs in a dark housing in front of the eyes. While wearing one of these, all you can see is the computer's graphic images. Remember, however, that Sutherland's original model displayed graphics as overlaying on the world around the user. This type of head-mounted display has some very exciting applications. For example, someone operating heavy machinery could call up important information about the equipment or the job without moving their eyes away from their work.

Building on Sutherland's design concept of a see-through display, UNC researchers have developed their own version of such a device. In the new UNC design, the LCDs are placed not vertically or at an angle in front of the user's eyes but horizontally, overhanging the helmet at about eyebrow level (see Figure 3-30). These LCDs, acquired from a pair of Seiko television sets, measure 2 inches diagonally and provide a resolution of 220 by 320 pixels.

The images displayed on the LCDs are projected downward, through a magnifying lens, onto a half-silvered mirror mounted at a 45-degree angle away from the user. Anyone wearing the helmet can see not only the reflected images on the mirror's surface, but also the "real world" beyond the glass. This display provides a horizontal view of approximately 25 degrees. Also, in this configuration, the majority of the control electronics are in a fanny pack worn around the user's waist, and the position/orientation tracking is handled by a Polhemus magnetic positioning system.

VPL EyePhone. Any discussion of head-mounted displays would be incomplete without VPL Research's EyePhone series (see Figure 3-31). The first commercially available stereoscopic head-mounted display for virtual reality applications, the EyePhone system uses color LCD displays with a resolution of 360 by 240 pixels and—using the LEEP stereoscopic wide-angle optics—provides a horizontal field of view measuring 100 degrees. A padded and counterweighted frame with side straps holds the display on the head.

A rubber seal like those on scuba diving masks serves to seat the display on the face and block out all ambient light (this rubber seal earned the EyePhone the nickname "the face sucker"). Position and orientation of the EyePhone system is measured using a Polhemus 3Space Isotrack magnetic positioning system. The entire weight of the EyePhone head-mounted display is only 4.25 pounds.

Two other head-mounted displays similar to the EyePhone are worth mentioning. The first, called the Flight Helmet, was developed

FIGURE 3-30   UNC see-through head-mounted display

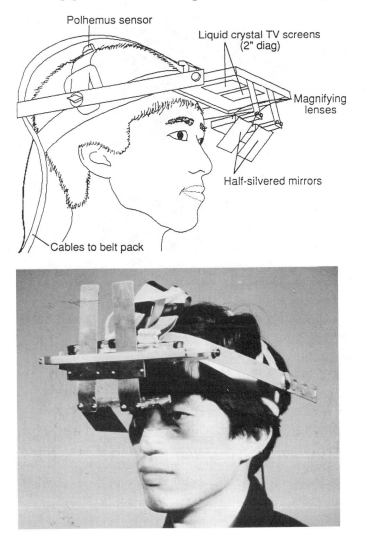

by Virtual Research, in Sunnyvale, California (see Figure 3-32). Weighing in at just under 4 pounds, the Flight Helmet has similar 360-by-240-pixel color LCDs and uses either magnetic position sensors or ultrasonic position trackers built by Logitech. The second, the

FIGURE 3-31   The EyePhone

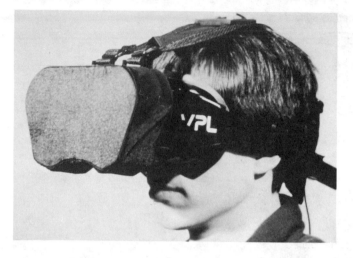

well-designed Visette, was developed by W Industries, of Great Britain, to be the principle display used in the Virtuality arcade game that has become so popular wherever it has appeared (see Color Plate 1). The Visette, perhaps the first publicly accessible virtual reality display system, has two color LCDs, each with a resolution of 276 by 372 pixels and an adjustable field of view measuring between 90 and 120 degrees. Position and orientation tracking is performed by an AC magnetic sensor called the Bird (developed by Ascension Technology) that is much like the Polhemus magnetic positioning system.

EyePhone LX and HRX. The EyePhone LX and EyePhone HRX are updated versions of VPL's original EyePhone system. Completely redesigned for greater comfort and display quality, the LX and HRX use color LCDs that provide a resolution of 422 by 238 pixels and 720 by 480 pixels, respectively. The LEEP optical system used in the original EyePhone has been replaced by proprietary compound Fresnel lenses and diffusion elements that only provide a horizontal field of view of 108 degrees, but weigh significantly less than their predecessors.

While the magnetic position sensors remain unchanged, the actual mounting system has been completely redesigned. Instead of a

FIGURE 3-32   The Flight Helmet

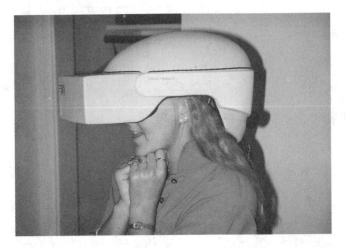

flexible piece of fabric running over the top of the head with a counterweight at the back, there is a more sturdy system called the Saturn Ring mount (see Figure 3-33). The entire weight of the LX system is only 2.5 pounds, just over half the weight of the original EyePhone.

FIGURE 3-33   The EyePhone HRX

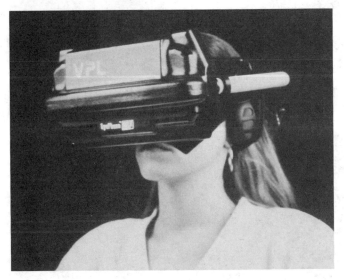

CAE fiber-optic head-mounted display. CAE Electronics, of Montreal, has developed a head-mounted display system that uses bundles of fiber-optic cable to display images (see Figure 3-34). Light-valve projectors feed images through these fiber bundles to the helmet, where they are projected through an optical system to produce a wide-angle stereo display. Beam splitters (half-silvered mirrors) located in front of each eye allow the user to view both real-world and computer-generated scenes simultaneously.

This system uses eye-tracking technology to move a high-resolution graphic inset over a low-resolution background. The inset measures 24 by 18 degrees and sits on top of a 130-by-65 degree background. As we noted earlier in the chapter, this dual-resolution display matches the requirements of rods and cones in the retina and reduces the computational burden of generating high-quality images.

The eye tracking is performed by projecting infrared light from light-emitting diodes (LEDs) along the perimeter of a thin, round glass window, into a mirror that reflects onto the user's eye. The light then reflects back off the mirror and into a camera mounted on the helmet. Image-processing hardware and software determine where the eye is looking by analyzing the LEDs reflection.

FIGURE 3-34   CAE Electronics fiber-optic head-mounted display

LEEPvideo System I: The Cyberface I. LEEP Systems/POP-Optix Labs, the developers of LEEP stereoscopic wide-angle optics, also designs some of the highest performance commercially available head-mounted displays. The LEEPvideo System I, also called the Cyberface I, is the company's first commercial virtual reality product, and it continues to set the standard for other commercial systems.

The Cyberface head-mounted display system is a monochromatic incandescent backlit video display system using twin LCDs with a resolution of 640 by 220 pixels and the LEEP optical system. However, rather than displaying images directly from a computer, the Cyberface is designed to display images gathered from video cameras. Two miniature video cameras mounted on a small head-shaped "puppet" feed images through a small electronics console to the Cyberface system (see Figure 3-35).

The easiest way to use this system to display computer-generated graphics is to remove the video cameras from the puppet head and point them at two monitors. Each monitor can display one eye's view. This technique, while appearing somewhat clunky, is actually more effective than sending images directly from a computer to the Cyberface because it avoids the calculation-intensive nature of LEEP video compression.

FIGURE 3-35   The Cyberface I and the Leep Puppet

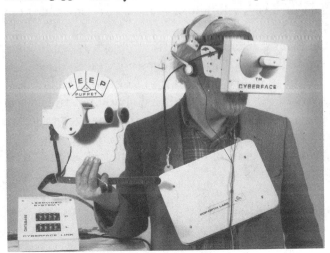

SIM EYE. Kaiser Electro-optics, of Carlsbad, California, has developed a high-resolution stereoscopic head-mounted display for military training and simulation applications called SIM EYE (SIMulation EYE). With applications focusing on simulation of night-vision goggles, mission scenarios, low-altitude flying, and out-of-the-cockpit-window scenes, SIM EYE is considered one of the most high-performance, cost-effective high-end systems commercially available.

SIM EYE is considerably different in appearance and functionality than the other displays described in this chapter. One-inch diameter monochromatic CRTs providing a resolution of 1280 by 1024 pixels are mounted on the sides of a lightweight composite helmet. Images are passed from the CRTs, through a complex optical system, to a round combiner in front of each eye. This allows the system to overlay computer-generated graphics onto the user's real-world surroundings.

Alternate Reality Vision System. One of the problems with most head-mounted displays is getting a full field of view from images shown on a small, flat, two-dimensional LCD or CRT display. Even with LEEP optics, the largest field of view available is about 108 degrees horizontal, which isn't even close to the over-250-degree horizontal field we can see without moving our head (see "Field of View," earlier in this chapter). However, a few years ago, Concept Vision Systems, of Conway, Washington, created a system that broke through this barrier.

The Alternate Reality Vision System (ARVIS) uses a combination of specially designed curved display screens and finely tuned contact lenses to create an enormous 240-by-120-degree field of view that immerses you in the image entirely. The contact lenses are of such high optical power—designed to make the images on the two concave display screens appear at the proper distance from your face—that you would never want to wear them outside of the ARVIS environment.

Concept Vision Systems promises to have a new head-mounted display by the end of 1992 that will be much more user friendly than the original. Not only will it not have contact lenses, but it will have a significantly higher resolution than most other systems (but until the company's patents are completed, they're not saying anything about the new technology other than that people will say, "It's so obvious, why didn't I think of it!").

Monocular Head-Mounted Displays

In the previous section, we explored stereoscopic head-mounted displays, including devices that allow the user to see both computer-generated images and the real world beyond. However, some researchers have also developed monocular (one-eyed) head-mounted displays that deserve mention, particularly the Private Eye.

Private Eye. Reflection Technologies, of Waltham, Massachusetts, has developed a unique monocular head-mounted display, which uses a rather innovative image-display technology. Known as the Private Eye, the entire system measures 1.2 by 1.3 by 3.5 inches and is suspended from a lightweight headband in front of one eye (see Figure 3-36). Wearers see what appears to be a 12-inch computer screen floating in midair about 2 feet in front of them.

Because our eyes can accommodate both the display and the real world around us, we can effectively use the Private Eye as a virtual overlay. The Private Eye can also display information or images that have little to do with our surroundings. Some people have even suggested that this device could be the perfect Walkman for watching TV or movies.

The Private Eye employs a strikingly effective means of creating images. Instead of using a miniature CRT or LCD, the image is created by a column of 280 red light-emitting diodes (LEDs). Opposite the column of LEDs is a mirror that rapidly pivots back and forth. As this mirror oscillates, each LED rapidly flickers on and off at a rate of 720 times per mirror swing cycle.

The blinking of the LEDs and the movement of the mirror is carefully synchronized and results in the appearance of a tiny screen with a resolution of 280 horizontal pixel lines by 720 pixel columns. You can adjust the display's small optical elements to change where the screen appears in space. For example, the screen, filled with

FIGURE 3-36   The Private Eye

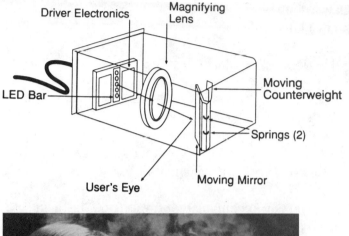

monochromatic red lines on a solid black background, could appear to be 9 inches away or 90.

While a single unit provides images to only one eye, two Private Eyes can be used simultaneously to produce a stereoscopic image, as was recently demonstrated by researchers in the Department of Computer Science at the University of Virginia.

Hughes Aircraft is presently developing an interesting application for the Private Eye system. Modern-day aircraft technicians must constantly access vast amounts of system documentation for repair and maintenance procedures while they work. But shifting their attention between the documentation and the mechanics is inefficient and potentially dangerous. The new system would allow technicians to see documentation "hands free" by floating it in front of their eyes using the Private Eye attached to a hip-mounted computer. Of course, when they don't need the information, technicians can flip the Private Eye up and out of the way.

Head-Coupled Displays

There's no denying that head-mounted displays, while effective, are just plain cumbersome. For virtual reality applications such as engineering or mathematical analysis, a more flexible device is preferred. For example, an architect might quickly tire of putting a head-mounted display on to observe a rendering of a building, then removing it to make a telephone call, then putting it back on.

The primary solution to this encumbrance problem is a head-coupled, rather than a head-mounted, display. The head-coupled display can be placed in front of the eyes with ease and removed just as quickly. As some VR scientists say, "No fuss, no muss!" Let's look at two types of head-coupled displays: the BOOM and the Fop.

Binocular Omni Orientation Monitor. In 1990 researchers from NASA's Ames Research Center developed the first head-coupled display and called it the Binocular Omni Orientation Monitor, or BOOM. The BOOM is now a product of Fake Space Labs, of Menlo Park, California. Other than the LEEP optics employed in the BOOM system, there are almost no similarities between head-mounted systems and this head-coupled device (see Figure 3-37).

Instead of the LCDs that have become standard in most head-mounted displays, the BOOM uses small CRTs as an image source. As we discussed earlier, CRTs can produce individual picture elements (pixels) considerably smaller than LCDs, so the images can be finer and contain better shading and smoothing. The Fake Space BOOM's CRTs measure about 2.5 inches diagonally and provide a resolution of 1280 by 500 pixels in color mode and 1280 by 1024 in monochrome mode.

The BOOM display is housed in a small black box attached to a two-section arm. You can look into this box through two eyeholes and move the box around by grabbing the handles attached to it.

FIGURE 3-37   Binocular Omni Orientation Monitor

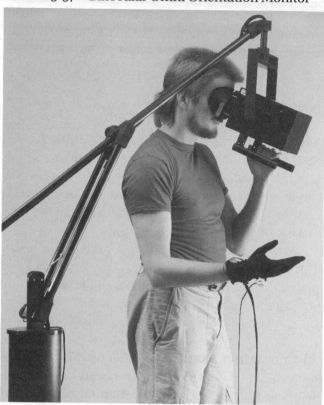

The entire system is carefully balanced so that when you let go of the display, the box hangs in space, waiting to be grabbed again.

As it turns out, this head-coupled display has proven to be better suited to most applications than head-mounted displays. Not only is the BOOM significantly easier to "put on" and "take off," but the mechanical position/orientation tracking handled by measuring changes in the joints of the armature is extremely precise. This precision is, of course, a tremendous benefit in engineering and scientific visualizations (see Chapter 8, *Architecture and Design,* and Chapter 12, *The Sciences*).

EyePhone XVR. While VPL Research's most recent addition to its list of commercial head-mounted displays is officially called the

EyePhone XVR, it's usually just called the Fop (see Figure 3-38). Aside from the fact that this system uses the same LCDs as the EyePhone LX, there are almost no similarities between this and the other VPL products.

The Fop lets the user view computer-generated images in two different ways. The first is as a normal head-mounted display, much like the EyePhones described earlier. The second is as a hand-held head-coupled display. The head-mounting structure is removed and replaced with a handle called the ZoomGrip. The position/orientation sensors are built directly into the display housing, so as you hold the display in hand and move it about, the images change. The nickname the Fop arose because people look as though they are looking through a pair of old-style opera glasses when using the

FIGURE 3-38   The EyePhone XVR

EyePhone XVR with the ZoomGrip. The entire device weighs only 2.5 pounds.

❋   ❋   ❋

The Power of Sight

Finally, we must look carefully at whether three-dimensional interactive displays are truly helpful. This question can't simply be answered with a yes or no. To begin with, because the field of virtual reality is still relatively young, research efforts are only now beginning to tackle the question of how effective or potentially dangerous virtual reality is (see Chapter 15, *Human Factors*). As when exploring any new technology, researchers must first acquire the necessary hardware and software before they can test it. But not until recently have the products' prices and availability arrived at a point where large numbers of scientists could obtain them.

Nonetheless, there is an enormous body of literature that shows that stereo displays are highly useful in interpreting some data. But virtual reality has many more elements than just stereoscopic displays. For example, take the concept of immersion. While there are a variety of tasks in which immersive displays are obviously helpful (such as molecular bonding or telepresence), there are many other areas in which it would either be inappropriate or simply overkill. For example, a word-processing program like the one we used to write this book or a simple database might actually be more confusing to use in a virtual environment.

However, as we've discussed, humans are spatial information processors. We see, hear, and move in three dimensions. Therefore, in general, any application that involves the evaluation of or interaction with data that represents either a physical object or an inherently three-dimensional phenomenon should benefit from the use of VR. As we've seen already (and will explore more fully in Part 3, *Applications in Virtual Reality*), architectural walk-throughs, air-traffic control, and most forms of entertainment fall into this category.

Another issue when discussing the usability of virtual reality is that of scope. A wide field of view might be detrimental to a task that focuses on a particular area, such as drawing technical illustrations, where distractions might be more of a problem than a solution. However, the stereoscopic view capability may still be quite useful. On the other hand, as we saw earlier, driving or exploring, which both require a wide visual scope alongside the ability to focus, would be dangerous or confusing with a narrow field of view.

Clearly, there's more to creating usable virtual realities than the visual display. In the next chapter, we'll look at sound and hearing, and how three-dimensional sound fields can aid in creating immersive virtual environments.

CHAPTER 4

Hearing

✿   ✿   ✿

We saw in the previous chapter how incredibly sensitive our sense of sight is and how we use it to gather an enormous amount of information about the real or virtual world around us. But sight is only one of many senses, and although we depend on sight a great deal, you may be surprised at how important our other senses are to us. Sound, for example, is crucial to most people's lives, although we usually don't consider it outside of listening to music or eavesdropping in on a conversation. Consider hearing a door opening in another room, a car approaching from behind, or a telephone ringing. In each of these examples, we couldn't respond appropriately without our sense of hearing.

Nonetheless, until just the past few years, work in virtual reality and computer-interface design has focused primarily on creating a better visual display or designing a more ergonomic mouse, and sound research was left to the music and audio industries. More recently, however, it has been demonstrated that using sound to supply alternative or supplementary information to a computer user can greatly increase the amount of information they can ingest. This is especially true in situations where visual cues are limited or non-existent, such as working with people who are blind or in low-light areas, but may be equally true in other, less restrictive applications.

For example, one of the goals of graphical user interfaces like the Macintosh or Windows operating system has been to create an officelike environment: a trash can over here, a file cabinet over there, and so on. It's a great approach, but the problem is that computer screens are too small, and they become cluttered with windows and icons.

Researchers are now looking at virtual reality interfaces that can extend your work space considerably by creating a three-dimensional virtual room. You could hang a message from your secretary in midair behind your peripheral vision until you needed it again (the equivalent of sticking it under a pile of papers on your desk). However, if you're like we are, you'd probably forget that it was there at all. One option might be a virtual sound attached to the memo that beeps every so often, reminding you not only that it's there, but of its exact location.

In this chapter, we look at sound: what it is, how we hear it, and how researchers are now using it for virtual reality applications. We also explore the differences between two- and three-dimensional sound and why creating a digitally synthesized 3-D sound field is as exciting a breakthrough as creating 3-D visual environments. Along the way, we look at some of the interesting applications of 3-D sound in virtual reality.

✿ ✿ ✿

Sound

All sounds, regardless of where they come from or what they sound like, are the result of some force causing an object to vibrate back and forth. These vibrations push the molecules in the air and cause them to collide into other molecules, which collide into other molecules, and so on. These collisions result in waves of air pressure that our ears turn into sound.

You can think of these waves as ripples in a pond of water. When you throw a pebble into a pond, small waves spread in all directions (see Figure 4-1). The waves are caused literally by water molecules striking other water molecules. The water doesn't really move outwards; only the general energy of the rippling wave. Similarly, in sound traveling through the air, the air doesn't really move; only the energy, passing as pressure from one molecule to another.

Of course, sound doesn't only travel through the air. Sound waves can pass through any medium, as long as it is dense enough (has enough molecules) to sustain the pressure. In fact, the speed at which sound travels through a given medium is a function of how densely packed the molecules in that medium are. The higher the density, the faster the sound travels. For example, sound moves through room-temperature air, a rather loosely packed medium, at about 340 meters per second; it moves through water, which is

FIGURE 4-1 ⟨ Waveforms

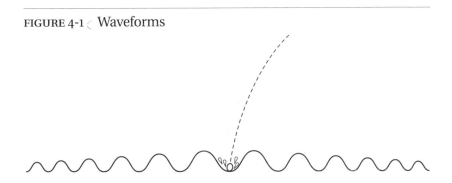

denser than air, at approximately 1,500 meters per second; and through hardened steel at more than 5,000 meters per second (which is why you can hear a train coming from far off by listening to the tracks).

The logical conclusion, then, is if there is no medium—such as in the vacuum of outer space—there is no sound. This was demonstrated in the seventeenth century by British physicist-chemist Robert Boyle. Boyle placed a bell inside a glass jar and, after sealing the container, pumped out all the air and rang the bell. No sound was heard. After refilling the jar with air, however, the sound could be heard again.

Sound waves are also like ripples in a pond in that they grow weaker as they progress from their source. The speed at which the sound (or water ripple) moves remains the same, but the intensity of the wave diminishes. This is why a whisper and a shout both travel at the same speed, but one can only be heard from close by.

Frequency and Amplitude

The curve shown in Figure 4-2 represents a sound wave. The height of a sound wave, commonly referred to as amplitude, is a measure of intensity or loudness. Amplitude is expressed in decibels (dB). Generally, when the physical intensity of a sound increases by 10 dB, its perceived loudness doubles. To give you a better idea of

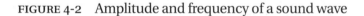

FIGURE 4-2   Amplitude and frequency of a sound wave

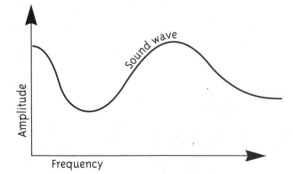

what decibel measurements are like, someone whispering is about 20 dB, normal speech is about 60 dB, and the roar of a subway train measures in at about 90 dB. Our threshold for pain is about 120 dB.

The number of wave peaks (or valleys, depending on how you look at it) that pass a fixed point each second is called the frequency of a sound wave. Frequency is expressed in a unit of measure called hertz (Hz). The frequency of a sound wave has a direct correlation to the sound's tone. Low frequencies are low tones, such as a rumbling train or a fog horn. High frequencies are high tones, such as whistles and screeches.

Echoes

If you let a single drop fall into a metal pot filled with water, you can see not only the ripple effects we talked about earlier, but also an interesting side effect: when the ripple hits the side of the pot, it reflects back at some angle. Part of the reflected wave returns back to the origin (where the drop of water fell). This reflection is called an echo.

Echos don't only happen with water, of course. All waves echo, including sound waves. You can hear an echo clearly when it bounces off a distant mountain (the "Heidi effect") or even if you clap your hands in an empty movie theatre. Many human-made and natural navigational aids have developed from this effect, such as the ability of a bat to hunt insects in darkness or a boat to locate fish in water (see "Echolocation," later in this chapter).

Human Audibility

As we noted earlier, the change in air pressure results from molecules moving slightly and bouncing into each other. A louder, more intense sound pushes the molecules harder and farther; a quiet sound pushes them very little. The human ear is extremely sensitive: it can detect air-pressure changes resulting from air molecules shifting one-tenth of their own diameter. To get a sense of how small that is, think of the smallest piece of dust imaginable floating in the air. An air molecule is about one hundred thousandth the size of that speck.

Figure 4-3 shows the range of auditory perception in human be-ings. Notice that the overall area of perception is bounded by two threshold curves, one delineating the lowest perceivable sound lev-els and the other delineating the threshold of pain. These measures

---

FIGURE 4-3   Human audibility

0 Threshold of hearing

10 Normal breathing

20 Leaves rustling in a breeze

30 Empty movie house

40 Residential neighborhood at night

50 Quiet restaurant

60 Two-person conversation

Beginning of danger level   70 Busy traffic

Annoying   80 Vacuum cleaner

90 Water at foot of Niagara Falls

Prolonged exposure can cause hearing loss   100 Subway train

120 Propeller plane at takeoff

130 Machine gun fire, close range

Threshold of pain   140 Jet at takeoff

160 Wind tunnel

are unique to human beings. For instance, bats are sensitive to frequencies in the sonar range and dogs are sensitive to sounds in the ultrasonic range. Young adults can hear sounds as low as 20 Hz and as high as 20,000 Hz.

In the simplest sense, we hear sounds by registering the vibrations of the sound waves in the ear. If you stand next to a speaker playing music loudly, you can often feel the rumbles of the low frequency sounds and the buzzing of the higher frequency sounds on your skin and clothes. The auditory system is basically a highly evolved extension of this same sense of touch.

✿   ✿   ✿

The Auditory Pathway

Now that we know something about sound and how it works, let's explore how humans hear sounds and how we can use them to create 3-D audio environments. To do this, we will follow the sound's path from when it first strikes the outer ear to when it registers in the brain.

The Outer Ear

When sound waves reach our ear, they initially strike the pinna, the curved appendage growing out from the sides of our head. The complex, curved surface of the pinna actually directs sound into the hole in the center. The pinna also has a specific role in locating where sounds are coming from (see "Sound Localization," later in this chapter). The hole at the base of the pinna is the start of the auditory canal.

The auditory canal measures approximately a centimeter in diameter and several centimeters in length, depending, of course, on the size of the head (see Figure 4-4). The shape of the canal acts as the first of several hearing enhancers. It is much like the funny-looking horns that people have stuck in their ears for hundreds of years to concentrate sound waves. The canal's shape increases the sound waves by about 10 dB in intensity by the time they hit the eardrum.

FIGURE 4-4   The human ear

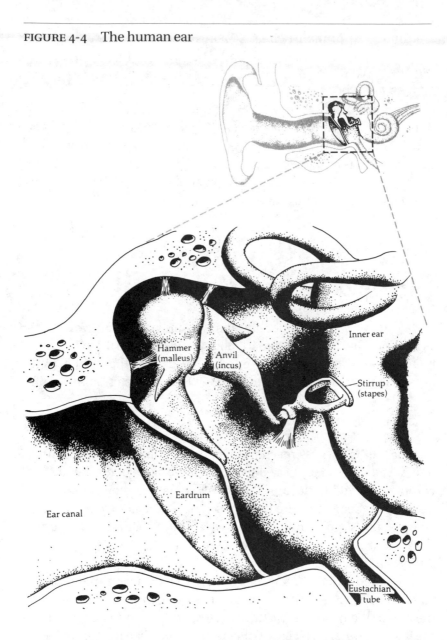

The eardrum sits at the back of the auditory canal, waiting for sound to hit. Its oval shape is structurally supported by an underlying ribbed skeleton similar to an umbrella. Just as sound makes the head of a microphone quiver, sound waves cause the eardrum to vibrate very quickly.

The Middle Ear

The middle ear consists of three tiny bones that form a bridge across an air-filled void. Named for their appearance, the hammer, anvil, and stirrup (or, actually, the malleus, the incus, and the stapes) are connected together by small ligaments. The first of the set, the hammer, is attached to the inside of the eardrum. As the eardrum vibrates, the hammer moves, too. This vibration is passed from the hammer to the anvil and from the anvil to the stirrup. The stirrup is firmly secured to the opening of the inner ear, the oval window.

The mystery of why the middle ear should be so complicated can be solved by seeing these bones not simply as transducers of sound waves, but also as a basic system of levers, which acts as the ear's second sound enhancer. The lever system, along with the difference in size between the eardrum (approximately 80 square millimeters) and the oval window (approximately 3 square millimeters), increases the molecule-sized sound waves that vibrate the eardrum by a factor of about thirty. Without this amplification, we would only be able to hear loud, intense sounds.

The middle ear can also act as a sound inhibitor. For example, when a very loud sound enters the ear, neuromuscular reflexes tighten the eardrum and rotate the stirrup to protect the ear from excessive noise.

The Inner Ear

The sound waves, after passing through and being amplified in the outer and middle ear, finally reach the inner ear, where they are translated into electrochemical signals that can be passed to the brain. In this section we discuss the inner ear in three parts: the cochlea, the organ of Corti, and the auditory nerve.

The cochlea. The cochlea is a spiral-shaped cavity in the skull that is filled with a fluid much like salt water. The entire length of the spiral is made up of three chambers: the vestibular canal, the tympanic canal, and the cochlear duct (see Figure 4-5). The center chamber, the cochlear duct, is smaller than the other two and is separated by membranes that stop fluids from passing between the chambers. However, at the apex of the spiral, the vestibular and tympanic canals actually connect through a small hole.

As we noted above, the stirrup is attached to a small membrane called the oval window, located at the base of the vestibular canal. The sound vibrations passed from the stirrup to the oval window are then transferred to the saline solution in the cochlea. The sound waves of pressure in the air are now waves of pressure in fluid. These waves pulse through the vestibular canal and back down through the tympanic canal. Another membrane located at the base of the tympanic canal, known as the round window, compensates for the displacement of fluid by bulging out into the air-filled space of the middle ear. In short, when the oval window pushes in, the round window pushes out.

FIGURE 4-5   The interior of the cochlea

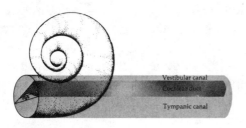

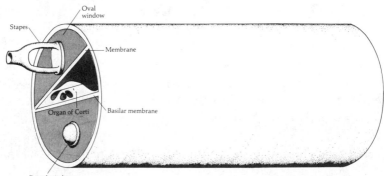

The shape of the membrane between the cochlear duct and the tympanic canal, known as the Basilar membrane, causes an interesting effect: the waveform that moves through the cochlea peaks at a specific place along the canal. This place is determined solely by the frequency of the original sound source. After the sound wave peaks, it quickly drops off and disappears (see Figure 4-6).

Although the idea of the distance that waveforms travel being dependent on frequency is somewhat nonintuitive, you can test this easily in a real-world experiment. First, rest your hand or forearm on a surface that is vibrating at a high frequency, such as an electric shaver or other small electric motor. Note that you can only feel the vibrations in a small area around the source. Next, place your hand or forearm on a low-frequency surface, such as a washing machine or a jack hammer. Now you can feel the vibrations all the way up your arm!

FIGURE 4-6   A waveform in the tympanic canal

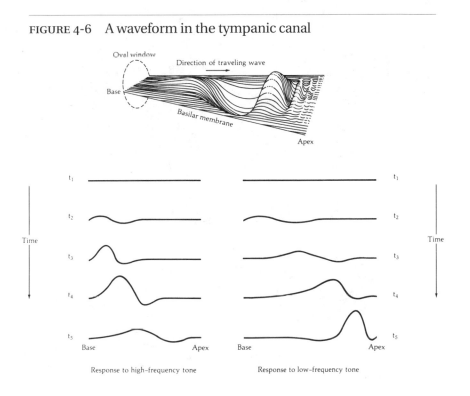

Response to high-frequency tone   Response to low-frequency tone

The organ of Corti. The mechanism that actually converts the fluid waveforms in the tympanic canal to electrochemical events lines the membrane between the cochlear duct and the tympanic canal (see Figure 4-7). This mechanism is the organ of Corti, named after its discoverer, Alfonso Corti.

Although the organ of Corti functions in a totally different manner than the retina of the eye, it performs the similar task of conveying information about waveforms to the brain. Instead of the retina's rods and cones, the organ of Corti has two regions of hair cells that protrude into the fluid of the cochlear duct. As pressure waves move through the fluid, these tiny hairs bend, triggering chemical reactions similar to those in the eye's photoreceptors. There are about 23,500 hair cells measuring sound waves throughout the cochlea.

FIGURE 4-7   The organ of Corti

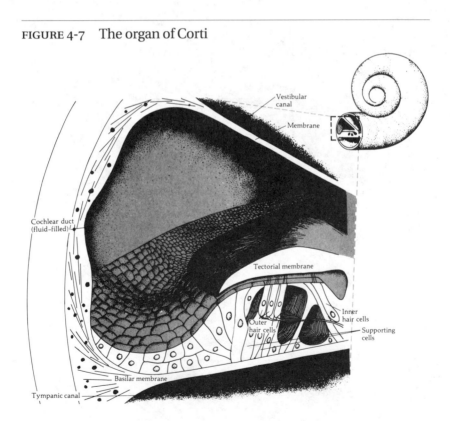

Frequency and intensity (wave amplitude) are easily extracted. The frequency of a sound wave, as we noted above, determines where along the tympanic canal (and therefore along the organ of Corti) the waveform peaks. The intensity of the sound wave determines how far the hair cells bend.

The auditory nerve. Again, similar to our visual system, neural impulses created by the flexing of the hair cells must be channeled to the auditory centers of the brain. The superhighway that carries these electrical impulses is called the auditory nerve. The auditory nerve consists of about 50,000 fibers, each of which is the axon of a nerve cell within the inner ear.

Information about the sounds we hear are conveyed along the auditory nerve from the inner ear to the brain. The auditory system is somewhat more complex than the visual system from this point. Suffice it to say that the path separates into a number of tracks at the cochlear nucleus and ultimately connects to the region of the brain known as the auditory cortex. For reference sake, if you cover your ear with your hand, you are also covering the auditory cortex.

Similar to the visual-information processing system, there are neurons within our auditory system that specialize in detecting specific characteristics of sound that reaches our eardrums. For example, some neurons specialize in sounds that originate in a particular direction, while others note how a tone changes over time. In general, the farther the neuron in the auditory pathway, the higher its level of specialization. A knowledge of how the brain processes sound is helpful in deciding how to build virtual worlds with complex sound cues.

Binaural cells. Until now, we've explored the human auditory system from the perspective of only one ear. That's because until this point in the auditory process, information from our left and right ears has remained separated, i.e. monaural. However, the brain combines the two signals at the cochlear nucleus, and the processing of auditory information becomes a binaural process.

Brain cells that compare information from each of the two ears are called binaural cells, and they play a critical role in determining where a sound originates within the 360-degree audio environment that surrounds us.

✿ ✿ ✿

Sound Localization

We both stand in constant amazement at how precise people's hearing is. Not just how much people can hear, but especially how well people can hear *where* something is in the environment around them. For example, if someone snaps their fingers behind you, you could probably turn around and immediately look at where the sound came from. This function of our hearing is called localization and is crucial to our understanding of how audio cues are used in virtual reality.

Sound localization is similar to seeing in three dimensions. You can actually create a three-dimensional audio "picture" of your environment in your head : that car is behind you, this person is to your left, and so on. This audio picture can be extremely effective in helping to create a sense of immersion in an environment. For example, bicyclists use audio cues to know what's coming up behind them. With practice, they can actually tell how close a car is and how far they had better move over to accommodate it.

And just as a person with sight in only one eye has difficulty extrapolating 3-D information while stationary, a person with hearing in only one ear often cannot tell exactly where a sound is coming from unless they pivot their head around for additional cues.

Extensive research has been conducted over the past three decades on the psychological and psychoacoustical models of directional and spatial perception. This research has shown that sound localization in humans is derived from three primary phenomena: time differences, intensity differences, and acoustic shadows. Each of these must be taken into account when synthesizing three-dimensional sounds on a computer.

Interaural time differences. If you can picture sound moving as a series of waves through space, it's easy to see that sound originating from a source to the left or right of a person arrives at each ear at slightly different times. For example, if the sound source is to the left of the head, the sound reaches the left ear prior to the right one. This is called interaural (between the ears) time difference. We experience the greatest interaural time differences when the sound source is directly to the side of the head (see Figure 4-8).

Note that when a sound source is directly in front or back of us, or above or below us, the interaural time difference is zero. In other words, in these cases we get almost no information about sound localization from this cue.

Interaural intensity differences. As we explained earlier in this chapter, sound intensity drops off with distance. With this in mind, it's easy to see that there are subtle differences in a sound wave's intensity between the two ears. This is called the interaural intensity difference. For example, a sound coming from our right side sounds louder in our right ear than in our left (see Figure 4-9).

A graph that plots sound intensity versus sound-source direction shows an interesting correlation in interaural intensity differences:

FIGURE 4-8   Interaural time differences

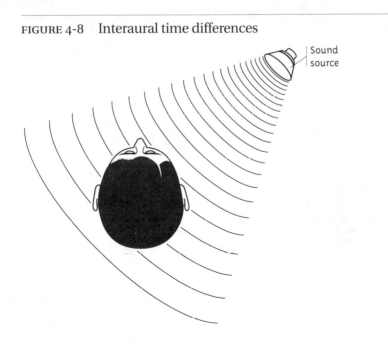

the dependence of intensity on frequency differences. Lower frequency sounds have less dramatic interaural-intensity differences than sounds with higher frequencies. For example, when you listen to an orchestra, the bass appears to have the same intensity in both ears, no matter where it is located; while there is a significant interaural intensity difference in the sound of a clarinet, depending on where it's located in comparison to your head.

The simplest explanation for this effect is that the length of a low-frequency sound wave is actually greater than the diameter of the human head. (In fact, a 100 Hz wavelength traveling through the air is actually about 10 feet long!) Consequently, our ears cannot easily measure the difference in wave intensity (amplitude) between one side of the head and the other. On the other hand, high-frequency sounds have wavelengths much smaller than the distance between our ears, so we can effectively measure differences in intensity.

Acoustic shadow. Another characteristic of high-frequency sounds is their ability to be easily blocked. For example, if you were

---

FIGURE 4-9   Interaural intensity differences

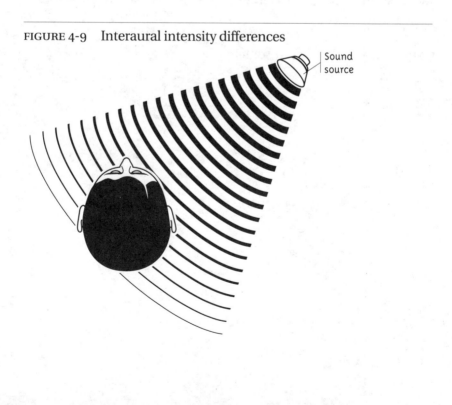

Sound
source

attending a loud outdoor rock concert and stood directly behind a tree, you would notice that the high-frequency guitar and cymbal sounds would drop off considerably, while the deep bass sounds would sound similar whether you were next to the tree or behind it. Indeed, an object needn't even be as large as a tree to deflect high-frequency sounds—a person's head does the trick, too. This effect is called acoustic shadow.

Although an acoustic shadow is similar to an interaural intensity difference, the brain seems to use slightly different criteria for discerning sound waves that have decreased from one side of the head to the other due to natural falloff than for discerning intensity differences due to acoustic shadow.

Additional Factors in Localization

Although interaural time difference, interaural intensity difference, and acoustic shadow are the three primary methods of sound localization, we shouldn't forget several other audiovisual cues that are often just as effective: visual aids, sound familiarity, echolocation, and the pinna. Each of these can both inform and misinform us of the environment around us.

Visual aids. Magicians rely almost exclusively on one basic feature of human nature: we tend to believe what we see. In fact, even if we know that what we're seeing can't be true, we're likely to talk ourselves into believing it. For example, take the trick of cutting someone in half onstage. It looks like the person is getting cut in half. Their screams sound as though they're getting cut in half. In fact, there doesn't seem to be any way for the person *not* to get cut in half. But, of course, they always (well, almost always!) come out of the box in one piece.

Our ability to localize sound also takes this human feature into account, in that when we see something that looks as if it is likely the source of a sound, we actually hear the sound coming from that direction. For example, ventriloquists don't really throw their voices; they just don't move their lips. When we see the dummy moving its lips, our brain makes some assumptions and "recalibrates" so that the sound appears to come from the dummy. Similarly, we hear the sound of voices coming from behind a movie screen as though it were coming precisely from the mouths of the movie characters.

Visual cues are also helpful in audio-ambiguous situations. For example, when the sound of a helicopter flying over a city echoes off buildings, it can be difficult to spot where the helicopter really is. We must see the helicopter to correctly localize the sound.

Sound familiarity. Our familiarity with the sound of an event is also helpful in localization. If you're familiar with cars that have mufflers, the first time you hear one without a muffler you're likely to think it's much closer than it really is. That's because we're used to cars sounding a certain way from a certain distance, and the mufflerless car is louder and harsher than the muffled one.

Movies sometimes also point out this audio/visual connection to us. For example, in some scenes, the distance at which the actors appear and the sound level at which you hear their voices may offer you very different cues. The actors might appear ten feet away, but sound as though they were right next to the microphone (which, in fact, they probably were in the over-dubbing process). And while most people generally follow their visual cues, this juxtaposition could cause some confusion.

Echolocation. As we noted earlier in this chapter, sound echoes are a natural way for us to get information about our environment. This is called echolocation. By evaluating the way we hear sound waves bouncing off the walls around us, we can get a sense of the spaciousness and content of a room. For example, there is a distinct difference between sounds in an empty warehouse and sounds in your living room. Also, if you're standing in a room, echolocation can help you figure out how close you are to the walls.

Of course, much of what is accomplished through echolocation is redundant with visual cues (you can probably *see* how close you are to a wall); in a virtual environment, however, sound cues may offer misinformation if they don't take echolocation into account. For example, architects working with an architectural walk-through of a symphony concert hall require precise echolocation cues. These cues depend on the size of the room, what's in it (a room full of people sounds very different than the same room without people), and the materials of the walls.

Nonetheless, note that echoes often appear to hinder sound localization more than they enhance it. The helicopter scenario described above is a good example.

The pinna. As we mentioned earlier, the pinnas play a critical role in our ability to localize sound. As acoustic energy approaches our ears, it first hits the pinna, where it is "colored," or "marked," while reflecting off of the irregular, folded surface. The particular manner in which the sounds are marked by the pinnas identifies the direction from which it originated.

While we don't recommend trying this experiment, if you were to switch pinna with your best friend, you would each experience considerable difficulty localizing sound sources. Each person's pinna is like a fingerprint, and when sound is colored differently, we no longer recognize the coding.

Errors in sound localization. Earlier in this section we talked about the potential for error in sound localization. This happens primarily when a sound hits both ears at the same time, as when the source is directly in front or back of us. However, while it's feasible that misjudgments in localizing an unobstructed sound can occur, it actually rarely does. The main reason for this is that our heads almost never remain totally still. And even the slightest deviation from midline positioning results in interaural time and intensity differences and, therefore, nonambiguous localization information.

The Cocktail Party Effect

Imagine standing in a room crowded with people talking in small groups. With some concentration, you can listen in on any one of these conversations, then shift your attention to another conversation, and so on around the room. This ability to "pull out" particular sounds from a bunch of ambient noise is known as the "cocktail party effect."

The interesting thing about this ability is that it only works with binaural hearing. If you loose the hearing in one ear, it's extremely difficult to make any sense from the barrage of sound. You can test this even more easily by recording the sound from a party from the middle of the room. Even if you record in stereo, the cocktail party effect doesn't work when you play the recording back.

✿   ✿   ✿

Computer-Generated Sound

While over the past thirty years a host of computer graphics experts have been pushing the boundaries of what computers can display, audio experts have been stretching computers in order to create more realistic (and surrealistic) sounds. In fact, if you listen to popular music radio stations, you may have heard their progress without even knowing it. Synthesizers and audio recording are now so advanced that we can create, edit, and play back sound through an almost entirely digital process. And digital means perfect.

Perfect sound means that you cannot tell the difference between the original and the copy; nor the difference between the copy and a computer-synthesized version. In this section, we'll explore how we can capture and create sound, and how computers are opening a whole new realm of three-dimensional sound. Then we'll look at the application of these sound fields in virtual realities.

Stereo Sound

A channel of sound carries information for one speaker. For example, each speaker in your home sound system or in a pair of headphones receives one channel of sound from the amplifier. In a monoaural (mono) system, like that on an old record or from a television program, there is only one channel of sound; it can be sent to two or more speakers, but the speakers all get the same information. Stereo sound, on the other hand, carries two channels of sound: the left channel and the right channel.

Imagine that you're wearing a pair of headphones and listening to a recorded tape of someone speaking. If the majority of the sound is coming from the left side, the voice appears to be on your left (see

"Interaural intensity differences" earlier in this chapter). If the two channels' volume levels switch, the voice appears to be on your right. If the sound is coming equally from both speakers, the sound appears to be directly in the middle of your head. Note that if sound is *only* coming from one side or the other, the brain no longer localizes the sound as coming from the left, right, or "inside."

3-D Sound

With basic recording and playback techniques, such as most stereo sound, any sense of sound localization is constricted to directly to the left, directly to the right, and somewhere in between. This "somewhere in between" may sound like it's coming from all around; however, when discussing three-dimensional sound localization, there's very little difference between sound appearing inside the head and sound appearing everywhere at once.

How, then, can we create a sound that appears from a particular place in our environment? How can we create a sound that appears to be behind us or above us or anywhere else in three-dimensional space? This problem is much like creating a three-dimensional visual effect even though we only have two eyes. All the subtle cues described in "Sound Localization" earlier in this chapter, such as interaural intensity differences and acoustic shadow, must be used to carefully craft the two sound channels that reach our ears.

Note that we've casually been using the word "appear" when talking about sound. Even though we don't see sound, VR researchers commonly speak as though we do. For example, sound is "displayed" with audio displays. We don't know where this tendency to use visual metaphors for aural experiences started, but it was long before virtual reality. In fact, you're probably familiar with comments such as, "Do you *see* what I'm saying?" and "*Watch* what happens when I turn the volume up."

Recording Sound in 3-D

Fred Wrightman and Doris Kistler have conducted extensive testing in displaying three-dimensional sound at the University of Wisconsin. A typical experiment goes as follows. A subject is seated in an anechoic (nonechoing) chamber. Next, small probe microphones are placed deep within each of the subject's ears, close to the eardrum. A tone is then played through one of 144 speakers positioned around the person's head, and the sound is recorded through the microphones (see Figure 4-10). This recording captures the tone after it has been affected by the head, the pinna, and the auditory canal. Another tone is played and recorded, and then another, and so on.

The second stage of the experiment is removing the microphones and playing the recorded tones back to the subject through a pair of headphones. As if by magic, the tones actually appear as though they are coming from the three-dimensional environment around the subject! Note that when a subject listens to a recording made from their own ears, they have no problem localizing the sound. However, when a recording made from one person's ears is played back for a difference person, the listener experiences a large number of inaccuracies in localization. Once again, this shows that our pinna and how we hear three-dimensional sound are truly as personal as our fingerprints.

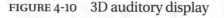

FIGURE 4-10   3D auditory display

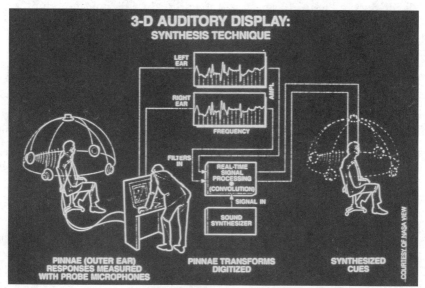

Of course, recording and playing back three-dir[...]
isn't limited to simple tones. Take, for example, the[...]
that Chris Currell, a leader in computer-generated[...]
founder of Virtual Audio Systems, conducts. He lead[...]
a room and seats them in a chair, placing a pair [...]
headphones on their head and a blindfold over their eyes. He then
proceeds to walk around the room, telling the person about the system, how it works, and how the demo will proceed. All of a sudden,
the door opens and four or five people loudly come into the room,
interrupting the demonstration. Obviously the demo can't continue,
so Chris tells the person to take the blindfold and headphones off.
And, much to the subject's surprise, the room is empty. In fact, the
room had been empty ever since the blindfold had been put on, and
the entire discourse and interruption have been recorded.

While this recording/playback process sounds like the answer to
the dream of three-dimensional virtual sound, it really isn't. Just as
movies (even 3-D movies) aren't really three-dimensional and interactive, a recorded audio tape can never truly be interactive either. In
reality, when you turn around, sounds that were behind you are now
in front of you. But when listening to a prerecorded audio tape with
headphones, sounds that are "behind" you always sound behind
you, no matter where you turn or look.

Virtual Sound

The trick to creating a truly three-dimensional, interactive sound
space is, of course, to use computers to generate sounds in real time
rather than rely on sounds that are prerecorded. Most of us rely so
heavily on our visual system that it's hard to even consider what a
sound space is. However, imagine a room with a table and couch in
it. On the table is a small radio, tuned to your favorite station. Wherever you are in the room, some of the sound reaches you directly
from the radio's speaker and some of the sound reaches you after
rippling through the air, bouncing off the walls and the couch.

In a virtual reality, you must be able to move anywhere in that
room and maintain the sense that the music is coming from the radio on the table. For example, if you turn away from the radio, the

_nd should be behind you, and so on. To do this, the computer must use a combination of position/orientation tracking and exquisitely difficult math.

Creating an Audio Earprint

We learned earlier that the curves and folds of the pinna are as unique as fingerprints. As acoustic energy reaches our ears, the pinnas color it, helping us to localize the sound in our environment. Researchers, including Klaus Genuit and Hans Gierlich, of Germany, and the aforementioned Fred Wrightman and Doris Kistler, have created mathematical models that represent the various sound modifications we rely on to hear sound in three dimensions. These models, which we think of as audio "earprints," are called head-related transfer functions (HRTFs).

Researchers can feed these head-related transfer functions, which are developed using techniques similar to the 144-speaker sphere described above, into a computer in the form of mathematical equations. The computer then acts as a filter: digitized sounds are generated by the computer or come in from another source, they get filtered using the appropriate HRTFs, and then are sent on to the headphones or speakers.

Convolvotron. Some of the most substantial work in this area has been conducted by NASA's Ames Research Center in collaboration with Scott Foster's Crystal River Engineering, of Groveland, California. The result of their research is a set of computer plug-in boards called the Convolvotron. The Convolvotron is an extremely powerful audio digital signal processor (DSP) that changes (convolves) an analog sound source using the HRTF to create a three-dimensional sound effect.

Sound that is computer synthesized or from an external source (like a compact disk) can be filtered through the Convolvotron and placed in space around the listener. For example, you could place a virtual wailing saxophone in one corner of a room and a drum in another part of the room, and then move them around. The three-dimensional audio cues are generated by the Convolvotron's filters and controlled by computer software.

Note that only 144 sound positions are measured in the audio sphere experiment. While it would appear that the Convolvotron could only create sounds in those same 144 positions, in fact any number of positions can be synthesized by interpolating values between each of the positions using linear weighting functions. In this way, the sound-space resolution is significantly higher than 144 positions in 360-degree space, and sound that moves from one place to another moves smoothly rather than jerking from one spot in space to another.

The Convolvatron can simulate up to four sound sources, either moving or static. A Polhemus magnetic positioning system (see "Position/Orientation Tracking" in Chapter 2, *Virtual Immersion*) tracks the user's movement, and information is passed to the computer to adjust the sound appropriately. The effect is that the three-dimensional audio environment is held stable as the user moves within it, and the combination of the three-dimensional sound and the position/orientation tracking creates an extremely realistic environment for the listener.

Virtual Audio Processing System. Virtual Audio Systems is creating a system for what will probably be the first mass-market application of three-dimensional sound: entertainment. Its Virtual Audio Processing System (VAPS) mixes the worlds of noninteractive binaural recording and Convolvotron-like signal processing to generate both live and recorded three-dimensional sound fields. Its literature states that "VAPS is used for recording music, sound effects, or dialog for a stereo format such as compact disk, VCR tape, video disk or broadcasting."

The concept is that in the not-so-distant future we will be able to listen to music and watch movies that include three-dimensional audio effects. A plane flying overhead will really sound as if it's overhead; an MTV guitarist might walk offscreen behind your couch; or a symphony might sound as if you were right onstage, near the violin section one moment and near the timpani the next. One of the amazing things about three-dimensional sound is that you can use the cocktail party effect in a way that you can't with simple stereo sound. As we mentioned earlier, if you record a party from the middle of a crowded room and try and listen to it later, all you'll hear is a barrage of sound; you can't pull conversations out of the crowd, the way you could if you were actually there. However, when the sound you're listening to is recorded or processed using a system like VAPS, you can actually direct your attention to a single conversation, just as if you were actually among a group of people. With a little imagination, you can see how the film and music business might be clamoring to move in this direction.

Once again, note that these recorded three-dimensional sounds are noninteractive. If you get up out of your chair while listening to a 3-D CD while wearing headphones, the saxophone player you heard behind you, remains behind—even if you turn to "face" him. The audio environment, although 3-D, does not remain stable vis-à-vis your position in it. However, with position tracking and real-time computer-generated sound, stable virtual sound spaces could be possible.

Virtual Audio Systems president Chris Currell claims that he is able to take a step further in the three-dimensional audio process and do away with headphones in some situations. By using transaural cross-talk cancellation techniques, his system (as well as some others, such as those developed by Roland Corporation) can stop right-channel information coming out of an ordinary stereo speaker from entering the left ear and vice versa. The more speakers used, the better the three-dimensional effect; but even two speakers will work. Nonetheless, headphones ultimately produce the best sound because they actually hold down the pinna and play the sound directly into the ear, avoiding double-coloration effects.

Complex Acoustic Environments

In most of the above experiments, binaural recordings made with the probe microphones were created within anechoic rooms. But when was the last time you were in an anechoic room? Researchers realized that if the goal was to create realistic three-dimensional sound, then they must study and recreate the complex acoustic cues found in reverberant environments. In other words, if you want to create sounds like those heard inside a room, the subtle echoes that the sound waves make must be taken into account.

Researchers have taken two paths to reach this effect. The first is to create head-related transfer functions through a similar probe-microphone recording process. The HRTFs that result are considerably more complex than the simple anechoic versions and carry with them proportionally larger computational requirements. Nonetheless, when you throw enough computing power at them, even these equations can be solved fast enough for real-time simulation.

Recently, a second method has come into use, similar to the three-dimensional computer-graphics method of ray tracing. Ray tracing is a process of tracing the path of light as it bounces off reflective surfaces. In ray tracing graphic images, each pixel in the image is traced to a corresponding point on an object and is then reflected to a light source, another reflective object, or off into space. A similar process is used in creating virtual sound

In ray tracing sound, extra sound sources are placed behind reflective surfaces (like walls, ceilings, and so on). The computer then figures out how loud these reflective sound sources should be at any given moment. The result is that sound appears to come from the reflector surface.

Both visual and aural ray tracing are extremely computation intensive. So as computers get more powerful and the algorithms for creating these three-dimensional illusions are refined, our ability to create dynamic three-dimensional environments will increase significantly. For example, researchers like Crystal River Engineering's Scott Foster can now create rooms and move walls around, giving the impression that the ceiling is lowering or that the room is getting longer, and so on. In the future, complex three-dimensional models, such as an entire office building or a busy street, will be modeled along with the extremely subtle yet powerful sound cues that accompany them.

✿ ✿ ✿

The Move Toward Sound

Five years ago, Foster thought it would be at least ten years before he'd be able to create interactive virtual sound so convincing as to be indistinguishable from reality. Three years later, the technology had moved so fast that he cut several years off his projection. Now researchers are finding that they can fool some of the people some of the time, and the prognosis for fooling the rest of us in the near future is good.

The development of three-dimensional interactive sound is farther along than its visual counterpart. Not only has the ability to create realistic (and hyperrealistic) sounds come a long way, but so has their inclusion in common technology. Personal computer manufacturers are recognizing the importance of sound and are beginning to incorporate it in their core operating systems. As time passes, there is little doubt that computer-generated sound will become as integral to computer technology as voice and music became to film almost seventy years ago.

CHAPTER 5

Feeling

❀   ❀   ❀

"By placing my hand on a person's lips and throat, I can gain an idea of many specific vibrations and interpret them: a boy's chuckle, a man's 'Whew!' of surprise, the 'Hem!' on annoyance or perplexity, the moan of pain, a scream, a whisper, a rasp, a sob, a choke, and a gasp. The utterances of animals, though wordless, are eloquent to me—a cat's purr, its mew, its angry, jerky, scolding spit; the dog's bow-wow of warning or joyous welcome, its yelp of despair and its contented snore."   —Helen Keller, 1908

It's 5:00 A.M. and you're sleeping peacefully while dreaming about sugar plum fairies or whatever it is that you dream about. All of a sudden: "BUZZZ!" Your alarm clock goes off with a vengeance. Rolling over, you begin to grope around on the nightstand for the alarm. Trying desperately not to open your eyes until the last possible moment, you begin the process of "looking" for the alarm clock with your hands. You first touch a tall, thin metal object with what feels like a lightbulb in it. Groping further, you feel a glass that, when you pick it up, you can tell is empty. Next, you bang your hand into a heavy, solid object that must be the telephone. Finally...small box shape, big dial on side, buttons on top. Yes! And...snooze...

Although our eyes provide us with the greatest amount of sensory information about our physical surroundings, our sense of touch is often the supplier of our most reliable information. It's easy to fool the eyes with optical illusions or simulated sensory data; we only have two eyes and two ears, and we can cover those easily enough with displays and earphones. Our skin, however, surrounds us and is often our primary interface with the outside world. Certainly, whenever there is a conflict in sensory data, touch most often clears up any confusion.

For example, in a dark room, what appears to be a shadow might actually painfully dent your shin when you walk into it. Without a thermometer, your only indication of air temperature on a clear morning may be opening a window and sticking your head out to feel the air. And if you've ever tried to put chains on a tire or thread a nut on a bolt when your hands were cold to the point of numbness, you know exactly how important the sense of touch can be in even basic tasks.

Fooling the Hands

These tasks get no easier in a virtual environment. While you can't bruise your leg on a virtual object, but you may not be able to tell where the object is in the room, either. If you're typing on a virtual keyboard (part of what some people envision as part of a future virtual office desk), it's important to know when your fingers are on the keys as opposed to above or below the keys. Similarly, if you're trying to find a smooth piece of virtual paper, you want to be able to feel its texture.

In virtual realities, the goal is to provide computer-generated sensory data in order to create three-dimensional environments. As you can see, a full-fledged virtual environment would be the poorer for lacking virtual touch. As we will see later in this chapter, virtual touch is helpful in some situations, such as basic manipulation of objects within the virtual environment. But in other situations, virtual touch is critical. For example, it has utmost importance in most telerobotics applications (see Chapter 14, *Telepresence*) and any use of virtual reality in a precision setting such as surgical simulation or the command and control of a jet airplane.

The key to virtual touch is some sort of material pressing against our skin, fooling us into believing that we are actually touching an object in space. Because our hands are our primary manipulators, researchers have focused primarily on fooling our hands and arms. In the future, we may even have virtual sensation in other parts of our bodies.

In this chapter, we look at how we use touch and feeling to interact with the world around us and how this sense is being used in creating virtual realities. As in the previous two chapters, we focus first on the mechanisms of how we feel things. This sets the stage for an exploration of virtual touch and the development of tools to create it.

✿   ✿   ✿

The Mechanisms of Touch

There are two principle systems that provide us with tactile information. The first, known as mechanoreceptors, are extremely sensitive mechanisms that measure pressure or deformation of the skin. Numbering in the hundreds of thousands, the mechanoreceptors are critical in providing information about texture. The second system primarily consists of the complex sets of muscles within our hands, which serve to not only move our fingers around an object but also to send information to the brain about the object itself. For example, you can discover the size, weight, and shape of an object by how hard your muscles have to work to hold it and where the fingers can move around it. This feedback from the muscles and tendons is called proprioception.

Together, the mechanoreceptors and proprioception make up the haptic system, and provide haptic cues that convey information about our tangible environment. In fact, it's interesting to note that while our hands are capable of providing extremely detailed information about any object they are in contact with, in many cases they cannot relay information unless we are moving our fingers. As pointed out in 1925 by David Katz, a pioneer in touch research, our ability to distinguish an object's spatial features is often diminished when the fingers are held stationary. You can get a good idea of this yourself by performing a simple exercise. Close your eyes and press a finger against a page of this book. Next, press the finger against some other flat surface. The feeling is almost exactly the same. Now if you press your finger against each of the surfaces and move it around slightly, you immediately sense the differences in texture.

We'll explore mechanoreceptors and tactile sensations first and then move on to the basics of proprioception.

Tactile Nerves

Because an understanding of the nerve structure helps us better understand the actual receptor cells, we will first look at how tactile signals are passed to the brain and then move back to seeing where those tactile signals come from. Again, although we have haptic sensations all over our body, for simplicity we'll focus on the hands.

Any tactile stimulation in our hands results in information being passed to the spinal cord through two principle nerve tracks: the median and ulnar nerves. These nerves, containing thousands of fibrous axons, originate at and provide information from different regions in the hand. The median nerve spreads out to cover a majority of the palm, all of the thumb, index, and middle fingers, and half of the fourth finger. The ulnar nerve covers the remainder of the palm, half of the fourth finger, and the pinky.

These two bundles of nerves contain two distinct nerve types: slowly and rapidly adapting fibers. Each of these are further broken down into punctate and diffuse fibers. These four nerve types connect to one or more mechanoreceptors in the skin, resulting in certain nerves carrying information about particular areas on the hand. This is similar to our optic system, which contains branching nerves that carry optical information.

Slowly and rapidly adapting fibers. If you briefly press a pencil eraser against the skin of your hand, two types of nerve fibers show activity. The first, known as slowly adapting fibers, responds as soon as the eraser is applied to the skin's surface and continues to show activity as long as the level of pressure is maintained. The second type of nerve fiber, the rapidly adapting fibers, responds with a rapid burst of activity as soon as the eraser is applied, but then reduces and levels off. When the pressure is released, the rapidly adapting fibers show a second burst of activity, again followed by a return to equilibrium.

Punctate and diffuse fibers. As we noted above, both slowly and rapidly adapting fibers are further subdivided into two additional categories. The first, known as punctate fibers, have small, oval-shaped receptive fields, sharply defined boundaries and relatively uniform sensitivity. Information coming from a punctate fiber can tell the brain almost exactly where the sensation is coming from.

Diffuse fibers, on the other hand, possess much larger receptive fields with vague boundaries. In fact, some of the diffuse-fiber receptive fields actually cover a whole finger as well as large regions of the palm. The larger the receptive field, the lower the ability to distinguish detailed characteristics. That is, if a diffuse nerve fiber is active, the brain may not be able to tell exactly where the sensation is coming from, but it might make a reasonable guess.

Each of the four fiber types—slowly and rapidly adapting punctate fibers and slowly and rapidly adapting diffuse fibers—delivers unique messages about tactile stimulation to the central nervous system. And each must be taken into account when building a system designed to fool the hands into thinking they're holding a virtual object.

Mechanoreceptors

Now that we know something about the nerves that convey tactile information to the brain, we can look at the cells that actually provide this information. These are the cells that need to be stimulated in virtual touch in order to synthesize tangible objects. The hairless portion of the human hand contains four different types of touch receptors, known as mechanoreceptors. Altogether there are approximately 17 million mechanoreceptor cells throughout the hand (see Figure 5-1), and each one is attached to one of the four types of nerve fibers listed above. Note that the reverse isn't necessarily true. That is, some nerve fibers are attached to more than one mechanoreceptor (which is why they can cover so large an area of the hand).

The four types of mechanoreceptors are Meissner corpuscles, Merkel disks, Ruffini endings, and Pacinian corpuscles. Yes, they have strange names. You would too if you were a mechanoreceptor. Each of these types of cells has a specific location and structure.

Meissner corpuscles. As you can see in the illustration on the next page, the touch receptors closest to the skin's surface are the Meissner corpuscles. Found just beneath the small grooves covering our palms and fingers, these receptors are oval shaped and are set with their longer axis perpendicular to the surface of the skin.

The Meissner corpuscles are connected to rapidly adapting fibers and consequently respond best to moving sources of stimulation, as when your finger caresses an object's surface. It's interesting to note that a preteen's fingertips have approximately ten times as many Meissner corpuscles per square millimeter as a fifty-year-old's. One's sense of touch diminishes with age.

Merkel disks. Descending into the depths of the skin, we next encounter a type of cell called the Merkel disk. Because the Merkel disk cells are connected to slow-adapting punctate fibers, it is currently believed that this type of touch receptor responds best when steady pressure is applied to the skin by a small object.

Ruffini endings. The third set of touch receptors, called Ruffini endings, are oriented parallel to the skin's surface, which makes

FIGURE 5-1   The skin

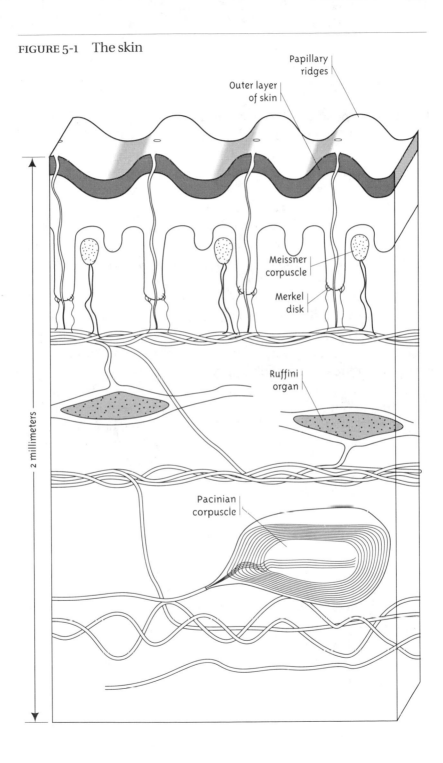

them excellent for supplying information regarding the stretching of the skin as well as steady pressure against the skin. Each Ruffini cell is connected to a slow-adapting diffuse nerve fiber.

Pacinian corpuscles. The most sensitive of all the tactile mechanoreceptors, the Pacinian corpuscles, are located the farthest from the surface of the skin. While these cells are found in the smallest numbers, they're also the largest in size. Oriented with their long axis parallel to the skin's surface, the corpuscles provide information through a single rapidly adapting diffuse nerve fiber.

The receptive field of a Pacinian corpuscle can measure as large as several centimeters, making accurate localization of stimulation sources difficult. You can test this for yourself with an easy experiment. Gently press an object such as a blade of grass or a paper clip against the palm of your hand. If you press hard enough to stretch the skin even slightly, the Merkel disks and Ruffini endings can tell the brain exactly where the sensation is. But if the touch is so light that only the Pacinian corpuscles can register it, you'll notice the tactile sensation but have only a very general sense of location.

Hair. In addition to the four different types of mechanoreceptors, attention must also be paid to the extensive network of free nerve endings, which can be found throughout our body's various layers of skin. In regions of the skin populated by hair follicles, these nerve endings wind around the root of the hairs so that even the minute movement of a single strand results in a neural stimulus.

Evaluation of Tactile Information

When tactile information reaches the brain, it passes through a number of filters similar to those used in the evaluation of visual and aural information. The amount of brain tissue dedicated to evaluating a piece of tactile information depends mostly on the location of the body this tissue is mapped to. For example, extremely sensitive areas such as the lips and hands have much larger representations in the brain than, say, the back.

The neuron filters in the somatosensory (touch and feel) cortex are extremely complex. For instance, some neurons fire only when a section of skin is pressed against an edge that runs in a particular direction. These same neurons remain inactive when contact is made in the same section of skin with an edge that runs in a different direction. And other neurons respond only when an object moves in a specific direction across an area of skin. As researchers discover more about how our brain uses tactile feedback to build mental models of the world around us, we will better understand how to create virtual worlds complete with tactile information.

❁   ❁   ❁

Discovery Through Touch

Now that we have a firm grasp on how we feel things, let's take a look at what sorts of things we can feel. Our haptic system provides two basic types of cues: mechanoreceptor cues and proprioceptive cues. And each of these has limits of sensitivity and acuity. Without a grasp of what types of signals our haptic system is trying to interpret, we don't stand a chance in trying to create virtual signals. If we want to generate the feeling of a virtual wooden cube, we need to know why we feel cubes the way we do: the shape, the texture, the weight, and so on.

Mechanoreceptor Cues

The mechanoreceptors are, perhaps, the most obvious mechanisms of touch. They inform us of the shape, texture, and temperature of every object we hold, feel, or bump against. They're also the most difficult to manipulate in virtual realities because they're extremely sensitive and very small.

Shape. One experiences tactile stimulation when there is a change in the condition of the skin. When you touch something, part of the skin is pushed or pulled, thus changing the resting state of the skin. The level of this skin disturbance varies greatly, depending on the an object's features. For example, if you roll a ball bearing or marble along the surface of a hard, flat table, assuming that you apply an equal amount of pressure during this process, the skin on your finger will be compressed equally because the object's topography is uniform. Our brains translate this equal pressure as a perfectly round shape. On the other hand, if you roll a small beach pebble between two fingers, the nonuniform topography of the object's surface compresses the skin at various levels. Your experience of varying amounts of stimulation across the surface of the fingers translates into a sense of what the pebble is shaped like.

Texture. Suppose you are ready to begin finishing a coffee table you have just built in your wood shop. At the hardware store, you run your fingers over the surfaces of the sandpaper samples on display. As you might know, the smaller and more densely packed the abrasive agent on the sandpaper, the smoother the finish, and, conversely, the larger and less densely packed the grain, the coarser the finish.

You can determine how coarse the sandpaper samples are because of the flexibility of the skin on the fingers. When you move your fingers over the abrasive surface, small sections of the skin are forced in between the grains. Mechanoreceptors register the irregular deformation of the skin as the finger moves.

As we'll see later in this chapter, creating tactile sensations in a virtual environment is extremely difficult.

Temperature. If you're a healthy individual, your skin temperature ranges somewhere around 33 degrees Celsius. When your skin comes in contact with an object, your skin temperature heats or cools to match the surface temperature of the object. If you touch an ice cube, the heat from your fingers transfers to the cold surface, melting the cube and leaving your fingers cold. You don't actually feel the temperature of the object, but rather the change in temperature within your skin.

Tactile Acuity

Just as visual acuity is a measure of how well we can focus on objects, tactile acuity is a measure of tactile precision. Tactile acuity is measured by noting how close together two separate points of tactile stimulation can be before they feel like only one point. This is known as the two-point threshold. Two-point thresholds have been studied extensively in different regions of the entire human body, with rather interesting results. For instance, the threshold measure on the average person's back is about 70 millimeters; on the forearm, 30 millimeters; and on the fingertips, 2 millimeters.

Also, as with the eyes, the regions of the human body that have the most acute sensitivity to tactile stimulation are those that have the highest density of mechanoreceptors and the greatest representation in the brain.

✿　✿　✿

Proprioceptive Feedback

In the previous section, we explored the world of tactile stimulus: texture, shape, temperature, and so on. Now we'll look at the other half of the haptic system: proprioception. Proprioceptive cues are pieces of information gathered from our muscles and tendons, such as "The object is small (I can fit it in my hand), heavy (it pulls my arm down), and round (my fingers can fit around it easily)." These cues can also tell us things like "If you push any harder you'll break the glass" and "That joint resists turning in that direction." Obviously, we'd be hard pressed to function in our world without any proprioceptive cues.

For the sake of simplicity, we'll break this short discussion of proprioception down into three basic elements: shape, force, and firmness. Each of these is crucial for the successful simulation of tangible virtual realities, just as they are crucial to our interacting with the real world.

Shape. Earlier in the chapter, we discussed our perception of shape through tactile stimulation. You can tell that a ball bearing is round when it presses into your skin equally wherever you roll it, whereas a rough pebble is odd shaped when it deforms the skin in different ways. However, much of the information we receive about the shapes of objects comes in the form of proprioceptive cues.

When you hold a cup in your hand, your fingers form a distinctive shape that tells the brain how large the cup is. If the cup is narrow, your fingers are very curled; if the cup is fat, your fingers are less curled. Although this type of cue seems negligible, it can be as important as our often-forgotten but much-needed peripheral vision. The process of finding the snooze button described at the beginning of this chapter was a process of evaluating proprioceptive cues for shape information.

Force. We refer to any sense of movement or potential movement as force. That is, when you're trying to hold on to a leashed dog, there is a force pulling away from you. Similarly, when you lift a heavy object, the force of gravity pulls the object down while you pull it up. When you shake someone's hand, some level of force is applied to your hand.

Force is critical in recognizing the world around us, and as we'll see in "Virtual Touch" below, it's just as critical in our virtual realities. Force informs us of object boundaries and is a major element when exploring the limits of movement. For example, without the force of resistance, we couldn't tell whether stretched rubber is still flexible or pulled to its breaking point.

Firmness. The third proprioceptive cue we'll look at is firmness. Imagine holding a bath sponge and an apple. If both of these objects are squeezed with equal force, one compresses more easily than the other. While the sponge provides little resistance, the apple provides a fair amount of resistance. The firmness of an object is the amount of resistance that counteracts your force. That is, when you grip a steering wheel, the wheel can be seen as "pushing back" at your hand, creating a resistance we sense as firmness.

The Tactile/Proprioceptive Relationship

The truth of the matter is that there is almost no way to really separate tactile from proprioceptive cues. The two work together. When we feel the firmness of an apple, we get tactile information from our mechanoreceptors that says, "there's a lot of pressure here." And we get proprioceptive information from our fingers and tendons that says, "we can't push much harder than this." The brain evaluates firmness using both these cues. Similarly, we can't find the texture of cloth without moving and exploring the surface with our fingers.

Obviously, the relationship between motor functions of the human body and our keen sense of touch is extremely important. In fact, the somatosensory cortex, which processes all haptic cues, is directly adjacent to the region of the brain that controls our motor functions. Neural relationships such as those between the haptic senses and motor functions or between the haptic and the visual senses are critical to our understanding of the brain and how it processes sensory information.

✿ ✿ ✿

Virtual Touch

Anyone who has tried one or more of the current virtual reality technologies can tell you that the most disconcerting element of that immersed environment is the lack of tangibility. You can see objects, though clumsy and crude, and you can hear sounds; but the absence of haptic feedback makes your world seem...fake. Even after you acclimate to the weightless floating, bobbing, and flying around within the virtual environment and become accustomed to the strange lag time and latency in the sights and sounds around you, you're in for quite a challenge when you attempt to reach out to pick up an object.

But we're getting ahead of ourselves. Let's start with the basics. For example, why are we even interested in virtual touch?

Up until now, we've discussed virtual reality as though being in a world just meant interacting by moving around, watching, and listening. And while this model of interaction seems very peaceful and Zen-like, our definition of interactivity is much less passive. Interacting with a virtual world means reaching out and grabbing it, manipulating it, and then watching and seeing how it responds. This type of interaction requires devices that can translate our body movements into computer commands. We will cover devices that do this, such as the DataGlove and the Dexterous Hand Master, in the next chapter.

However, the ability to reach out and touch something turns out not to be enough. As we've seen in this chapter, in the real world, when you reach out and touch something, it touches you back. But how can computers touch us? Because we're already familiar with music synthesizers, it's easy to imagine computers making sound. Similarly, we're well accustomed to computer graphics. But outside of giant computer-controlled robot arms, it's hard to imagine computers touching us.

The Importance of Touch

Nonetheless, this sense of the world touching and pushing back is crucial to the realism of some computer simulations. Earlier we commented on the difficulty of screwing a nut on a bolt when your fingers are numb. Imagine how much more difficult and frustrating it would be to not feel anything in your hand when you pick something up. If you pick up a virtual chair, you get no tactile sensation of it being in your hand, nor any proprioceptive sensation of the chair's weight. If you reach out to turn a virtual water faucet, there's no way to tell when your hand is actually touching the faucet, much less tell when you've successfully turned it.

Until recently, virtual reality researchers have used sound cues to signal contact. That is, when you reached out and touched an object in virtual space (again, we'll cover gestural input more in Chapter 6, *Recognition*), you heard a beep or click or some other cue telling you you'd made contact with the object.

However, simple touch/not-touch cues can only go so far. Although you can turn on a virtual lightswitch without worrying about how the switch feels, you can't tighten a screw without feedback. If you're attempting to manipulate a model of two molecules in three-dimensional space, it's helpful to have haptic cues that represent the forces at work, such as the relative bond strengths within the molecular components. And without proprioceptive cues, there's no way to tell when you've run into a wall or put your virtual hand right through another virtual person (what scientists call boundary detection).

✿   ✿   ✿

Tactile and Force Feedback Devices

In order to create the sensations of virtual touch, researchers have developed tactile and force feedback devices. Although they come in all shapes and sizes, they all do roughly the same thing: push against our hands or arms in order to register a mechanoreceptive or proprioceptive cue. However, the task of developing technologies capable of generating anything more than rudimentary haptic sensations is one of the most difficult challenges virtual reality researchers are encountering.

Author Diane Ackerman eloquently outlined the complexity of the challenge in her book *A Natural History of the Senses:* "Research suggests that, although there are four main types of receptors, there are many others along a wide spectrum of response. After all, our palette of feelings through touch is more elaborate than just hot, cold, pain, and pressure. Many touch receptors combine to produce what we call a twinge. Consider all the varieties of pain, irritation, abrasion; all the textures of lick, pat, wipe, fondle, knead; all the prickling, bruising, tingling, brushing, scratching, banging, fumbling, kissing, nudging. Chalking your hands before you climb onto uneven parallel bars. A plunge into an icy farm pond on a summer day when the air temperature and the body temperature are both the same. The feel of a sweat bee delicately licking moist beads from your ankle. Pulling a foot out of the mud. The squish of wet sand between the toes. Pressing on an angel food cake. The near orgasmic caravan of pleasure, shiver, pain, and relief that we call a back scratch."

While most applications of tactile feedback systems won't require such a diverse selection of sensations, even a simple scenario, like the feeling of holding a child's building block in your hand or moving your fingers over the edge of a table, offers significant technical challenges. Nonetheless, even though the history of virtual touch is even younger than that of virtual sound, researchers are already achieving some exciting results. In the mid-1980s, US Air Force researchers were sewing piezoelectric crystals into the tips of gloves, which, when exposed to a mild electrical current, would vibrate. While tactile stimulation of this type yields little discernable detail, this particular application was enough to validate a pilot's pushing a button on a virtual cockpit display.

For the sake of clarity, we should point out the difference between tactile and force feedback. As we've discussed, tactile sensations occur, in most cases, through the mechanoreceptors in our skin (mechanoreceptor cues). Force feedback, on the other hand, can be thought of as actual restraint or forces acting on the fingers or hand (proprioceptive cues). These sensations are registered in the muscles, tendons, and joints. It would require an extremely strange set of circumstances to experience some form of force feedback without tactile feedback as well.

In this last section of the chapter, we explore some of the force feedback and tactile feedback systems developed over the past ten years. Many of these systems are simply prototypes or works in progress, but show significant promise for near-future application. Several of these are built around gestural input devices like the DataGlove from VPL Research.

Argonne Remote Manipulator. Years before virtual reality exploded onto the world's high-technology scene, there existed a wide range of tasks requiring some form of tactile or force feedback cues, perhaps the most famous being the ability to control a robotic arm when handling radioactive material. You may have seen pictures or movies in which a lab-coated scientist stands behind a lead shield, his hand gripping some sort of metal device attached to a robot's arm in another room.

A device developed specifically for this use is the Model E3 Argonne Remote Manipulator, known simply as the ARM (see Figure 5-2). Originally designed by engineers at Argonne National Laboratories, the ARM is a long, multijoint arm that is suspended from the ceiling. The device provides basic control and force feedback to

FIGURE 5-2   The Argonne Remote Manipulator

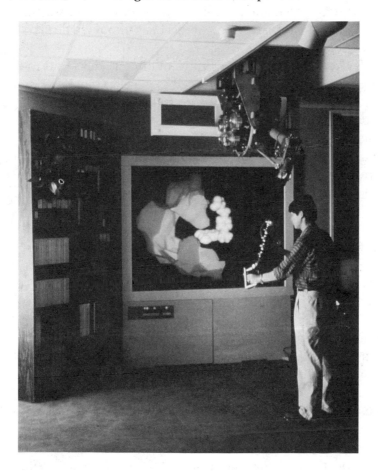

the user's hand, wrist, elbow, and shoulder along three axes (x,y, and z) and three torques. This is commonly referred to as six degrees of freedom (similar to the six degrees of freedom for position sensors discussed in Chapter 2, *Virtual Immersion*).

Two ARM systems have found their way to the University of North Carolina at Chapel Hill, where they are being used to investigate molecular modeling and docking. Using custom-developed software to drive the ARM, chemists are actually able to *feel* how well two molecules fit together, taking into account such factors as the molecule's complex three-dimensional geometry, electrostatic and van der Waals forces, hydrogen bonding, and so on. They can hold on to one molecule and manipulate it around another while watching the pair on a video display screen or in a head-mounted display.

Portable Dextrous Master. With the advent of more dexterous robotic hands, researchers have been forced to develop more precise tracking of finger motion rather than the crude (but effective) wrist, elbow, shoulder movement allowed by the ARM. Human finger movements are then passed on to the robot's arm and fingers. However, in most cases, the device worn on the human hand does not provide any form of force feedback. That means that there's no way to tell when the robot's hand makes contact with some object, and the remote robotic hand may penetrate or dislodge the manipulated object, often resulting in damage. While various techniques have been employed to prevent this from occurring, such as pressure sensors within the robotic fingers, there are obvious benefits to be gained from simply passing on haptic cues to the human operator.

As we noted earlier, the problem of boundary detection also extends to virtual reality technology. While one may be able to see a virtual hand come in contact with a virtual object, these objects have no physical mass; they are merely graphic representations of a numeric database that describes a three-dimensional object. For example, grasping a virtual ball is nearly impossible because your fingers aren't restrained at the ball's boundaries. You're left grasping in midair, waiting for the computer to figure out if you want to hold the ball, push it away, or reach through it.

The Portable Dextrous Master, designed to be used with a VPL DataGlove, conveys force feedback to the human hand through pistonlike cylinders mounted on ball joints (see Figure 5-3). The system works by passing force feedback information from a robot hand's sensors to the Portable Dextrous Master. A computer controls the amount of air pressure that enters or is released from the piston. These pistons press against ball joints mounted in the palm of the hand. While this system seems quite simple, the device imparts surprisingly realistic feelings that virtual or remote objects are being grasped in the hand.

PER-Force Handcontroller. Cybernet Systems, of Ann Arbor, Michigan, recently introduced a versatile six-degree-of-freedom force feedback hand controller similar in some ways to the ARM. The system, called the PER-Force Handcontroller, is a compact robotlike arm with a motorized joystick and six small brushless DC motors providing force feedback at the joints of the arm (see Figure 5-4).

Rather than being developed for a particular robotic system or for a limited range of tasks, the PER-Force is designed to be universal and can be easily customized to a broad selection of systems and

FIGURE 5-3   Portable Dextrous Master

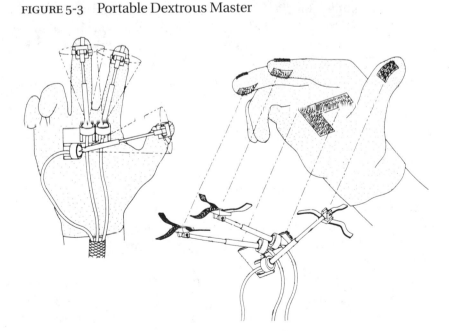

FIGURE 5-4   The PER-Force Handcontroller

uses. For example, the device can be used to control a large crane, either real or virtual. By providing force feedback to your hand and arm on a one-to-one ratio continuously, the PER-Force keeps your hand from moving faster than the arm of the crane. Of course, this ratio can be altered; for example, to let slower movements of the controller result in the slave arm traveling greater distances.

Another potential application of this force feedback system is in aircraft flight or training. The PER-Force could help the pilot maintain a precise preplanned course by applying force to the pilot's hand from the direction in which the aircraft is veering off course. This, in effect, would cause the pilot's hand to move in the direction necessary to correct the wandering. Because the system is so customizable, the controller handle could potentially even be replaced with a steering wheel for remote driving applications.

TeleTact tactile/force feedback system. The United Kingdom's Advanced Robotics Research Center, in conjunction with Airmuscle Ltd., has developed a unique system for supplying tactile stimulation to the hand using arrays of miniature air pockets that can be rapidly inflated and deflated. This system has been developed into a commercial product called the TeleTact tactile/force feedback system.

The TeleTact system consists of two Lycra gloves: the Data Aquisition Glove (DAG) and the TeleTact Glove. The DAG contains an array of twenty force-sensitive resistors (FSRs) distributed on the underside of the fingers and hand as shown in Figure 5-5. When you put this glove on and grasp a real object, the force-sensitive resistors register distinct force patterns. These force patterns are in turn converted to twenty proportional electrical values and stored in computer memory. Developers can use this data to create "templates" of how an object feels by touching it with the DAG. For example, a small square block produces tactile sensations in the

---

FIGURE 5-5   The TeleTact Data Acquisition Glove

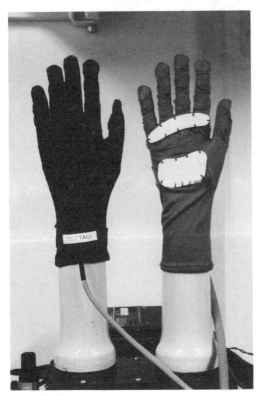

hand dramatically different from those produced by a baseball or broom handle. Thus, the DAG would register significantly different measurements.

Having stored such information, you can now, in effect, play back the data. Glove number two, the actual TeleTact Glove, contains arrays of air bladders distributed about the underside of the fingers, thumb, and palm (see Figure 5-6). Each air bladder's position corresponds to the location of a Data Acquisition Glove force-sensitive resistor. The presently available TeleTact Glove is designed to be worn inside of a VPL DataGlove.

The differing shapes and sizes of the bladders accommodate the

---

FIGURE 5-6   The TeleTact Glove

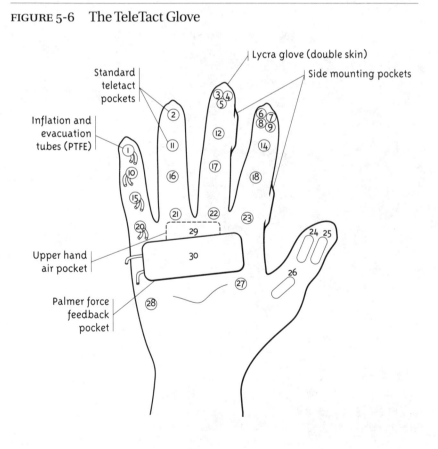

varying levels of sensitivity of the corresponding regions of the palm, fingers, and thumb. During use, as when a virtual hand comes in contact with a virtual object, force patterns acquired from the FSR array are retrieved from the host system's memory. These values are compared to the measured pressure within a bladder. A silent compressor, designed specifically for the TeleTact system, provides compressed air to the air bladders through microcapillary tubing. Two miniature solenoid valves, one to introduce more air and the other to allow pressure to escape, are provided for each bladder. Depending on the result of the value comparison, the appropriate inflation/deflation response is invoked, creating a particular tactile sensation.

Begej Glove Controller. Begej Corporation, of Littleton, Colorado, under a contract with NASA's Johnson Space Center, is currently fabricating a three-finger glovelike exoskeleton that can provide tactile and force feedback cues. The system's principle use will be in the control of remotely operated (teleoperated) dexterous robot hands. In the glove controller, each of two fingers and the thumb contains three joints. Force feedback is provided, at each joint, through a small mechanism that applies resistance to the finger. Each joint also contains a force sensor and mechanical position sensor.

Located in the tips of the glove controller's fingers and thumb is a forty-eight-channel array of tactile display elements, referred to as taxels (this play on words stems from the computer graphics term pixel or picture element, denoting the smallest discernable visual element in a computer screen). Tactile sensors in the robot's fingers generate electrical signals when contact is made with the surface of an object. These signals are, in turn, used to drive the taxel arrays. Existing prototypes include a fingertip display approximately the size of a thick sewing thimble and incorporating thirty-seven taxels.

TiNi Alloy tactile feedback system. An innovative means of providing tactile stimulation has been developed by TiNi (pronounced "Tye-Nye") Alloy, of San Leandro, California. This method involves the use of shape-memory alloys, more commonly known as memory metals. These alloys assume one shape when initially cast but remain flexible enough to be formed into other shapes. When heated again, the alloy reassumes the shape in which it was originally cast.

Imagine a small piece of wire composed of this alloy wrapped in a spiral around a pencil. If you heat the wire until it glows red, then cool it, the wire remembers this spiral shape. You can then straighten the wire out or shape it differently. But when you heat it (let's say you drop it in a cup of hot water), the wire rapidly assumes the spiral shape.

TiNi Alloy's tactile feedback system exploits this same physical characteristic in an alloy called nitinol. A piece of metal called a tactor is held in the off position (in this case down) by a thin, semistiff beam of metal with a 90-degree bend near one end (see Figure 5-7). A length of shape-memory alloy wire (nitinol) is anchored at one end atop a small base positioned on top of the beam. The other end is laced through the other end of the beam just before the 90-degree bend. When the wire is heated with electrical current, it contracts, pulling the free end of the metal beam up.

An early tactile display prototype that used this design incorporated an array of thirty tactors. When the tactors are pulsed with an electrical charge (in effect, heating the metal), the capped end of the metal beam projects out through a small hole in the top of the array (Figure 5-8). By pulsing various combinations of these tactors at different times, simple textures and physical features can be created. For example, you can activate one line of tactors starting at one end of your finger, then successively moving to the next line, and the next, and so on. This creates a tactile effect that feels roughly like running your finger over the edge of a desk.

More recently, the tactors have been altered in size and complexity so that the entire tactile display can fit on a finger or be incorporated into a glove. Xtensory, of Scotts Valley, California, has worked with TiNi Alloy's memory-metal systems to create usable applications like the Tactools package.

Sandpaper system. One recent device for generating haptic feedback, created by a research group including the MIT Media Lab's Margaret Minsky and the University of North Carolina's Ming Ouhyoung uses a force-feedback joystick to simulate the texture and mass of virtual objects. The Sandpaper system, named for its simulation of variable textured sandpaper among other things, is a powerful dem-

FIGURE 5-7   Side view of a TiNi tactor

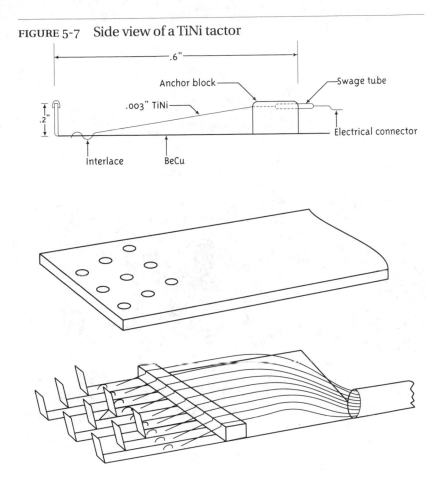

onstration that computers can create realistic haptic displays.

In one experiment, subjects easily ranked three swatches of virtual sandpaper according to roughness. In another, the joystick was made to feel like a stick in a bucket of molasses, a bucket of ice, and a bucket of bricks. The experience of switching between one proprioceptive environment and another is somewhat uncanny, but you get used to it quickly.

Each of these environments is simulated by small motors attached to the joystick, which offer force and resistance as you move the joystick. For example, when moving over a grooved bumpy surface, the motors are controlled so that the joystick is pulled toward

FIGURE 5-8   Prototype tactile feedback array

the low areas. As you move over a bump, the resistance in your hand grows until your reach the top, at which point the joystick pulls you into the next valley.

❀   ❀   ❀

Does Force Feedback Really Help?

Of course, the predominant question in the minds of both developers of tactile/force feedback technologies and potential users is whether or not such haptic displays truly aid in perception, particularly when they're used in the evaluation of complex data. Extensive research conducted at the University of North Carolina reveals that such systems do, in fact, aid in the perception and understanding of force fields and virtual environments containing impenetrable objects. For example, if you're studying magnetic repulsion and attraction, there's almost no reason to use a virtual environment without a force feedback system. Similarly, if you need to know how firm the virtual ball in your hand is, you need it to "push back" at you.

The actual measure of these performance gains varies with the individual application. Research on the use of the ARM system conducted under the direction of Fred Brooks at the University of North Carolina indicates a performance improvement approximately twofold over those situations that used only graphic displays.

Other observations have included performance enhancements on the order of 2.2 times for simple positioning tasks, while complex multidimensional molecular positioning tasks show an increase of about 1.7 times. Researchers are quick to point out that the rate at which haptic displays are updated (similar to a graphic frame-refresh rate) is critical to both the verisimilitude and the effectiveness of these force and tactile feedback systems.

Nonetheless, whatever the statistics say, a virtual reality with no sense of touch is simply disconcerting and difficult to be in for any great length of time. We live in a world that pushes back at us, verifying sight and sound, and any attempt to create (or recreate) a world must generally include the important sensation of haptic cues.

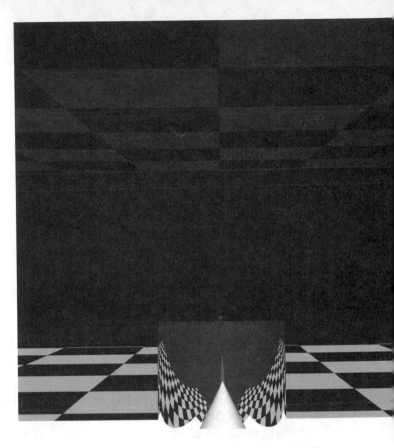

CHAPTER 6

Recognition

❁   ❁   ❁

In the field of computer science, any information that comes out of a computer—be it text, numbers, punch cards, or a stereoscopic virtual environment—is called output. The other side of the equation, information that is fed into the computer, is called input. You rarely see one without the other, and computer scientists tend to talk about them together, as input-output, or I/O (pronounced "eye-oh"). We've spent the last three chapters talking almost exclusively about the output side of the equation: computer-generated sight, sound, and haptic feedback. Now it's time to look at how we control the computer in virtual realities—that is, how we input our commands.

Traditionally, people have controlled computers using everything from switches and dials to punched paper tape, keyboards, light pens, and mice (the electronic kind, not the organic ones!). But a paradigm shift in computer interfaces as large as the one from the two-dimensional computer to virtual reality requires a major shift in input design as well. The old tools just don't cut it. When considering the particular demands of input in a virtual environment, perhaps Thomas Furness, of the University of Washington, said it best during hearings before the US Senate Subcommittee on Science, Technology, and Space, when he stated that "the keyboard is the invention of the devil."

Imagine trying to type a command like "make me travel slowly forward and to the left" on a standard computer keyboard. A mouse makes this kind of thing easy if you're only working in two dimensions, but in a three-dimensional world, it's significantly easier simply to point in the direction you want to go.

Similarly, some applications let you simply point to something, such as a graphic representation of a molecule or some unknown virtual object, and ask, "What is that?" This sort of interaction is only possible when a computer can recognize your gestures and physical commands.

In this chapter, we'll take a brief look at the various input devices that have been developed so far for use with virtual reality. The four primary types of input devices are gloves, three-dimensional mice, body input, and voice recognition.

Note that at the time we go to press, none of these devices includes tactile or force feedback controls (although as we noted in the previous chapter, researchers have been working on combining the DataGlove with tactile feedback). Consequently, if you touch an object in three-dimensional space, your hand is likely to simply press through it. Similarly, you can walk through walls or fly through floors without a hitch. Let's see how.

❋ ❋ ❋

Gloves

Our hands are intermediaries between our brain and the world around us. When we want to take a book off a shelf and open it, we use our hands. When we want to turn a box over to see the other side, we use our hands. Almost every time we want to manipulate our environment precisely, we use our hands. So it's no wonder that researchers have turned first to hand-gesture input for manipulating virtual reality. The best method developed so far for translating the movements of the hands into computer-input signals is a glovelike apparatus that surrounds the hand.

Although the several types of glove input devices we'll discuss in this section each works slightly differently, they all have a common thread: when you move your hand, the glove picks up the movement and sends an electronic signal to the computer. This signal is translated into the motions of a virtual hand. In fact, you can usually see your virtual hand floating in the virtual world, moving in time with your real hand. This aids in the hand-eye coordination necessary for any attempt at three-dimensional positioning in the virtual environment. For example, if you want to reach out to grab a virtual graph of a mathematical equation (see Chapter 12, *The Sciences*) you need to know where your hand is in relation to the object.

DataGlove

The first major glove input device, developed by VPL Research, is called the DataGlove. This device is used all over the world in research laboratories and product-development sights in many different applications, from architectural walk-throughs to manipulating molecules. We'll look at some of these applications in the next section of the book. While the glove looks simple, the technology that enables it is relatively complex (see Figure 6-1). The glove itself is made of lightweight Lycra and fits rather snugly around the hand. The system that measures finger and hand movement consists of a position/orientation sensor and a set of sheathed fiber-optic cables that run along the back of each finger.

The fiber-optic cables act as sensors to measure the flex and extension of each finger (including the thumb). Each cable originates at a small electronics board plugged into the front of a control box. Each fiber leads from the interface board, through a long section of flexible web conduit, to a wrist anchor on the glove. From here, the fiber-optic cable runs up the back of the hand and over one knuckle on each finger and then loops back to the wrist anchor and the interface board.

Within the interface board, one end of each fiber-optic cable is equipped with a light-emitting diode (LED), and the opposite end is connected to a photosensor. The control unit converts the light energy received by the photosensor into quantifiable electrical signals (see Figure 6-2). When you bend a finger while wearing the DataGlove, the LED's light that is traveling through the fiber-optic cable escapes through small scores or cuts in the cable's sheath. The more the knuckle bends, the larger the hole in that knuckle's cable that light can escape through. And the more light that escapes, the less light reaches the photosensor, which lowers the electrical signal.

A computer can interpret the deluge of light-signal data to figure out which fingers and knuckles are bending and how much they're

FIGURE 6-1   The VPL DataGlove

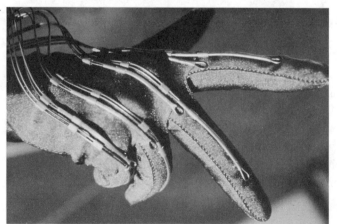

FIGURE 6-2   VPL DataGlove exploded view

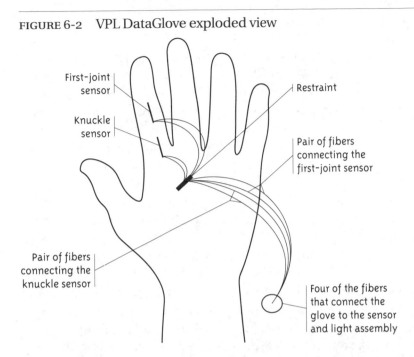

First-joint sensor

Knuckle sensor

Restraint

Pair of fibers connecting the first-joint sensor

Pair of fibers connecting the knuckle sensor

Four of the fibers that connect the glove to the sensor and light assembly

bent. Each finger has a minimum of two cables, one at the lower knuckle and one at the middle knuckle (except for the thumb, of course, which only has two knuckles). A third and fourth fiber-optic cable are sometimes added for additional accuracy. But no matter how many cables you add, this method only measures the movements made by the fingers. The second measurement tool in the DataGlove is a magnetic position/orientation sensor, such as the Polhemus magnetic positioning system described in earlier chapters. This sensor measures the absolute position (x, y, and z) and orientation (roll, pitch, and yaw) of the hand. Between these two measurement methods, the computer can track almost any movement that the hand can make.

The DataGlove is remarkably simple to use. After slipping this snug glove on, you first run several calibration measurements by making a series of gestures. The gestures—such as a fist, a flat hand, and a flat hand with a bent thumb—provide the computer with sample data that describes the spectrum of your hand's range of motion. That is, the computer learns the shape and limitations of your particular hand.

After the computer is calibrated to your hand, how you actually use the glove depends on how the computer software is designed. Typically, you can fly around the environment using various hand gestures. For example, you can fly by pointing with your index finger in the direction you want to go. Flying backwards is easy: just point with two fingers. Some systems let you transport yourself to a different place in the environment by making a quick hand gesture, like a fist. In fact, in systems where there is a limited area for physical movement, this sort of navigation is necessary. By flying in virtual space, you can actually tour an entire architectural model while sitting in a chair.

Additional enhancements can and have been made to virtual systems in which the speed of travel depends on factors such as how far away your hand is from your body or the placement of your thumb. At this time, too little research has focused on exploring appropriate user interfaces for virtual movement and interaction. The result is that most researchers use whatever navigation methods seem reasonable to them. We'll discuss these sorts of interface decisions further in Chapter 15, *Human Factors*.

The PowerGlove

The DataGlove is not inexpensive, reflecting the price of each of its components. However, lower-cost models are already appearing on the scene. The most prominent has been the Mattel PowerGlove, developed in a joint arrangement between VPL and Abrams-Gentile Entertainment and manufactured by Mattel (see Figure 6-3). Although this glove was originally sold as a game controller for the Nintendo Home Entertainment System, because of its relative cost, the PowerGlove has also quickly found its way into a number of virtual reality research facilities around the world. Aside from costing approximately a hundredth of the DataGlove, the PowerGlove is also more rugged and easy to use.

Other than the function itself, there are almost no similarities between the PowerGlove and the higher-end DataGlove. First of all, the flex-measuring and position-sensing technologies are completely

FIGURE 6-3   The Mattel PowerGlove

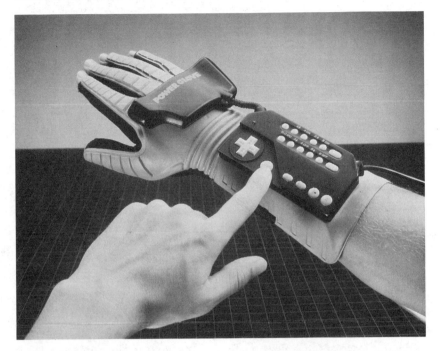

different. The PowerGlove's flex sensors are very simple in design. A small strip of mylar plastic is coated with an electrically conductive ink and placed along the length of each finger. When the fingers are kept straight, a small electrical current passing through the ink remains stable. When a finger is bent, the computer can measure the change in the ink's electrical resistance.

While the DataGlove uses magnetic position and orientation tracking, the PowerGlove uses the simpler ultrasonic positioning technique (described in Chapter 2, *Virtual Immersion*). Each PowerGlove is equipped with two ultrasonic transmitters located on the back of the glove, one on the right side and one on the left. These "clickers"—as they are often called—point outward toward the tips of the fingers. Receivers placed around a television or monitor pick up the ultrasonic signals, translating them into a position in space.

As we noted earlier, the PowerGlove was originally designed as a toy to be used in conjunction with video games. For example, a child wearing a PowerGlove can physically engage in on-screen action, whether it's punching in a boxing game or slashing in a sword-fighting game. However, researchers soon realized that this same glove could be used for architectural walk-throughs, scientific visualization, or any number of applications.

In fact, the only problem is that the PowerGlove is limited in a number of ways. First, the ultrasonic transmitters must be facing the receivers in order for the system to work. This is referred to as line-of-sight transmission. In addition, this line of sight must be free of any major obstructions or else the ultrasonic clicks won't reach the transmitters. This is a limiting factor in many applications, as you can't turn around or grab an object behind you. The second limitation is the accuracy in measuring finger-joint angles. The painted mylar approach can never be as accurate as the fiber-optic cables described above or the mechanical joints described below. While these limitations are hardly noticed in most video games, they can be stumbling blocks in higher-end applications. Clearly, you get what you pay for in this business.

Note that the PowerGlove is no longer manufactured by Mattel. In an industry where the average lifetime of a toy is about a year, the PowerGlove lived for nearly three years, generating over $100 million. The market for physically interactive applications certainly appears to be strong.

Dexterous Hand Master

Beth Marcus, of Exos Inc., in Burlington, Massachusetts, saw the need for an extremely high-precision hand input device and knew that neither the DataGlove nor the PowerGlove would suffice. Moving away from the slip-on glove design, she developed an exoskeleton called the Dexterous Hand Master (DHM). Unlike the DataGlove and the PowerGlove, the DHM uses mechanical linkages to track the complex motions of the human finger joints (see Figure 6-4).

The DHM exoskeleton is attached to the fingers using velcro straps, and attached to each finger joint is a device called a Hall effect sensor (see Figure 6-5). This sensor is a tiny semiconductor that changes the amount of its output voltage in proportion to the strength of a magnetic field around it, which originates from an arm on the opposite side of the hinge. As the fingers and the hand move,

FIGURE 6-4   The Dexterous Hand Master

the sensors measure each of the finger-joint angles. These measurements are sent through wires to the computer, which translates the sensor data into hand-movement and gestural-control commands.

One major difference between the DHM and other current systems is that it also measures the radial-ulnar deviation (side to side motion) of each finger. In addition, the standard DHM configuration also takes into account the fact that the fingers of the human hand actually have three joints, not two.

Although the Dexterous Hand Master is rather clunky to work with, its precision makes it extremely useful for controlling dexterous robotic hands, such as those mentioned in Chapter 5, *Feeling*. Indeed, any application that requires a high level of control and

FIGURE 6-5   Functional diagram of the Dexterous Hand Master

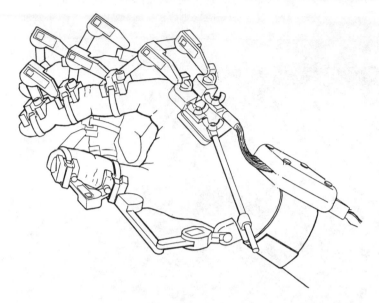

precision, such as the training of robotic hands for pick and place tasks or accurate interaction with virtual objects, may require this sort of system.

Talking Glove

Yet another glovelike gesture-recognition device was developed by James Kramer while he was an electrical engineering graduate student at Stanford University, along with Larry Leifer, a professor of electrical engineering at Stanford and director of rehabilitation research and development at the Palo Alto Veterans Administration Medical Center. Called the Talking Glove, the device was designed to be used as a speaking aide for nonvocal deaf and deaf-blind individuals, though it has also been used in both virtual reality and stroke rehabilitation applications. This multicomponent system converts finger-spelled words into synthesized speech (see Figure 6-6).

The designers of the Talking Glove approached flex measurement from an innovative angle. Instead of using fiber-optic cables,

FIGURE 6-6   The Talking Glove

mechanical joints, or variable resistance paint on plastic strips, the Talking Glove uses extremely thin strain gauges enclosed in the glove's material to measure how much the fingers bend. Each hand can be fitted with up to twenty-two sensors: three bend sensors and one abduction sensor per finger and thumb, plus seven to measure the hand's yaw and pitch at the wrist joint.

This award-winning device includes a small electronic unit worn on a waist belt that interprets the strain gauges' output and converts the gestures into signals that are passed to a voice-generation system. This system actually creates the sound of each word and plays it through a small speaker worn beneath the user's shirt. Anyone listening can reply by typing a message on a small keypad and display.

Although the Talking Glove was developed for a specific purpose (sign-language finger-spelling translation), it can be used in a number of applications, including those involving virtual reality. James Kramer has developed a more refined version, which may be more useful in virtual reality work, called the CyberGlove (see Figure 6-7).

FIGURE 6-7   The CyberGlove

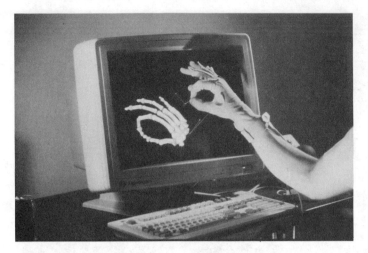

❀ ❀ ❀

The Evolution of the Mouse

The mouse, that attachment to personal computers that has become so popular since the release of the Macintosh computer and the Windows operating system, has actually been around a lot longer than most people think. First developed at Stanford Research Institute (now SRI International) in the 1960s, the mouse slowly crept into general use via Xerox PARC (Palo Alto Research Center) and other research facilities. The idea is simple: a small ball is placed inside a device that is rolled around a table. Sensors measure how far the ball has rolled forward, backward, or side to side, and the computer translates these movements into horizontal and vertical coordinate movements of an on-screen cursor. We have no idea why this device was called a mouse. Some people have noted that it's as difficult to control as a live mouse; others comment on the taillike wire that runs from the mouse to the computer. Some members of the graphic arts field, who have had to do very precise work with computers, began to call this device a "hand-held brick," which perhaps is a better term for it.

Nonetheless, it is surprisingly easy for most people to map the rolling of this plastic brick around on a table into cursor movements on a screen, at least for general movements. Moving the mouse forward and to the right makes the cursor move to the upper-right part of the screen, and so on.

Researchers are now looking at using a similar paradigm for working within three dimensional computer work spaces like virtual environments. In this section, we'll look at three versions of three-dimensional "mice" and how they work.

3Ball

Polhemus Navigation Sciences has developed a three-dimensional input device based on their popular Polhemus magnetic positioning system (see "Position/Orientation Tracking" in Chapter 2, *Virtual Immersion*). Called the 3Ball, the device is simply a no. 3 billiard ball—Polhemus literally bought cases of nothing but no. 3 balls from a billiard company—hollowed out to house a magnetic triaxial sensor (see Figure 6-8). This simple design also includes a flattened area so that the ball doesn't roll when it's set down and a small button that can be pressed ("clicked") to select objects and specify commands.

You can move a cursor or object around in a virtual reality by holding the 3Ball in your hand and moving it about. While it's somewhat tiring to maneuver a billiard ball (even a mostly hollow one) in midair, this method works well for short-term tasks, such as those involving navigation and manipulation.

Logitech 2D/6D Mouse

If you are building a three-dimensional model with a computer-aided design system, it may be helpful to move between working in a two-dimensional setting (with a mouse and a flat computer screen) and a three-dimensional setting. For example, if you want to turn the model around to see the back side, you might want to pull a BOOM or other display device in front of your eyes and then switch to a three-dimensional mouse to select the exact position in space

FIGURE 6-8   The 3Ball

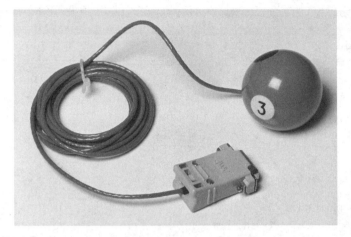

that you want as the new perspective. Logitech has combined a two- and a three-dimensional mouse into one in the 2D/6D Mouse.

The combination is somewhat simple: they've added ultrasonic position sensing to a standard mouse. As shown in Figure 6-9, the 2D/6D Mouse consists of two parts. First, a triangle with three ultra-sonic transmitters is placed on the desktop in front of the mouse. Second, three corresponding microphones are attached to a normal desktop mouse. These microphones sample signals from the trans-mitters fifty times per second, providing information to the com-puter about where the mouse is located (see "Ultrasonic" in Chapter 2, *Virtual Immersion*).

The 2D/6D mouse can function as a normal desktop pointing device. Then, when you lift it off the desktop, the system tracks it in three-dimensional space. You can manipulate the three-dimensional space displayed on a screen or in a stereoscopic display. Once again, the computer software must be configured for this sort of device, and different software publishers may provide various features that make three-dimensional mouse controls especially advantageous.

The Spaceball

A number of virtual reality hardware vendors have been promot-ing the use of a force/torque control ball called the Spaceball (see

FIGURE 6-9   The Logitech 2D/6D Mouse

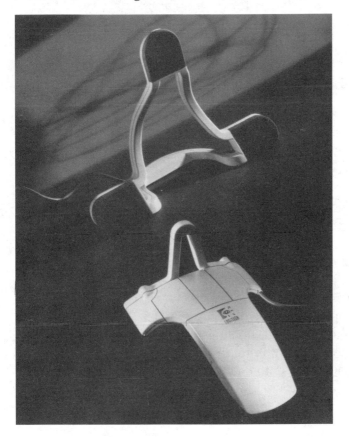

Figure 6-10). The device is relatively simple: a small ball is attached to a base with a series of control buttons. You can move through or control something in the virtual environment by twisting the ball or applying soft directional movements such as pulling it up, pushing it down, moving it forward and backward, and so on. You can also click on the buttons that are located both on the ball and in front of it to select different operating modes or control an object's movement.

The Spaceball is almost as simple a technology as the mouse. Six infrared LEDs are mounted on a small plastic pillar inside a hollow ball. Also inside the ball are infrared photosensors that can sense where the light from the LEDs is shining. Each LED represents one

FIGURE 6-10   The Spaceball

degree of freedom: up/down, left/right, forward/back, and pitch, yaw, and roll. When you grasp the ball and move it in a particular direction, the photosensors register the movement and relay this information to a processor that issues a movement command to the computer.

The Spaceball has several qualities that make it particularly good for use with virtual reality. Primarily, it is extremely easy to use and intuitive. You simply grab the ball and move it in the direction you want to travel. Also, because it sits on a desk, you don't have to hold it in midair while working in three dimensions, as you would a mouse.

✿   ✿   ✿

Body Recognition

A single hand floating in cyberspace is hardly a good representation of a person. And if we are truly looking at creating immersive virtual reality, then there is clearly a need for full-body recognition. That is, the computer must be able to recognize where our entire body is, what our arms are doing, what our facial expression is, and how we move through space. Researchers began to explore the possibilities of full-body computer input some years ago, but only recently have potential commercial systems been developed.

Myron Kreuger outlined the need for these sorts of recognition systems in the 1970s in his book *Artificial Reality*. His recent sequel, *Artificial Reality II*, describes his projects from the past twenty years, many of which used a form of body recognition called image extraction. Even though this method, which uses video cameras to locate and interpret the body's movements, has been used the longest, it is still years away from becoming a viable product. Because of this, we will hold off discussing image extraction until Chapter 17, *The Future of Virtual Reality*.

Let's look at two recently developed products that have shown some interesting results and how they might be used.

The DataSuit

VPL Research has addressed the need for full-body recognition by designing a whole-body computer input device called the Data-Suit (see Figure 6-11). The DataSuit uses the same fiber-optic flex-sensing technology as the DataGlove, but instead of ten or fifteen cables on the hand measuring five fingers, the DataSuit uses up to fifty different joints on the human body. This includes the knees, the arms, the torso, and the feet. It also employs four Polhemus trackers: one one each hand, one on the head (on the EyePhones), and another mounted on the back of the suit.

The DataSuit isn't really a commercial package at this point for several reasons. First of all, it's much too cumbersome. Also, the calibration process of the suit is very complex. Instead of creating a for-sale product, VPL has used the DataSuit to conduct its own research, while taking on a few commercial jobs. For example, animators for a Hollywood movie wanted their graphics computer to "know" how humans move. VPL Research put someone in a DataSuit and had them move around, tracking and recording the data signals passed back to the computer. This information could later be used to help the computer create humanlike movement.

In a virtual reality, a DataSuit, or something like it, could be helpful for conveying nonverbal communication or controlling complex robotic tasks. Because various parts of the body can be mapped differently, a foot movement might control a lighting system, a particular body position might signal the computer to change

FIGURE 6-11   The VPL DataSuit

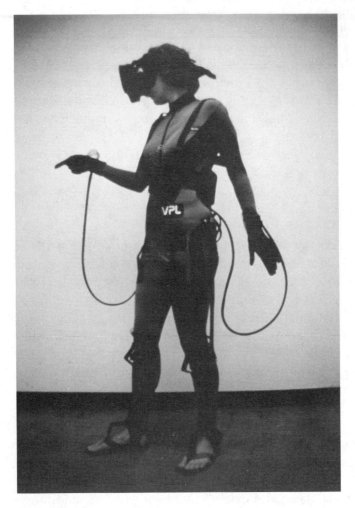

scenes, or a nod of the head might be translated into a robotic arm's movement. This might seem complex, but you'd be surprised at how quickly we are able to adapt to strange body mappings.

The Waldo

In addition to a high-profile reputation in motion picture special effects and character design, Rick Lazzarini and his firm, the Char-

COLOR PLATE 1   The Visette

The W Industries' Visette is probably the most widely available headmounted device (see Chapter 3, *Seeing*). It is used in the Virtuality games (see Chapter 9, *Entertainment*).

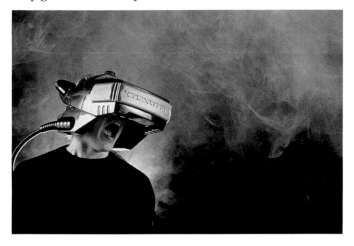

COLOR PLATE 2   Image from *The Lawnmower Man*

The movie *The Lawnmower Man* was the first major motion picture to discuss virtual reality, its technology and its implications.

COLOR PLATE 3 Visualizing Weather Patterns
Weather patterns over the Los Angeles area can be seen in a variety
of formats in a virtual environment, including smog bubbles.

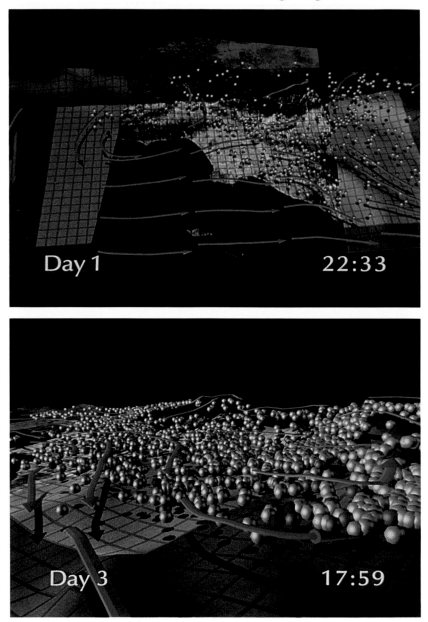

COLOR PLATE 4   The USAF Super Cockpit
An early application of virtual reality, the USAF Super Cockpit provides pilots with a virtual representation of their surroundings.

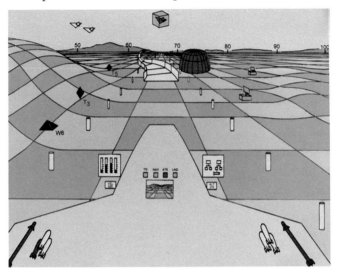

COLOR PLATE 5   W industries' Virtuality
This virtual reality arcade system lets you play a variety of different games, including Dactyl Nightmare (see Chapter 9, *Entertainment*).

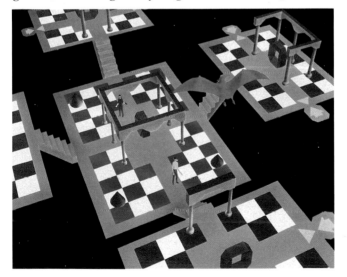

COLOR PLATE 5   Art gallery

Each picture in this virtual art museum, created by Sense8 Corporation, acts as a portal into a new virtual world (see Chapter 16, *Social considerations*).

acter Shop, in Van Nuys, California, have been developing a reputation for constructing some of the most advanced systems available for tracking movements of the human body. These systems do not have set product names and are manufactured one at a time depending on the client's particular need. For example, one client wanted a system that could track facial movements. Someone wearing this system, called the Waldo, could control a video-game character's facial expressions by making facial movements themselves. The Waldo uses several types of sensors to track movements of various facial muscles and the jaw (see Figure 6-12). The information from these sensors is sent to the simulation software, which in turn instructs the character's face to move.

❊   ❊   ❊

Voice Recognition

Aside from a wide gamut of nonverbal facial expressions and gestures, the spoken word is the most basic form of communication between human beings. Studies have shown that speech is also the

FIGURE 6-12   The Waldo

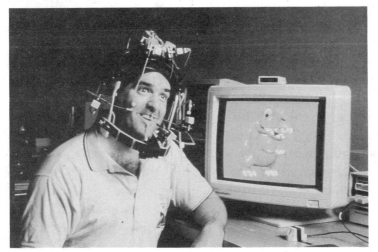

most rapid form of communication, no matter how fast you can type. As such, a considerable amount of research has been conducted in the area of voice-recognition technology in an attempt to let people use computers more intuitively and quickly. This mission is, of course, parallel with that of virtual reality technology. The two can clearly go hand in hand.

We use spoken language all the time in manipulating our natural environment, often including general phrases such as "Move that there" or "Go down the street three blocks." In virtual reality environments, we can use these sorts of phrases to make known our intentions. For example, we can point at a box and ask, "What's that?" Through position/orientation sensing, the computer can tell where we're pointing and can respond to the question in one way or another. Commands can quickly be barked at the computer through a microphone, such as "Open door" or "Make me small."

There are over twenty companies in North America alone that offer voice-recognition products. These systems range in cost from hundreds to millions of dollars and work with a wide range of computers. In all but a few cases, these systems employ the use of various pattern-recognition technologies in order to understand the spoken word.

Pattern Recognition

The problem with computers, as we noted earlier, is that they're incredibly dumb. In fact, at a base level, you could say that the only thing they really understand is "on" and "off." Every piece of information that goes through wires into their metal and plastic cases must somehow be translated into on and off signals: millions of zeros and ones. This is what digital processing is all about.

When faced with the challenge of trying to get computers to understand what people say, scientists must first get the voice into the computer and translate it into a digital signal using an analog-to-digital signal converter. Like a baby, the computer doesn't understand the words when it "hears" them. But, again like a baby, the computer can learn to recognize the sounds over time.

Training the system. Initially the user "trains" the computer's voice-recognition system by repeatedly speaking words into a microphone and telling the computer (through the keyboard or other traditional input device) what the words mean. For example, a doctor can say the word *prescription* into the microphone and the computer can connect the word to the action (filling in a prescription form, checking a prescription, or whatever).

Note that the computer doesn't actually understand the word, but rather the *sound* of the word. If the doctor says a word while sitting straight up in a chair and then later says the word while slumping lazily in the chair, the sound of the word may be different enough that the computer can't understand it. Why? Because, as opposed to a baby learning to understand a word's meaning, the computer is only programmed to find a digital replica of the sound it was trained with.

Most voice-recognition systems let you repeat a word several times in the training process, and they encourage you to say it in various ways (quickly, slowly, loudly, softly, and so on). This lets the system capture a variety of patterns for each word or phrase so that the computer has a better chance at understanding it if it's not spoken exactly the same every time. Each of these patterns is stored away in the computer's memory for later comparison. Clearly, the more versions, or templates, of a spoken word available for comparing to a voice command, the better.

Vocabulary. Voice-recognition research began in the mid 1970s when a number of companies, including AT&T and IBM, began to develop software to support voice recognition on large, mainframe computers. One of the first operational systems, developed by IBM, was based on an IBM 370 computer and was actually capable of taking simple dictation. The problem was that very few could afford the primitive system's $10 million price tag. It was much like an expensive secretary who could only take simple dictation—and very slowly at that.

Several years later, the algorithms were simplified enough to allow their use on much smaller personal computers (which had, of course, gotten significantly more powerful). However, systems today are still functioning with vocabularies in the range of—at most—a few thousand words. And most systems are limited to a vocabulary in the hundreds of words. Nonetheless, because you generally get to choose the words, the systems are reasonable for most task-specific work. That is, a doctor can get by with a hundred key words unless he expects the computer to take dictation. A mechanic can use the system to speak commands to the computer while her hands are too burdened with tools to reach the keyboard and, similarly, doesn't need a wide vocabulary to get the job done.

Limitations

There are two limitations with voice-recognition technology: appropriate use and natural language. Appropriate use refers to when it should and should not be used. While the addition of voice-recognition capabilities to a computer can help in many tasks, there are many instances in which this technology actually reduces efficiency. For example, in a computer-aided design system, it's faster to simply draw a line than to tell the computer, "Starting with a base point at this screen coordinate, extend and connect to screen point such and such." On the other hand, entering orders on the trading floor of a stock exchange or aiding in an assembly-line process, voice-recognition capabilities can have a significant impact on productivity. It's for this reason that a significant amount of work in voice-recognition research has been carried out by and for brokerage houses and those that help supply them with information, such as Shearson, Lehmann, Hutton, and Rueters.

The second limitation, natural language, refers to the problems that voice-recognition systems have with understanding words in everyday usage. Because the computer is attempting to match sounds, it can easily confuse commands. For example, if you say "Pet the dog," it may think you're saying "Bet the dog." There's almost no difference in sound, but a great difference in meaning. Voice-recognition systems can be combined with other computer systems that look for context and that understand some common sense notions (such as, people usually pet dogs rather than take them to Las Vegas). The voice-recognition systems also have problems with words said quickly in succession, causing all sorts of problems ("Send an e-mail to me" could be understood as "Send any male to knee").

Lip reading. Scientists have been working hard at getting past the natural-language limitation of voice recognition, as it's a substantial barrier in many applications of the technology. Automatic language-translation systems, for example, are near impossible without the ability to quickly and clearly understand every word and meaning correctly. An expert system that helps voice-recognition programs understand probable meaning based on context and common sense is one method of tackling this problem. Another method that has been looked at in some research laboratories is lip reading.

A system at MIT's Media Lab is based on the idea that there are sixteen basic lip positions used in the English language. If a video camera is aimed at a person's lips when he or she is speaking, the computer can attempt to figure out which of the sixteen lip positions are being used at any moment. That information can be added to the audio data to gain a better recognition of the words. That is, the computer can "see" the difference in lip movements between "gnat" and "mat."

However, although this technology has been shown to be effective in some limited circumstances (and it makes for a great demonstration), its future is questionable due to its major limitations: processing speed and line-of-sight requirements (you must be facing the camera at all times for it to work correctly).

❁   ❁   ❁

Computer Recognition

A common mistake made by a number of people working with technology is to ignore common sense and a healthy analysis and just grab the hottest new product for every project. These people might get very excited about technologies like voice recognition or glove-based manipulation, without thinking about how helpful they really are in the majority of applications. Voice recognition, while extremely useful in situations where the computer operator can't

operate a keyboard with his or her hands, is often more of a hindrance than a benefit. Your desktop computer voice-recognition
system might pick up the sound of paper rumpling or trucks going
by the window as spoken commands, causing it to do some very
strange things!

Similarly, as noted earlier, holding a mouse in midair is certainly
not something we'd want to do for a long time, nor is having to carefully fit our hands into a glove every time we wanted to manipulate
something in a three-dimensional environment. The answer, perhaps, is to have a number of different control devices and be able to
use any of them at will. But this, too, has its challenges.

However, one thing *is* clear: working in three-dimensional virtual
realities requires some sort of three-dimensional input device as
much as working on a two-dimensional screen requires a mouse. It's
not essential, but we wouldn't want to go back to the days when it
wasn't available.

PART III

Applications of Virtual Reality

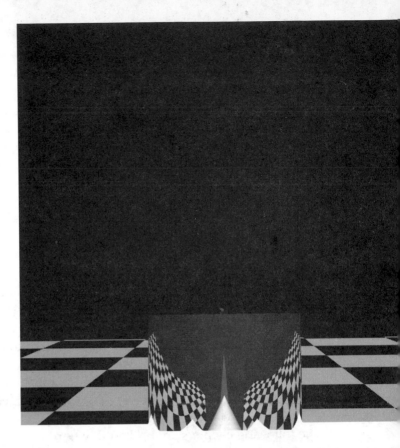

CHAPTER 7

Real World Virtual Reality

✿　　✿　　✿

Over the course of the past five chapters, we've explored virtual reality technology, how it works, and what tools researchers have developed to make it work. But who cares about a technology without an application? Just saying "Sure, that's interesting" isn't good enough. The tools must be taken in hand (so to speak) and used productively. In the next seven chapters, we will look at real-world applications of virtual

183

reality. Some are presently in development, and others are actually being used. Some are still only ideas.

It's tempting to throw ourselves overboard and fantasize about the possibilities of virtual reality without any regard to reason or the limits of technology. This is, in our opinion, what the media has done in sensationalistic articles, movies, and news stories over the past several years. Everyone loves a parade, but people's imaginations have become so aroused by these wild stories that they expect more from virtual reality than can be delivered in the near future.

So let's take a moment and remember where we are at this stage of the technology. As we described in the earlier chapters, the images are cartoonlike in complexity; head-mounted displays are, even at 2.5 pounds in the best cases, a bit on the heavy side; and the resolutions provided by the commonly used imaging devices (mostly LCDs) are significantly lower than that necessary to provide crisp, detailed pictures. Plus, computer hardware is being pushed to the limits of its performance, and it's still not fast enough.

However, even with all these restrictions, some incredible applications for the technology have been developed, from education to engineering, from science to entertainment.

The following chapters are broken down into seven categories: architecture and design, entertainment, health and medicine, education, the sciences, information control, and telepresence. However, please note that the applications in one chapter may also be used in another area and that the applications we're describing are only a small handful of the many uses of virtual reality being developed or planned today. Virtual reality, in many ways, is like the theatre or movies, where every field and area of expertise unites into a synthesis greater than the whole. Let's see it happen.

CHAPTER 8

Architecture and Design

❖ ❖ ❖

We've given examples of architects and designers using virtual reality throughout earlier chapters because it's both the easiest application to understand and it's one of the first applications of virtual reality to have actually come to fruition. From California to New York, from Tokyo to Berlin, architects and designers have used immersive and nonimmersive three-dimensional modeling programs for the past few years to help bridge the gap between the vision and the finished product. In this chapter, we'll take a look at how virtual reality can be used in these fields and particularly at how it is now being used for designing buildings and aircraft.

❀   ❀   ❀

Computer-Aided Design

Computer-aided design (CAD) has had a significant impact on the speed with which people can create designs and design prototypes in many fields, from architecture to industrial design to interior design. The idea of using computers for design work was first demonstrated to the scientific community in the 1960s by Ivan Sutherland with a program called Sketchpad. This was the first program that let people create graphic images on a screen using a hand-held object such as a pen rather than by entering numbers with a keyboard into a computer (see Figure 8-1). In his 1977 book,

FIGURE 8-1   Sutherland's Sketchpad

The Home Computer Revolution, Ted Nelson called Sketchpad "the most important computer program ever written."

The advent of computer graphics opened the doors for a number of real-world computer uses, including computer-aided design. CAD was an obvious application in its synthesis of the precision and calculation skills of a computer with the graphical interface of blueprints and modeling designs. But even though CAD had the potential to be used by thousands of people, for the first fifteen years of its existence, it remained an extremely expensive technology owned only by very large companies for use on big, mainframe computers.

All that changed in the 1980s, when Autodesk first introduced AutoCAD. Company founder John Walker believed that it was not only possible to present the capabilities of these large CAD systems at significantly lower costs, but that this relatively inexpensive program could run on inexpensive desktop computers. In retrospect, we can see that the immense success of the product clearly validated his belief.

Nonetheless, while AutoCAD brought computer-aided design to an affordable level, a number of limitations still exist. The first is the complexity of symbols. If you're an architect or designer, chances are you can easily visualize the three-dimensional objects represented on a blueprint. For the uninitiated, however, this is literally impossible. So it is not surprising that architects frequently encounter significant difficulties in sharing design concepts with clients, who rarely can understand what the building will look like when complete. The complexity of a two-dimensional blueprint also increases the possibility of errors in designs, which more often than not reveal themselves only after the construction process has begun.

A second limitation in the CAD process, one which has been described several times in earlier chapters, has to do with how you can (or cannot) manipulate these images. With a standard CAD system, to rotate or move an element or the entire design, you must translate your wishes into a series of typed commands or movements in three separate axes. For example, to rotate along the X axis, turn this dial, for the Y axis, turn this dial, and so on.

When researchers were looking for prime targets for virtual reality applications, they hit the jackpot with computer-aided design.

People who worked with CAD systems had to contend with complex, nonintuitive symbols, three-dimensional objects represented in two-dimensional space, and methods of manipulation that had little to do with normal "hands-on" interaction. Virtual reality opened the door for designers to freely explore their designs, without the barriers of screen or paper.

Virtual reality can act as a powerful visualization tool with which to explore, analyze, create, and manipulate designs. There may always be a need for traditional coordinate-based CAD systems. In fact, CAD systems are an integral part of building virtual realities at this point. However, virtual reality technology is an increasingly helpful supplement to CAD systems, with the number of specific case studies involving the use of virtual interface technology growing rapidly. The results of these studies clearly demonstrate that virtual reality is indeed a highly useful tool for evaluation of designs, minimizing last minute surprises and increasing creativity.

✿   ✿   ✿

Aircraft Design

The Advanced Technology Center at Boeing Aircraft in Seattle is commonly credited with having developed the first industrial application of virtual reality. Boeing uses virtual reality to prototype CATIA (a sophisticated high-end CAD program) models of new aircraft, including the tilt rotor transport called the VS-X (Figure 8-2). This system is a powerful aid in studying and comparing aircraft designs for operability, maintainability, and manufacturability while the design still exists only in digital form. Not only is the virtual reality interface an aid to the design process, it also means that performance simulations can be carried out without having to laboriously build physical models.

To create a prototype, designers load digital CAD "blueprints" into two computer workstations. Each computer is responsible for creating the image for one eye's view, and the user views the images through a set of VPL EyePhones. Instead of looking at blueprints or even a two-dimensional rendering of the design on a flat screen or

FIGURE 8-2   The Boeing VS-X

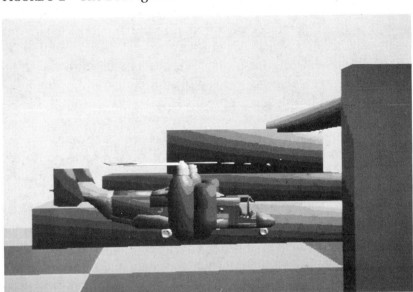

on paper, designers can experience the model as though a full-scale mock-up of the aircraft were parked in the design lab.

The designer has a number of ways that he or she can move within and around the model. The first method is to simply walk in the desired direction of travel. The magnetic position/orientation sensing tracks designers as they walk around, and the screens in the goggles are updated appropriately. Of course, movement is limited to only 3 or 4 feet in any one direction because of the multitude of cables connecting the person to the computer-graphics hardware.

A second movement option is to use hand gestures conveyed through a glovelike I/O device. While seated or standing, the designer can simply slip on the DataGlove and point in the desired direction of travel. The system is programmed to understand certain gestures: point with one finger to go forward, two to travel backwards, thumb up to enlarge the scale of the model, and so on. Of course, people using a virtual reality system will generally use both methods of movement, often in an avant-garde dancelike combination of hand gestures and body movements.

Remember that the computer is updating the display depending on where the designer is located and oriented in the virtual reality. If the person enters the aircraft simulation in the cockpit facing the control panel, he or she needs only to physically turn around to see down the aisle into the passenger compartment. Because there is no boundary detection, designers can quickly walk or fly (*flying* is the accepted term for moving through hand gestures) around the airplane, through its walls, or wherever they want to go.

The Boeing system is not only designed to be an exploratory virtual reality (see Chapter 1, *Silicon Mirage*, for a discussion on the three levels of virtual reality); it is interactive as well. Using the DataGlove, the designer can quickly and simply reach out to grab objects in the virtual environment. For example, if you were using this system, you could reach out and manipulate cockpit controls, open and close hatches, and reposition seats, windows, and overhead storage bins. As you perform these tasks, the computer model of the aircraft updates appropriately. Because these sorts of manipulations are still somewhat difficult, a small icon in the shape of a hand is provided within the model for the necessary hand-eye coordination. As you move your hand, this floating hand moves in the virtual space.

Another application for virtual reality presently under consideration by the Boeing group is crew station ergonomic studies. Their reasoning: why wait for a mock-up to be built, only then to discover that the controls need to be positioned differently or that the wings need to be more visible? With virtual reality, such discoveries can be made well before the design ever leaves the engineer's work area. In fact, a number of engineers can enter the same model of the aircraft at the same time.

❀   ❀   ❀

Architectural Walk-through

The cost savings in using virtual reality to explore designs can be seen perhaps no better than in architecture. And there is perhaps no better place to look for these architectural models than at the University of North Carolina. Over the past four years, architects and computer scientists have used virtual reality to evaluate the designs of several new structures on campus, including portions of a church and Sitterson Hall, the building that presently houses the school's Department of Computer Science (see Figure 8-3). Before even a single spade of dirt had been turned in the construction process, these structures had been carefully explored through models called architectural walk-throughs.

The system is similar to that at Boeing. First blueprints of a structure are defined using AutoCAD and other CAD programs. They're

FIGURE 8-3   A virtual model and the finished product

then loaded into a high-end computer-graphics workstation that renders the images (creates a three-dimensional image from two-dimensional data). Engineers and architects can then wear head-mounted displays to gain a stereoscopic three-dimensional view of the building.

In order to make walking through the building as natural as pos-sible, researchers at the University of North Carolina developed the system around a treadmill with handlebars (see Figure 8-4). To move forward in the virtual environment, the user simply walks forward on the treadmill. To turn corners and explore connecting rooms and hallways, the user simply turns the handlebars in the desired direc-tion of travel while walking. It's very simple to adapt to this combi-nation of movements taken from walking and bicycling.

When walking around in the building, you can control your rate of movement by adjusting your own walking speed. Again, this is in-tuitive and just like the real world. Plus, while moving through the model, you can freely move your head from side to side and up and down to look around you. And when you turn around, you can even

FIGURE 8-4   The UNC walk-through treadmill

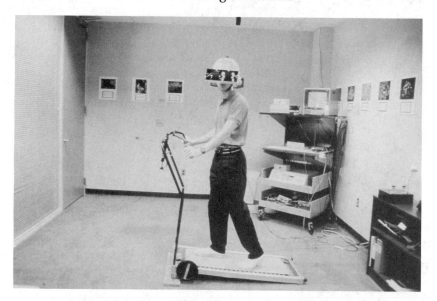

see objects and features within the model grow smaller as you pass and move farther away.

Besides being just plain interesting, this method of exploring architectural designs has a number of advantages over traditional methods. First seeing the designs on a simple desktop monitor or on paper does not accurately relay a correct sense of the model's spaciousness. Second, there is almost no good way to evaluate the design short of creating a large, detailed model of the building and poking your head into it. With virtual reality, the model can be explored naturally, relatively inexpensively, and quickly. Plus, if you're a prospective owner of the building, you have the ability to "kick the tires" of the building prior to giving your final approval.

The UNC computer scientists, who would later inhabit Sitterson Hall, took the architect's plans and created a walk-through. By virtually touring the building, the scientists uncovered a number of design flaws that had been missed during the evaluation of the designs on a standard workstation monitor and on paper. In fact, after the walk-through, the future occupants decided that two walls in the lobby area were too close together. The building's architect was apparently unconvinced of the change (after all, who were these computer scientists anyway?) until he actually toured the model with the head-mounted display. Actually seeing the full scale model convinced him to change the lobby design.

It's almost inconceivable to change an element of a building after it has been erected. Moving that wall would have cost an incredible amount of money. But changing the position of a wall, staircase, or window before the designs are complete, while still working with a CAD model, is a trivial task incurring minimal cost.

❊   ❊   ❊

Acoustical Evaluation

Whether designing concert halls or houses, architects have long struggled with acoustic challenges. The problem is that it is simply impossible to determine the acoustics of a building with any significant detail prior to its construction. Miniature models can be made, construction-materials analysis can be performed, but when it comes right down to it, building acoustics are extremely difficult to calculate. Computers have been brought in to create simulations of the buildings, but because of the computational burdens of such tasks, real-time simulations have, until recently, been limited to free-field rooms (rooms without echoes). These simulations are academic at best and have little meaning in the real world.

However, research conducted at NASA Ames Research Center and Crystal River Engineering has resulted in the development of powerful digital signal processing systems that support the real-time simulation of acoustical factors such as reflecting surfaces (walls) and sound absorption by a variety of different surface materials. As we saw in Chapter 4, *Hearing*, these acoustic displays can be delivered through high-quality headphones to give the effect of a three-dimensional sound field. Furthermore, they can be correlated and stabilized with visual models of the environment. Thus, if you see a virtual dog barking at you, the sound of the bark comes from that direction, too.

Not only does this ability to mix sound and sight together add an increased level of realism to the overall simulation, it lets architects work on both visual and acoustic challenges at the same time. A virtual walk-through of a concert hall could then include a virtual string quartet onstage. How do they sound from the back of the auditorium? How is the sound different when the hall is filled with an audience? What if we place sound reflectors on the ceiling? These sorts of questions will be more easily answered in the near future by using virtual reality technology, such as the Convolvotron.

✿   ✿   ✿

The Virtual Kitchen

If you've ever wanted to design the kitchen of your dreams, you are going to love Matsushita's new virtual reality system. Having to choose between thousands of appliances that come in various colors, sizes, and costs is difficult enough, but trying to make sure the ones you like will fit together in your kitchen space is almost impossible. Matsushita, the Japanese equivalent to American companies like General Electric or Maytag, has developed a virtual reality system that can help.

Using VPL Research's glove and goggle technology, the system lets you create a CAD model of your kitchen on computers. This model is then downloaded to a Silicon Graphics workstation for real-time rendering of the images. When you place the EyePhones and DataGlove on, you can walk though your virtual kitchen, placing appliances here, moving them there, changing the color of the refrigerator, requesting a smaller microwave oven, and so on. The design is completed before even ordering a single ice cube tray.

If you don't know where to start, you can tour kitchen sets predesigned by Matsushita decorators (referred to as "system kitchens") to get a feel for the combinations recommended by the dealer. Then, once again, you can alter whatever you want, from adjusting the cabinet height to child proofing the cabinets. During this process, the customer can use hand gestures to fly around the computer model, positioning themselves to view the design from any angle or perspective. The user viewpoint can even be scaled to let the customer view the model from the perspective of a child. Is the cookie jar within reach?

❁   ❁   ❁

Designing the Future

Riots in South Central Los Angeles in April 1992 left over $500 million in property damages to the neighborhoods. When the fires burned out, and the riots dispersed, urban planners at the University of California Los Angeles offered to help reconstruct the area as part of a new project using virtual reality technology as a city planning tool. In just a few months, a team of students under Bill Jepson, director of computing at the Graduate School of Architecture and Urban Planning, built a large scale virtual environment showing buildings, street intersections, and zoning restrictions on Silicon Graphics computer workstations. City planners, local residents, and officials can now use this system to understand who owns the neighborhoods, what kinds of stores fill the buildings, and how best to rebuild the damaged areas.

In a recent *San Francisco Chronicle* article, Jepson said, "Flying overhead, you can highlight all the liquor stores in red, then point to one of the buildings and see who owns the store, when they got their liquor license, and what the assessed valuation of the building is." Virtual reality technology can bring together massive amounts of information such as zoning, valuation, and city records, and present it in a way that would otherwise be totally baffling.

Similar work is also being performed in Germany, where architects are working with VPL Research to aid in the reconstruction of East Berlin. Entire models of cities or neighborhoods are incredibly difficult to build and require intense computation to work with, but the payoff is great. By building our futures in virtual environments, whether they be airplanes or buildings or even cities, we can experiment while the ideas are still malleable and communicate them easily to those who don't speak the obscure language of designers.

SILICON MIRAGE

CHAPTER 9

Entertainment

❀   ❀   ❀

Besides the military, the largest investors in virtual reality technologies clearly come from the entertainment sector. Film studios, amusement parks, makers of video games, and toy manufacturers have made it clear that virtual reality shows great promise to be the next major wave in the evolution of recreation. Of course, high technology in the entertainment industry is nothing new. You can see examples of the latest

197

computer and communications technology in nearly everything from simple home computer games to rides at amusement parks.

Technology appears to make magic, and people will pay all sorts of money to escape a dull day and partake in magic. For this reason, almost no one argues that the most profitable applications of virtual reality—in both the short and long term—will be entertainment.

In this chapter, we'll explore some of the more interesting applications of virtual reality in entertainment and then look at where the industry may be going. Keep in mind that these systems all consist of fully immersive visual displays. That is, they each use some sort of head-mounted display device that incorporates position and orientation tracking.

❀ ❀ ❀

Virtual Racquetball

We saw in the last chapter that Autodesk is one of the primary movers and shakers of the computer-aided-design world. But aside from the popular AutoCAD, they have also put a great deal of time and money into the research and development of virtual reality. It was by way of demonstrating their achievements in this field that Autodesk created the Virtual Raquetball game (see Figure 9-1).

Perhaps it was fitting that one of the first publicly demonstrated entertainment applications of virtual reality should be so similar to one of the first computer games to use computer graphics: Pong. But, where Pong is two dimensional, extremely basic, and becomes monotonous quickly, Virtual Raquetball is three dimensional and fascinating. Like Pong, however, it's still extremely basic.

Through a pair of VPL EyePhones and a DataGlove, you become immersed in a computer-generated, three-dimensional racquetball court. You can then hold a real racquetball racquet that has been outfitted with a Polhemus magnetic positioning system. As you swing the racquet, a computer-generated representation of a racquet makes exactly the same movements in the virtual space. The game begins when a ball is served from behind you. It flies past your virtual body and bounces off the far wall. You then attempt to strike the ball back

FIGURE 9-1   Virtual Racquetball

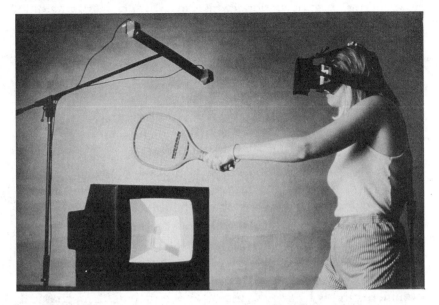

to the far wall with the virtual racquet. While the dimensions of the virtual court are by no means comparable to a real court, the game is still highly engaging.

Playing racquetball inside a three-dimensional cartoon is certainly less than satisfying at this point. However, we're fascinated by how people react on the virtual court. Although the crude, weighty display is a constant reminder that the game is virtual, action on the court can, in fact, invoke a strong emotional reaction from the user. This reaction is identical to the way one reacts to a similar event in the real world. For example, when the virtual ball comes too close to you, you really duck out of the way!

✿ ✿ ✿

The High Cycle

Another entertainment application developed and demonstrated early on by Autodesk is called the High Cycle (see Figure 9-2). The

idea was developed around another activity: riding a stationary bicycle. Although riding stationary bicycles provides a great aerobic
workout, it can be extremely boring. However, if you augment the
experience with a head-mounted display and headphones, you can
pretend you are riding through a desert landscape or along a bike
path next to a lake, or wherever you choose.

In the Autodesk demonstration, if you pedal fast enough through
the virtual environment, your viewpoint from within the model begins to rise as though you were taking flight. The flying effect
continues until the rate of pedaling decreases, at which point your
bicycle lowers and you land back on the ground. It was this fun feature that earned it the name "High Cycle."

Researchers at the University of North Carolina expanded on the
bicycling concept and altered a ten-speed mountain bike to supply
force feedback to simulate variations in the slope of the road and
the type of terrain in the virtual environment. With a pair of VPL
EyePhones on your head, you can steer through the virtual environment simply by turning the bike's handlebars. A mechanical

FIGURE 9-2   The High Cycle

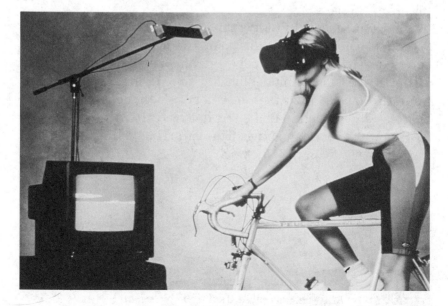

encoder measures the rotation of the handle bars and passes the information back to the computer, which calculates the scene you're seeing. The force feedback is supplied by a computer-controlled eddy-current resistance device called the RaceMate CompuTrainer. As you pedal up a hill, the CompuTrainer increases the resistance on the rear wheel, which, in turn, requires more effort to pedal. Therefore, if you pedal up a steep grade, the amount of effort required to turn the pedals is much greater than that required to pedal downhill.

Perhaps the best feature of virtual cycling is the ability to pass landmarks. The system can be programmed to include everything from flocks of birds flying overhead to billboards along the roadway. People find that when bicycling along the path, it's nice to have landmarks to gauge how far you've traveled as well as create distance goals for endurance ("If I can just make it to that tree up ahead...").

Although wearing a head-mounted display is not the most comfortable way to relax or exercise, the varied scenery makes up for the inconvenience. Plus, researchers have pointed out that navigating through a virtual environment by bicycle is significantly easier and more natural than using special hand gestures with a glovelike I/O device. A stationary bike takes almost no effort to figure out. You simply jump on, pedal, and steer.

✿　✿　✿

Virtuality

The only places you'll see Virtual Raquetball or the High Cycle these days is at a conference or in the laboratory. However, virtual reality has made a move out of the lab and into the marketplace with the British company W Industries' introduction of a game called Virtuality. This commercial system was developed specifically for use in video arcades. Actually, the original game, completed in 1988, was called the Giraffe. But this prototype suffered the fate of many commercial applications: it was abandoned due to limits in functionality and safety.

Once Virtuality was finally released, it quickly grew in popularity, and is now burning holes in the pockets of a growing number of youths and adults throughout Europe, Asia, and the United States. W Industries offers two models of the Virtuality game to choose from: a stand-up version, the Virtuality SU1000, and a sit-down version, the Virtuality SD1000 (see Figures 9-3 and 9-4).

The designers of Virtuality realized that for a virtual reality game to become popular, it had to be made as easy to use as possible. Considering all the clunky headgear and wiring that clutters most virtual reality laboratories, this wasn't an easy task. Nonetheless, Vir-

FIGURE 9-3   Virtuality SU1000

tuality does a good job of keeping all the wires and displays in align-ment, so that they hardly ever get tangled. To use the stand-up version, you first step onto a small circular platform and lock a safety ring around your waist. This safety ring serves two purposes: it keeps you from walking off the platform (remember that while you're wearing a head-mounted display, you can't see the real world around you), and it serves as a handhold if you suddenly become disoriented (see Chapter 15, *Human Factors*).

Next, you put on an LCD-based stereoscopic head-mounted dis-play. This display, called the Visette, along with the technology to

FIGURE 9-4   Virtuality SD1000

create it, was discussed in Chapter 3, *Seeing*. W Industries avoided using an input device based on a glove, as it would be cumbersome and difficult in an arcade setting. Instead, they created a small hand-held pointing device that looks somewhat like a pistol grip and trigger with no barrel. The two buttons on the "gun" control movement and fighting. When you point this lightweight "gun," you can see a virtual hand holding some virtual weapon in your display. Pulling the trigger button activates the weapon (usually a gun of some sort), and pressing the movement button moves you in the direction you're pointing.

Dactyl Nightmare

Note that once the actual hardware is installed (the computers in the back room, the headgear and so on in the arcade), you can load up a number of different games to play on the machine. This is different than most arcade-based video games that are programmed to only play one game. One available game scenario for Virtuality is called Dactyl Nightmare. Putting on the head-mounted display, you find yourself on a game field with a main floor and a set of four raised platforms connected to the main floor by stairs (see Color Plate 5). An assortment of geometric shapes are scattered around the game—mostly for decoration, although they can help as hiding places for the players. The objective of the game is simply to hunt down your opponent and shoot him before being shot yourself.

Meanwhile, as the game goes on, a pterodactyl circles above the game, randomly dive bombing and trying to grab you (the representation of your virtual body) with its claws. If successful, the creature carries your virtual body high above the playing level where it then drops you. While still somewhat simple compared to many video games, Virtuality is exceedingly fun to play.

More Virtuality Games

The second version of Virtuality, the sit-down unit, uses an identical head-mounted display, but the actual gaming scenarios are quite different. These sit-down versions are used for such games as piloting a simulated fighter aircraft or driving a race car around a track. Of course, any game that requires sitting down while playing would benefit from this version of the hardware.

The method of moving and shooting is slightly different, depending on which game you're playing. With the fighter-aircraft simulator, you use two joysticks, one for each hand. The joysticks control movement, and buttons on the joysticks control shooting. In this game, you must search for the enemy aircraft while piloting your aircraft over simulated playing areas, such as a sea coast, mountainous regions, and small towns.

✿   ✿   ✿

Need a Partner?

Today most commercial virtual reality systems can support more than one user at any given time within the same virtual environment. This ability to support multiple users adds an exciting new dimension to the discussion of entertainment applications. For example, in the Virtual Raquetball game described earlier, you could play the game against the computer (the computer has some "intelligence" about how to play) or you could play against someone else wearing the appropriate equipment. Again, this other person could be in the next room or the next county. It only depends on how the computers are networked.

Similarly, the Virtuality games are usually played against a partner. In the arcade near us, two hardware setups are arranged about 20 feet from each other, and each player can hear the shouting or mumbling of the opponent from "outside" in the real world. We've even started to see tournaments set up, pitting the best Virtuality players against each other. As the game often costs as much as a dollar a minute, you can imagine how much it costs to get good enough to win one of these tournaments.

But the possibilities of shared virtual realities go far beyond these simple games. There might come a time in the next few years when you play a game of tennis with a friend in Britain via the telephone lines (one of you would have to wake up very early). Or perhaps you'd be interested in purchasing a membership at a centrally located virtual golf club, conveniently accessible at your home? The technologies necessary to support such applications are not as far off as you might think. As we go to press, they're either currently available or under development.

❀   ❀   ❀

The Future of Entertainment

It's rare that a handfull of new technology demonstrations makes so many people in an industry sit up and smile. But that seems to be what has happened in the world of toy manufacturers and game makers. Almost every electronic game company is now developing products that include virtual reality technology as a home entertainment system. These systems, which should retail at under $2000, will start appearing around the end of 1993.

But what happens after that? What sorts of entertainment applications are likely to appear in the future? Let's take a look at a few products that we expect to see in the next few years.

Interactive Music Videos

We don't know about you, but we grew up playing air guitar and singing (poorly) over rock and roll albums in our bedrooms. Avid imaginations set us on a stage full of musicians, with screaming fans surrounding us. Fortunately we grew out of this activity, but we do admit that every once in a while we have that secret urge to be rock and roll megastars again. In the not-too-distant future, virtual reality will help us out.

When you place the lightweight head-mounted display on, you can see the stage below you and ten thousand teenagers waiting to hear you play. In your hands you have a virtual guitar or drum sticks or a bass or a cello or whatever you fancy playing. It doesn't matter that you never learned to play the instrument; the computer does that for you. All you need to do is strum appropriately. This is the setting for the ultimate music video: the one that you are part of. The lights dim and you begin your solo (don't worry, it always goes well).

While some people feel this scenario could be just another step in the shrinking of our imagination, others just can't wait to get their hands on the technology. It's a ways off yet, but we're convinced that it's inevitable.

Exercise Machines

Earlier in this chapter, we looked at the High Cycle as an innovative way to relieve the boredom of indoor exercising. Of course, bicycling isn't the only thing that people will do in virtual environments. Rowing machines could be fitted so that you can see yourself on the lake, the water glistening in the sunrise. The harder you row, the faster you move across the lake. Similarly, you could be on a virtual rowing shell along with several other virtual rowers. For the person who needs the urging of a coach, perhaps you'd hear a voice yelling from behind you, "Faster, Faster! You're slowing down! Push it for a hundred more meters."

Jogging or walking is clearly good exercise, but is painfully dull on a treadmill. Perhaps you will be able to purchase various virtual routes, such as "Walking along the Thames" or "A Jog Through New York City Streets." No doubt the latter would be the more challenging of the two. Stair-stepping machines or any other workout activity could also be spiced up with virtual reality. Even with low-quality images, the technology could help relieve the monotony and keep you coming back for more.

Interactive Theater

But virtual entertainment isn't all sitting or exercising at home. MCA/Universal Studios is now working with VPL Research to develop a three-dimensional movie theater that would play "voomies" (a reversal of the word *movie*). Between fifty and two hundred people would come together at a voomie theatre, don head-mounted displays, and navigate their way through whatever voomie was playing that night. At first, the experience probably won't be fully interactive, but that's clearly the goal. Instead, voomies will be second-stage, or exploratory, virtual realities, where audience members can move through the environment and watch the action from their own unique perspectives.

Plans at this time call for one person, called a changeling, to act as an emcee for the entertainment. The changeling would be trained to keep everyone involved with the action in the voomie, a task that may approach that of corralling herds in the Old West. Each person would be like a ghost in the virtual world, able to watch and explore, but unable to be seen by anyone else. Perhaps later, when computing power is great enough, the entire audience may be able to interact and take part in the voomie.

Voomies won't be "coming to a theatre near you" anytime soon. There may be one in Tokyo (home of MCA's parent company, Matsushita) by the end of 1993 and another soon after in Los Angeles. But widespread distribution will depend a great deal on how successful the initial ventures are. The capital investment for this kind of theatre is a mixed bag: there's no need to build large rooms for a 60-foot screen, but computers powerful enough to generate images for each audience member are extremely expensive.

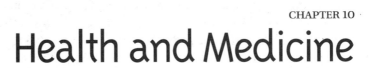

SILICON MIRAGE

CHAPTER 10

Health and Medicine

✿　　✿　　✿

It's been said that members of the medical community are similar to auto mechanics. Certainly, both professions specialize in preventative maintenance and in repairing the nonfunctional. And in the pursuit of these objcctives, professionals from both camps use a number of tools for analysis and adjustment, not to mention cutting and sewing back together. But where the drive shaft and transmission mechanisms in a car are always in the same place for a given model, the human body is significantly more variable and complex. Organs like the kidneys and the liver can shift into non-standard places, making them difficult to locate; different people come in different sizes and proportions, sometimes requiring special tools for those who fall outside the range of the average person; and the body is so interconnected that damage in one place may affect the functionality of the entire system.

Thus, where a wrench and a solid understanding of auto mechanics can go far in fixing an engine, the human body generally demands a more complex approach. Virtual reality technology is beginning to be used in various medical and health-related areas and is already showing great promise in becoming a standard tool in some medical processes. Let's look at two areas that are currently getting attention: radiation therapy planning and surgical simulation.

✿   ✿   ✿

Radiation Therapy Planning

The continuing battle to develop new and effective treatments for cancer has spawned a number of promising new technologies. One in particular is the use of radiation to destroy tumors. The underlying concept is to position several radiation beams in such a way that they travel through healthy tissue causing no damage but destroy the cancerous tissue at the exact spot at which the beams intersect. You don't have to be a specialist in this area of medicine to understand the difficulties associated with this task.

The radiologist must possess a comprehensive understanding of the complex three-dimensional layout of the human anatomy, as well as the spatial interrelationships between the various anatomical structures. For instance, if you could look through the body from a particular angle, what organs would your line of sight pass through? Obviously, great care must be taken in preparation of the treatment, including the orientation of each radiation beam, its cross-sectional shape, and the dosage of radiation delivered.

Of course, bodies aren't transparent, and a radiologist can't simply look through the body to make his or her calculations. Instead, conventional treatment-planning strategies typically involve indentifying the location and geometry of the target anatomical structures by using a number of two-dimensional X rays. Thus, the beam configurations are completed for only those two-dimensional slices. The result is a less-than-optimal balance between overall tumor volume and the distribution of the dosage. As a result, these treatments are often either less than adequate or overly destructive.

Recent advances in technology allow the person who is planning the procedure to sit at a computer workstation and view a computerized model of the patient's body along with beam information. But this method, too, has its limitations. Although it's possible to achieve a high level of precision with these computer systems, the actual task of positioning a series of radiation beams in such a way that they all intersect at the same spot in three-dimensional space can be challenging.

Now researchers at the University of North Carolina, focusing on the anatomical exploration portion of radiation treatment planning, have developed an alternate planning method that uses virtual reality technology. Instead of sitting before a standard video display terminal and manipulating the image, the practitioner dons an LCD-based stereoscopic head-mounted display and actually walks around a stabilized graphic model of the patient (see Figure 10-1), viewing areas of interest from any angle.

The UNC radiation planning system not only lets you explore the actual layout of a patient's internal organs, but also visualize and manually interact with graphical representations of the radiation beams. This interaction is handled through a hand-held positioning device. Using this system, you can position yourself anywhere around the virtual body, including at a beam's point of origin, and actually see the exact spot with which the beam will come in contact. Manipulating several beams becomes easier and more intuitive in this three-dimensional virtual environment. In this way, the normally difficult procedure of beam positioning becomes a relatively simple task of aiming.

FIGURE 10-1   UNC radiation therapy treatment system

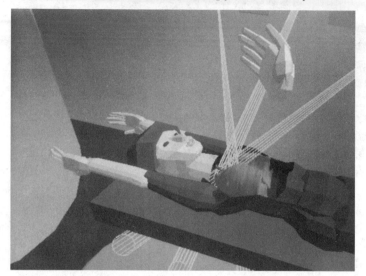

❁   ❁   ❁

Surgical Simulation

Simulators create environments that simulate real life experience. In some ways, the traditional simulators are basic forms of virtual reality, though a number of differences exist. Traditional simulators can be used to train airplane pilots or the crews of boats. However, while simulator technologies have existed for a number of years, until recently, little of the work conducted with this technology has been focused on the medical industry. This is due to a number of reasons, including the immense complexity of the human anatomy and the computational requirements required to simulate it.

Now, however, researchers are having some success in approaching the idea of medical simulation from a new perspective: virtual reality. Although the ability to generate complete virtual replicas of the human body is still many years away, virtual reality researchers are now beginning to develop a number of highly innovative medical applications. Perhaps one of the most significant and promising is currently being developed by Richard Satava of the Silas B. Hayes Army Community Hospital at Fort Ord, California, in conjunction with VPL Research.

Intended for eventual use as both a teaching tool and a method of practicing surgical procedures, initial models have focused solely on the abdominal area (see Figure 10-2). Although the virtual abdomen is cartoonish in appearance, due to current limits in computer power and head-mounted-display resolution, the simulation is realistic in its anatomical and technical accuracy and the interactivity with the model's internal organs is excellent. For example, you can grasp and manipulate instruments such as virtual scalpels and clamps, applying them where appropriate in the model.

Because virtual reality lets you explore a model from any angle, anatomical structures can be evaluated in ways not possible in the real world. For example, medical students could carefully study the digestive tract without actually performing surgery on a living person or dissecting a cadaver. Instead, a virtual body might allow students to explore the anatomy by journeying through the body, starting inside the esophagus, down into the stomach, through the duodenum, and into the bile duct. This sort of interactive virtual exploration not only obviates the need for major surgical procedures, it also offers significantly more flexibility and opportunity in the study.

Clearly, a virtual cadaver could be an incredibly useful tool in learning about the body, how it works, and how to repair it. From anatomical interrelationships to practicing difficult operations, a virtual surgical simulator is a powerful tool. And despite the limitations of current hardware and software systems, the basic framework for a fully interactive virtual simulator has already been developed. Now it's only a matter of time before the necessary components are available to make the simulation more realistic.

※　※　※

Virtual Health

Health and medicine is an enormous field, ranging far beyond radiation treatments and anatomy. And there are at least as many

Figure 10-2   Virtual surgery

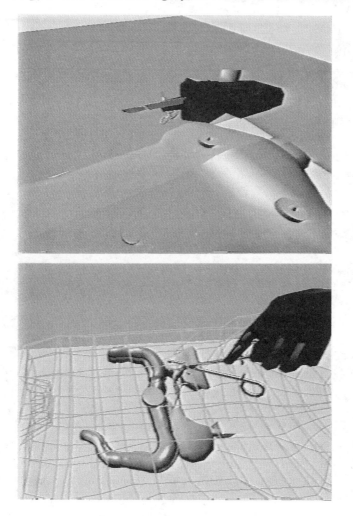

ways to apply virtual reality technology as there are professions, procedures, and methods under the medical umbrella. Some medical areas are extremely subtle and have been traditionally difficult to work with. For example, studying the range of motion in a human hand or arm is a difficult task. Hands and arms come in different shapes, sizes, and flexibilities. If you have an injury in one of your hands, you may go into physical therapy to recover strength and dexterity in the hand. But how can your physical therapist best measure your progress? Greenleaf Systems, of Palo Alto, California, is tackling this problem by using virtual reality technology (though not virtual reality itself). Greenleaf uses the DataGlove to register and record movement in the fingers and hand with a degree of accuracy not possible with traditional methods.

Other medical issues are much more obvious. Take, for example, the concerns of someone with a degenerative nerve disease or other paralyzing disorder. Virtual reality holds a significant potential for freeing the minds of the severely physically handicapped and allowing them a greater measure of functionality despite the reduced or nonexistent use of limbs. For example, integrating eye tracking, voice recognition, and a small tongue-operated joystick can open tremendous doors for someone who is limited to moving his or her eyes and tongue. Navigation through and interaction with nearly any of the virtual environments described in these chapters can easily be accomplished with these devices, which means that interactive, three-dimensional worlds that educate, entertain, and enable are all accessible to someone who might not otherwise be able to participate.

The vast number of possibilities in applying virtual reality technology to medicine and health—from the perspectives of both preventative maintenance and repair—is mind boggling. And although it may be years before the technology is able to contribute in any significant way, the present-day development of virtual reality medical systems shows great promise for the future.

SILICON MIRAGE

CHAPTER 11

Education

What if...? The question is asked so often as we're growing up: What if I could explore the moon? What if I could see atoms? What if I could shrink down in size and walk around inside a computer chip? But when we asked this as children, the answer was always, "You can't." Well, times have changed, and virtual reality makes possible what yesterday was only a dream. Asking questions is an integral part of our education as we grow. However, reading science textbooks is a relatively inefficient form of learning, and listening to lectures in a classroom can only go so far. However, learning by experience—by actually doing or seeing or hearing—is not only efficient, but can be fun, too.

Virtual reality lets students ask "What if...?" and then find out by trying. In this chapter, we'll look at a few examples of how virtual reality has begun to be used in education, as well as some ways that we think it will be used in the not-too-distant future. While you're reading, imagine yourself as a child in school, with this technology at your fingertips. We think you'll find that whatever field you're studying or have studied, especially if it has to do with three-dimensional or complex phenomena, there is a significant potential for applying virtual reality.

✿ ✿ ✿

The Virtual Physics Lab

Physics was always an area in which we had a lot of what if's. While trying desperately to comprehend such enticing topics as gravity, moments of inertia, complex interactions between colliding objects, and a hundred other concepts, we knew that if we could *visualize* what was going on, we'd have a reasonable time of understanding it. Apparently we weren't alone. Researchers at the University of Houston and NASA's Johnson Space Center, under the direction of R. Bowen Loften, have developed a virtual reality system called the Virtual Physics Laboratory. The goal of the project is to let students experiment within a simulated physics laboratory and to control the physical properties of objects within the lab (Figure 11-1).

There are many different experiments that can be performed now, and the system is growing every day. Presently, while using the system, students can easily experiment and control phenomena such as the magnitude and direction of gravity, properties of elastic and inelastic collisions between two bodies, and coefficients of friction. Changing or adding elements in the environment helps students understand what's going on. For example, tracers can be applied to several flying objects that have varying size and mass in

FIGURE 11-1   The Virtual Physics Lab

order to show the objects' trajectories. Plus, time can be frozen at any time, so that the students can perform detailed observations of a phenomenon that varies over time.

The system's underlying hardware consists of a pair of high-end Silicon Graphics workstations generating images for a VPL Eye-Phone LX. Students interact and navigate within the virtual environment by using a VPL DataGlove. As we go to press, researchers are finishing the development of Virtual Physics Lab, and preparing it for high-school and college students.

❁   ❁   ❁

Planetary Exploration

Although a trip to a planetarium or observatory could make for an exciting field trip, we think a trip to Mars or Venus would be truly fascinating. What would the ground look like? How large are the mountains? The valleys? What kind of weather would there be? People have been pondering what it would be like to walk on a different planet ever since the planets were discovered in the night sky. Now virtual reality offers us a chance to find out.

Researchers such as Mike McGreevy at NASA's Ames Research Center are working on a project called Visualization for Planetary Exploration in which they take topographical data generated from satellites and space probes and create three-dimensional models of portions of a planet surface. For example, they have taken data retrieved from flybys of Mars and Miranda, a moon orbiting the planet Uranus, and created a virtual environment that can be explored (Figure 11-2).

This sort of re-creation of a planetary surface is not easy, but the benefits are significant. The images are generated with high-end Silicon Graphics computer graphics workstations and viewed through head-mounted displays such as the EyePhones or the other displays described in Chapter 3, *Seeing*. This planetary exploration system lets you fly over mountains and down into valleys, freely exploring any aspect of the simulation that you choose. The images, like most virtual reality applications today, are still relatively crude. But with better display devices and more powerful image-processing units, the sensation of being on the planet will be impressive. Of course, you wouldn't feel the difference in gravity or the drastic temperature changes, but in the future you might be able to combine this simulation with the Virtual Physics Lab. How does the change in gravity affect a virtual ball thrown in the air?

FIGURE 11-2   The virtual Martian surface

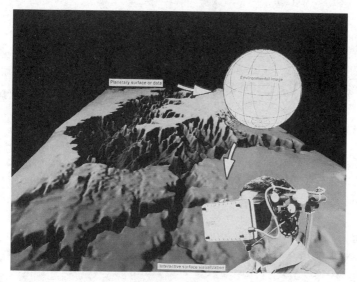

Other than as a educational tool, the Virtual Planetary Exploration system may someday be used for mission planning and training in the eventual exploration and possible colonization of the planet Mars.

❀   ❀   ❀

Back to Basics

Flipping through a course listing at a university is like reading a list of future virtual reality applications: art, astronomy, architecture, geophysics, mathematics, physics, all the way through zoology! Any subject that studies three-dimensional objects or ideas is well-suited to virtual reality.

Let's take a look at a few areas that we think are likely to embrace virtual reality and how they'll use it. Note that unless otherwise mentioned, most of these applications are not currently in development.

Archeology. Nearly every group currently conducting large-scale archaeological studies of ruins uses some sort of CAD program to track and archive every aspect of the excavation, from the dimensions of the structures to the placement of the artifacts found within them. The Center for the Study of Architecture at Bryn Mawr is currently creating archives of some of the great archaeological monuments around the world using computer-aided design programs. These three-dimensional models could easily be adapted into virtual environments that students could explore.

A classroom of students could potentially take a virtual field trip to the ruins of Carthage in the morning and move on to visit a virtual reconstruction of the city in the afternoon. Perhaps the next day a student would go to the school library where he or she could fly first through the halls of the pyramids of Egypt and then through the pyramids of Mexico. Or perhaps explore the acropolis and Parthenon as it existed in 433 B.C., and then flip to its present condition and back again. What are the similarities? How are they different? What if...?

These visits would never be as good as visiting the places themselves but would be significantly more enlightening to a student than simply seeing a photograph in a book or seeing a video tape.

Biology. In the movie *E.T.*, the little extraterrestrial aborts a potential slaughter of doomed frogs, causing havoc in the classroom. Science teachers and students alike may not have to worry about this sort of activity in the future, when virtual anatomical studies let people poke and prod their way through frogs, pigs, and even humans without having to kill anything. Not only would students be able to see how organs are placed within the body, but they could also take tours through the gastrointestinal tract, into the brain, or through the parts of the ear.

Anatomy isn't the only element of biology that lends itself to virtual reality applications. Students of the future might fly through a virtual cell, reaching out and pointing at objects, asking the computer, "What is that?" The mitochondria (or whatever) would light up, and the computer would read a recorded description. Or genetic modeling might be understood well enough so that a student could change genes in a virtual DNA molecule and then tell the computer to use that DNA to build a three-dimensional life-form.

Chemistry. As we mentioned back in Chapter 5, *Feeling*, molecules are of particular interest to researchers at the University of North Carolina, where they are using three-dimensional environments and force-feedback systems to aid in the visualization of complex molecules. If you've ever taken a chemistry class, you know that there are many different ways to display molecules, from colored spheres to ball-and-stick models to simple line drawings. But aside from actually building physical models of these representations, you are usually limited to viewing them on a piece of paper or on a computer screen.

The application developed at the University of North Carolina lets you build a three-dimensional model and then fly around within it to examine how the molecule really looks. You can even change how the molecule is represented, depending on what you're trying to understand about it. For example, if you're focusing on the bonds between atoms, you could make those the predominant items in the virtual environment. You can make yourself bigger and fit the molecule in your hand or make yourself tiny so that the molecule looks as if it'd fill a whole room. Then, using an input device like the DataGlove or a Polhemus tracker, you can reach out and move the molecule, turning it around, and so on.

❈   ❈   ❈

Simulation and Training

In many cases, providing someone with hands-on training in a particular task is too difficult, too costly, or just plain impossible. This is clearly the case in training airline pilots to handle difficult situations such as a sudden loss of fuel or a wind shear. Trying to recreate these events while flying a real airplane is not only difficult but potentially disastrous. Instead, the airline industry has turned to using high-quality flight simulators that provide pilots with the look and feel of taking off, flying, and landing, even though they remain stationary on the ground (see Figure 11-3).

FIGURE 11-3   Current flight simulators

One of the great things about flight simulators is that pilots can try many more flights each day than they could in an actual aircraft. As soon as they land, they can restart the simulation to try the flight again, perhaps this time taking off in heavy fog or landing on an icy runway. Many of these flight simulators are not usually considered virtual reality, as the cockpit is real and the view outside the windows (projected onto screens) is computer generated. The simulation feels immersive, though, and pilots often walk away with sweaty palms. More recently, however, flight simulators have been built that use virtual reality technology, such as head-mounted displays. In fact, each branch of the military is presently developing or using a head-mounted display to help train pilots in a lab setting.

However, simulators could be potentially used in many other fields, as well. In the last chapter, we looked at how surgeons could practice a difficult operation before attempting it in a life-threatening situation. A military operation that involved sending troops into an unfamiliar place, like a foreign embassy, might have a better chance of success if each of the soldiers had explored a virtual model of that building beforehand. Studying a blueprint is one thing, but actually visiting (even if it is virtual) is much better.

There are hundreds more jobs that could benefit from training in a virtual environment, from automobile construction and aircraft maintenance to the control of nuclear reactors or giant cranes. People benefit whenever they can learn by actually performing the job, and if they can perform that job in a safe space, then it's all the better. Plus, virtual reality applications could create learning environments that would be impossible otherwise. For example, a person might be able to freeze the simulation in the middle of a difficult procedure and ask the computer for advice or additional information.

✿   ✿   ✿

What If

Although our editors insisted that we limit the scope of this chapter to how virtual reality can be used in education, in many ways this whole book is about that. Anytime you see a new perspective or use a new tool to tackle a problem, you are, in effect, learning. In this way, virtual reality can be a powerful teacher in every field. And in the future, as more people are able to answer the question, "What if...?," we may see great progress in how quickly and how well people learn.

SILICON MIRAGE

CHAPTER 12

The Sciences

The history of science has been a journey of un-
covering the invisible elements of our universe. You
already know that when you throw a ball through the
air it travels along a curved path. But at first glance it's
difficult to define what, exactly, that curve is. Physics
reveals that a ball always follows a perfect parabolic
path, unless other forces act upon it. A series of numbers gathered by astronomers, chemists, or biologists

may also appear random until we decipher the mathematical function beneath them, encountering perhaps an equation of great simplicity. And in the last hundred years, these scientific unearthings have dramatically increased in number and changed in style. In fact, this century has been a time of radically surpassing the limits of our own senses to explore far beyond what we can see, hear, and touch.

Now virtual reality technologies are beginning to take us to an even greater level of understanding by enabling us to create three-dimensional, interactive simulations of scientific phenomena. In this chapter, we'll look at three areas in which scientists are exploring the use of virtual reality: aerodynamics, mathematical modeling, and astronomy. In each of these areas, scientists are increasing their ability to uncover and decipher the mysteries of our everyday world.

✿   ✿   ✿

Virtual Aerodynamics

There are a number of instances in which an object or surface must be designed such that it creates a minimal disturbance in its surrounding environment. For examples, designers try to make automobiles sleek so that air will move smoothly and easily around them, thus reducing drag and increasing gas mileage. Other designers have similar objectives in building new aircraft wings or sailboat keels. However, the dynamics of how air or fluid moves around an object is an extremely complex phenomenon, requiring a level of computation that was not available until recently.

Traditionally, automobile, aircraft, or sailboat designers have used a number of different methods to visualize the complex turbulent flow patterns that these objects create. Perhaps the best known method is the wind or water tunnel. Each of these tunnels works in basically the same manner. First, the object or structure under investigation is placed inside the tunnel apparatus. Depending on what is being explored, this tunnel may be small enough to fit on a desktop or large enough to fill a multistory building. Next, the object is surrounded by a current of air or water, perhaps supplied by a fan or a propeller of sorts. Then, during the procedure, smoke or dye is injected into the flow field at a point upwind (or upstream) of the object. The smoke or dye acts as a flow visualization tool. That is, whereas scientists can't see the air or water move, they can see the smoke or dye move through the surrounding medium, giving them the information they need. Of course, in a real life situation, it may be the object that moves, rather than the air or water around it. However, the results are ultimately the same.

Another technique involves covering the surface of the object under examination with tufts or streamers. These items are anchored at one end, allowing the other to hang free. As water or air passes over the surface of the object, the free end of the tuft or streamer is caught up in the flow. The direction in which this free end points indicates the direction of flow for that particular region of the object's surface.

Clearly there are drawbacks and limitations inherent in both methods of testing. Creating a model or prototype is time-consuming and expensive. And a scaled model, no matter how carefully constructed, may still have radically different performance characteristics, throwing off the accuracy of your results. Plus, examining the flow field closely is problematic, at best. Studying a model from within a closed wind tunnel would be not only difficult but uncomfortable (if not lethal) and would corrupt the results. Consequently, the search for alternatives that provide the same—if not more—information has long been a dream of aerodynamic researchers.

The Virtual Windtunnel

As we noted earlier, there is an extreme computational burden when calculating the changes in magnitude and direction of air movement over time (called flow fields) around even basic geometric shapes. Displaying that information to human eyes makes the problem even more difficult. Rendering a computerized image is made all the more complex because the computer must be able to rapidly store and retrieve massive amounts of data. In fact, the amount of data generated by a single three-dimensional computational fluid-dynamics simulation can generate several thousand megabytes of data (over ten billion pieces of information).

However, with the aid of supercomputers, researchers at NASA's Ames Research Center have finally been able to actively pursue several alternatives for aerodynamic testing. One of those projects is called the Virtual Windtunnel (see Figure 12-1).

The Virtual Windtunnel lets you visualize a simulated flow field as though you were actually standing inside a wind tunnel. Of course, a principle difference between the real and virtual windtunnels is that while you receive the visual sensation of being present in the simulation, the flow field is not disturbed, and so the experiment is not corrupted. The project's objective is to let engineers analyze the complex three-dimensional nature and effect of multiple vortices, areas of recirculation, and the chaotic flows during vortex breakdown, all of which are extremely difficult to visualize through normal numerical simulations.

In one use of the Virtual Windtunnel, a CAD model of a space shuttle is loaded into the system. At this point, the complex turbu-

FIGURE 12-1   The Virtual Windtunnel

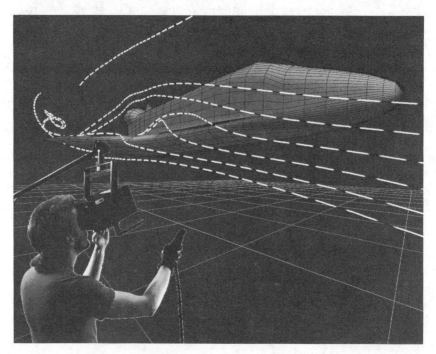

lent flow-field information describing the environment around the model has been resolved on a supercomputer, but it is only an enormous set of numbers (again, billions of them). A Fake Space BOOM (see Chapter 3, *Seeing*) is used to view the model. As with other systems we've talked about, the model remains stabilized as the user changes his or her perspective.

You can reveal the patterns of water or air flow in the model by injecting tracers into the flow field on command. The tracers flow out of a small graphical icon in the virtual environment and—like smoke or dye—flow past the object, showing the twists and turns that the air or fluid would take. Positioning this tracer icon near the space shuttle is easy using a DataGlove (see Chapter 6, *Recognition*) with a magnetic positioning sensor. As you move your hand, the icon follows along, allowing natural control of the placement of the streamlines within the simulation. When the icon is positioned where you want, a gesture with the gloved hand stabilizes it so that the user is free to view the resulting tracer patterns from any angle or position.

By executing another hand gesture, the single line of tracers transforms into a set of tracers, called a rake. This lets you see a number of flow patterns simultaneously. The simulation can also be stopped at any time to let you fly through a specific vortex or swirl in order to study the phenomenon in greater detail.

✿   ✿   ✿

Mathematical Modeling

Stephen Wolfram knew it all along: mathematical equations are most easily understood by visualizing them. That is, if you put an equation or a set of numbers in front of someone, it's rare that they'll understand it immediately. But a graphic representation of an equation is significantly more intuitive and understandable (see Figure 12-2). So Wolfram created the software program Mathematica, a powerful tool for visualizing math.

However, Mathematica only goes so far. You can create three-dimensional images on-screen. You can move them around and look

FIGURE 12-2   Visualizing math

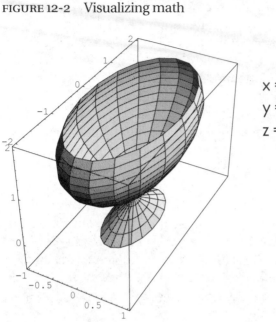

$$x = \cos t \cdot \sin u$$
$$y = 2 \cdot \sin t \cdot \sin u$$
$$z = u$$

at them from varying perspectives. But at times it's helpful to actually immerse yourself in a graphic, especially one that involves a
number of different variables. Virtual reality has the potential to create these sorts of mathematical environments, letting you fly
through three-dimensional representations of equations, exploring
their intricacies, and interacting with them.

Why would anyone want to do this? It turns out that interacting
with an equation can be educational. Some equations, especially
some fractals, actually require three-dimensional viewing to make
their subtleties understandable. Other equations would be simply
easier to understand if you could reach out and play with them. For
example, imagine standing in a large virtual room that contains an
enormous mathematical graph. Seeing the graph in three-dimensional space would be one thing, especially as you could walk or fly
around it, but imagine actually reaching out and grabbing part of
the graph and moving it. As you move the graph, you can watch how
the rest of the function changes. Or, similarly, perhaps you could

reach out and turn a huge virtual dial, changing the value of a variable, and watch the graph change.

These sorts of virtual mathematical modeling are presently only in early development but may someday prove to radically alter how students and mathematicians work with complex equations.

✿   ✿   ✿

Virtual Astronomy

Late at night, staring up into the heavens, we can't help but be amazed at how large and complex the universe is. Of the thousands of stars you might see in the night sky, many small points of light are actually immense galaxies, each located thousands of light years from us and from each other, and each containing millions of stars themselves. It's difficult to remember sometimes that all those galaxies and stars are situated in a vast three-dimensional structure. In fact, some scientists and philosophers once thought that the stars were all an equal distance away from the Earth, attached to a spherical firmament surrounding our planet. Even now, with all our complex computerized tools, astronomers still have difficulty understanding how pieces of the heavens appear in three dimensions.

In order to better understand the complex layout of various portions of the universe, researchers Margaret Geller and John Huchra at the Harvard-Smithsonian Center for Astrophysics and the National Center for Supercomputing Applications have been using virtual reality in order to explore complex astronomical data. Their principle objective has been to map the positions of all of the galaxies within approximately five hundred light years of the Earth. This is a monumental task, considering that in the ten years the project has been under way, about thirteen thousand galaxies have been catalogued.

Within the region being investigated is a pattern of galaxies referred to as the stick man, which is part part of the "great wall" of galaxies that have been observed by the two researchers since the early 1980s (see Figure 12-3). In the initial stages of building the

FIGURE 12-3   The stick man pattern of galaxies

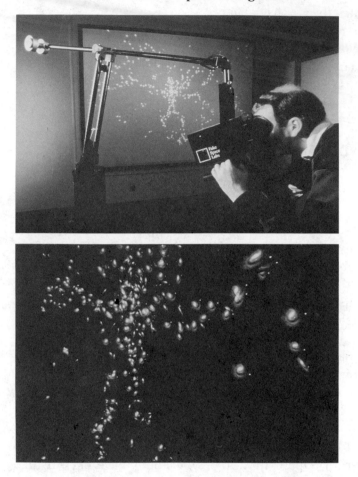

virtual environment, the complexity of the astronomical data has been reduced to mapping 935 points, each of which represents a single spiral galaxy.

Seeing all this astronomical data in a two-dimensional medium like a computer screen or on paper is almost meaningless. But when you step into the virtual environment and are immersed in the data, the patterns start to become clear. To view the data, the researchers have made use of a Fake Space BOOM connected to a high-end computer graphics workstation. By moving the BOOM display around and navigating within the environment, the researchers are able to view the galaxy structures from any angle or perspective. This allows them to gain insight into the structural layout and placements of the galaxies. What does the cluster look like from this angle? How about from over here? Reports by the researchers indicate that this manner of visualizing the data significantly enhances the traditional methods of statistical analysis.

❁   ❁   ❁

Visualizing Science

In attempting to understand and describe the phenomenological world around us, scientists are using computers to create trillions of pieces of data each year. But organizing that data in such a way that it is useful is a truly difficult task. Much of the information comes from events that are inherently three dimensional, but are typically represented as either streams of numbers or two-dimensional graphs. Now virtual reality is offering a method to visualize three-dimensional data in a three-dimensional medium.

We've seen in earlier chapters that researchers are beginning to use virtual reality to explore biology and chemistry. Now scientists are looking at using it to work with many different areas, including materials stress, electrical engineering, and nanotechnology. In the future, scientists may explore the geology of our planet by flying into virtual representations of gathered data. Or they'll simulate genetic experiments in a virtual world that gives them quick feedback before attempting the procedure in a real-world setting. Whatever the future holds, scientists will certainly be on the cutting edge of where virtual reality is going.

SILICON MIRAGE

CHAPTER 13

Information Control

✤   ✤   ✤

If you can keep five thousand numbers in your head and see trends and relationships between them within seconds, you can just skip this chapter. Typically, humans are extremely poor in mental processes that include a great deal of information, whether it be numbers or names or pieces of data. A librarian at a large library reigns over an immense quantity of information, but it's a rare librarian who can quickly answer the question, "Tell me the publisher and call number for every book ever written by Isaac Asimov."

Instead, we've developed tools that let us manipulate information in various ways. Written language is one of the most basic forms of information control. That is, we can extend the capabilities of our memory by writing information in a symbolic form such as letters and numbers. In Chapter 3, *Seeing*, we looked at Watson and Crick's model of DNA and saw how it acted as an extension to their ability to create mental models of information. Now computers are our most powerful data processors, and they act as extensions of our minds by manipulating and presenting vast fields of information in humanly understandable forms.

As we've seen, one of the most powerful ways that computers can present information is through virtual reality technologies. In this chapter, we'll look at some of the ways that virtual reality is being developed to present large and complex sets of data in forms more easily digestible.

❂   ❂   ❂

Financial Visualization

Some of the most complex and demanding information environments involve understanding and manipulating the nonstop flow of financial data from around the world. Professional traders on the floor of a stock exchange, investment planners, and fund managers must all contend with dozens of two-dimensional displays teeming with constantly changing alphanumeric information. The highly aggressive nature of their businesses results in a stressful environment that requires quick decision making based on both specific knowledge and an understanding of the big picture. Of course, there are those people who thrive in such a setting, but for most, this is a sure way to drown in a sea of information.

Virtual reality developers have begun to create systems that can take the inundation of complex financial data and present it in a more easily accessible three-dimensional environment. Let's take a look at two systems that are currently being used: *n*-Vision and Capri.

n-Vision

Reseachers Clifford Beshers and Steven Feiner at Columbia University have developed a virtual reality system known as *n*-Vision that lets you visualize sets of complex, multivariable data. Their focus so far has been the financial market, working with call options and butterfly spreads. A call option is an option to buy a stock or commodity at a specified price (the call price) within a specified period of time. Buying and selling call options is a complicated business. For example, determining the value of a European call option typically requires thinking about both foreign and domestic interest rates, volatility (the measure of an option's price fluctuation tendencies), strike price (the specified price at which an option may be exercised), spot (the current selling price of the commodity), and the time remaining in which the option can be exercised.

Trying to keep five or six variables in mind is extraordinarily difficult, and it's easy to make a mistake by not taking a pertinent variable into account. Analysts can visualize one or more of these variables by placing them on a graph. But as we discussed back in Chapter 3, *Seeing*, while we can easily graph two or three variables at a time, it's difficult to graph four or more without the use of three-dimensional equipment. And when it comes to graphing many variables concurrently, virtual reality technology becomes the best possible solution.

The *n*-Vision system uses an innovative method to help in visualizing the complex data by reusing spatial dimensions to allow additional variables to be visualized and controlled. The technique involves taking one three-dimensional coordinate system and a surface within it (which represents a function of two of the many variables mentioned above) and nesting it in one or more levels of a three-dimensional coordinate system that represent the other variables (see Figure 13-1).

The surface inside the nested coordinate system represents a combination of every variable in the financial equation. You can fly around the graphic or make it larger to inspect portions of it, or you can adjust the placement of the nested coordinate system, which

FIGURE 13-1   Nested coordinate systems in the *n*-Vision system

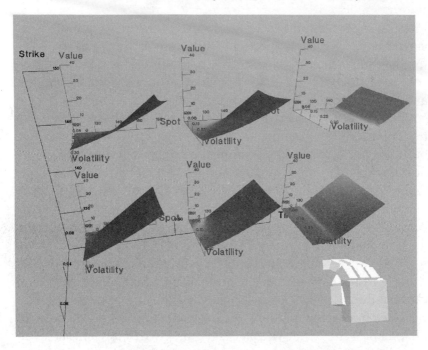

alters the value of the variables. To move the nested coordinate system, you wear a DataGlove (see Chapter 6, *Recognition*) and literally grab it and drag it around within the larger, outer coordinate system. The net result is that by using *n*-Vision you can see trends and other features of the data that would have been difficult to visualize otherwise.

Capri

Maxus Systems International of New York is credited with the development of the first commercial use of virtual reality in the field of high finance and money management. Developed for TIAA-CREF, the $106 billion college teachers' pension fund, the system lets the fund managers track Pacific Rim markets in an easy, highly intuitive manner.

The system, known as Capri, displays financial market information in such a way that it is relatively easy to understand. The Capri virtual world consists of a grid much like a giant checkerboard. One side of the grid is labeled with a series of industry groups, such as financials, utilities, automotive, pulp, and so on. An adjoining side is labeled with the names of various stock exchanges in such places as Tokyo, Hong Kong, Singapore, and Thailand. Located within each square on this grid is a collection of chips. Each chip represents a particular security, and its position within the grid clearly indicates which market and industry the stock falls in.

Each of these chips also has characteristics that help an analyst understand more about it. For example, the color of the chip indicates its price performance; red denotes that the stock is down from the day before, blue represents a rise, and so on. A spinning chip indicates that the security has features that are considered more appealing than others in that industry. For example, a security with a better price-to-earnings ratio or one that is considered undervalued might spin. Also, a stock that is blinking indicates that it has the potential to be simultaneously bought and sold in different markets. This may enable an investor to profit from a difference in market prices in two or more locations. Additionally, the position of the chip above or below the grid reflects the stock's measure of activity against other chips in the same industry.

Remember that all this information has traditionally been communicated from computers or ticker tape machines in an alphanumeric form, then painstakingly translated into a number of charts and graphs for analysis and comparison. Capri lets financial analysists bypass several steps and gain a greater understanding of the important information without getting lost in the numbers.

Other than watching as the chips blink, turn color, and spin in various locations, you can navigate through the virtual financial market grid to learn more about each security as needed. When you first enter the Capri system, you are directly above the grid, looking down on the whole scene. Then, using a Spaceball (see Chapter 6, *Recognition*), you can swoop down into the grid, moving your head around to view the grid from any angle. If you want to learn more about that spinning blue chip on the other side of the grid, you simply fly over to it, click once on the Spaceball button, and up pops a list of specific information regarding that stock.

Obviously, the concept of visualizing financial information is not limited to only chips on a checkerboard. For example, some virtual reality researchers have suggested representing each stock or security as a stalk of wheat or grass. These stalks could be separated according to market and industry, and if the stock is showing an upward trend in value it might glow a bright red and get taller. Similarly, perhaps it would glow blue and shrink when it's lowering in value. Market trends and price fluctuations would move across vast fields of the virtual stalks, looking like wind through a farmer's field. With such a setup, you could walk through patches of commodity stalks, grabbing a handful of tall red stocks and throwing away the small blue ones in your virtual arms.

❈ ❈ ❈

Visualizing Information

The fast-paced finance scene is not the only place where people need to gain an understanding of large sets of complex data. Some meteorologists gather immense numbers of pressure, temperature, and wind readings in an attempt to predict the world's weather patterns. Others who study tornadoes and hurricanes build elaborate mathematical equations based on millions of air current readings. Sociologists exploring the demographics of a nation are confronted with a deluge of information that must be carefully sifted through in order to perceive the bigger picture.

Virtual reality technology can help these professionals—and others—by generating multi-dimensional, interactive worlds that represent the data. Plus, virtual reality is flexible enough to display different sorts of information in different ways, letting you work in the manner most intuitive and helpful to you. Let's look at two other virtual reality systems, one currently in the prototype stage and another still in the very early stages of design.

Software Visualization

Writing software programs to control a single computer is complex enough; writing programs to control a number of computers connected over a large network can be a nightmare. But these sorts of systems are not uncommon: regional electric power or telephone companies rely on the efficient and continuous functionality of thousands of computer processors to provide their services. Using virtual reality technology, researchers at the University of Tokyo and the Tokyo Electric Power Company have been working on a partial solution to the problems that arise in the programming of these complex software systems.

The traditional method of building these systems involves using sets of two-dimensional flow charts and timing charts. A flow chart shows the relationships between the large number of processes, and a timing chart shows the precise timing between the processes in the flow chart and the computer processors in the network. This new virtual reality system is based on the idea that it would be helpful to combine the two sets of charts into one three-dimensional graphic environment (see Figure 13-2).

This virtual environment can represent the processes and the processors, along with the complex interrelationships that programmers must carefully map out. According to the developers, this 3-D repre-

FIGURE 13-2   Three-dimensional flow charts

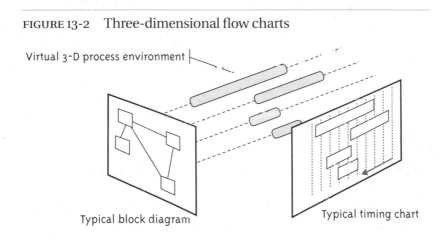

Virtual 3-D process environment

Typical block diagram

Typical timing chart

sentation provides an increased capability for the direct and intuitive understanding and planning of these complicated relationships.

You can interact with and manipulate this programming environment by using a DataGlove (see Chapter 6, *Recognition*). For example, you can reach out and grab the entire model and turn it in space to view the process flow from various angles. At the time of this writing, the researchers are reporting that using this system has reduced the effort on large-scale programming tasks by half.

Air Traffic Control

Air traffic control is yet another field in which human operators must make decisions based on rapidly changing data. An air traffic controller typically must assimilate a number of alphanumeric codes and symbols displayed on a two-dimensional radar screen. Remember that these people are attempting to understand and control the sometimes complex relationships between airplanes in a three-dimensional airspace. Obviously, when there are dozens of aircraft moving at hundreds of miles per hour within close proximity to each other, things happen fast, and a simple mistake can cost lives.

By changing the manner in which the radar information is displayed, the job of the air traffic controller could be made less taxing, and the process of directing aircraft could be made significantly safer. Virtual reality offers a perfect interface for displaying this three-dimensional information. The controller could quickly ascertain the relationships and speed of aircraft in a highly intuitive way: simply by seeing miniature representations of the airplane flying through a virtual airspace environment. To get a different view of the airspace around an airport, the controller could fly around to different locations in the environment, perhaps flying closer to one airplane to gather more information about its airspeed and altitude. In addition, this sort of system could include communications control. For example, an air traffic controller might simply point at a representation of an airplane to open a radio communication link with it.

Note that this sort of system is not even close to the prototype stage and is still only under consideration by some foreign countries. However, the system is potentially so powerful that we expect it to be developed within the next ten years. (However, having it approved by the federal government may be even more complex that building the virtual reality system!)

✿   ✿   ✿

Virtual Information

A computer is a particularly interesting tool because we can make it act like thousands of other tools. And, as a hammer is an extension of our arm, the computer can be an extension to our imagination. Computers can juggle large quantities of information in a way that our brains can't and present it in a way that our eyes or ears can understand. In the years to come, we as a species will be required to make decisions based on more and more available information. And virtual reality might very well be the one tool that enables us to easily and quickly decipher the codes and patterns in the deluge.

www – information highway coded in HTML transitioning to virtual information coded in VRML

CHAPTER 14

Telepresence

✿   ✿   ✿

"If only I could be in two places at once!" We've all heard it said and probably said it ourselves. But to some extent we already can be in two places at once or at least create the illusion that we are. For example, while you're talking on the telephone to someone, it is as though your ears were in some remote place. You can hear what's going on miles away and then create sound (through the telephone) without actually being there. Similarly, watching a security video monitor like those installed in banks is like seeing what's going on someplace else while not actually being there yourself. Perhaps you can even control where you're "looking" by electronically controlling where the remote video camera is pointed.

These technologies, which we've come to take for granted, are the core of a technology which is called telepresence: the conveying of a feeling that you're present in one place while you're actually in another. Although some people argue that telepresence has no relevance to virtual reality, we disagree. But a distinction must be made: virtual reality refers to experiencing a computer-generated three-dimensional environment, while telepresence refers to experiencing a real but remote environment. That remote environment might be across the room or across the ocean; it might be under the ocean or on another planet. Of course, definitions can never be this black and white. There may even be telepresence applications that require a mixture of direct input from a real source (e.g., a mine shaft) combined with computer-generated input (e.g., a virtual overlay showing where mineral deposits are likely to be found).

We'll look at two forms of telepresence in this chapter: telerobotics and teleconferencing. Both of these are particularly close to virtual reality, from the technology they use to the feelings they generate. There are so many other applications of telepresence, including a number of variations on telerobotics, that a whole book could be written on them alone. We'll explore some of the typical applications of the technology to give you a good idea of what is possible.

✿ ✿ ✿

Telerobotics

There are a number of instances where something needs to be accomplished in an environment in which human beings were not meant to dwell. For example, changing cooling rods inside a nuclear reactor, constructing a pipeline at the bottom of the ocean, or handling highly unstable explosive ordnance. Each of these situations requires the flexibility, judgment, and dexterity of a human being to be successful, but some aspect of the environment makes a person's presence either extremely dangerous or downright impossible.

Although a fully functional autonomous robot system might someday be able to carry out these sorts of tasks, the current state of artificial intelligence provides nowhere near the level of complexity necessary to carry out even simple tasks, such as reaching around an unexpected obstruction, stepping over a log, or exploring the interior of a shipwreck. Instead, researchers around the world are developing systems that let a human operator at a remote task site control a robot. This process, which combines the power and flexibility of a robot with the intelligence, perception, and motor skills of a human being, is called telerobotics.

System Features

A telerobotic system is, on the surface, relatively simple. A robot that contains video cameras for eyes and microphones for ears sends information to a person wearing a stereoscopic display and headphones. Everything the robot sees, the human operator sees. Everything within hearing range of the robot is passed to the operator. There are often other sources of information, too, such as tactile and force feedback sensors in the robot. If the robot has a mechanical hand, there may be sensors in the fingers of the hand that can pass haptic feedback to the human (see Chapter 5, *Feeling*).

The human operator controls the robot in a number of ways. First, position/orientation tracking on the person's head may control where the robot looks. When the operator looks to the left, the robot's head (or cameras, or whatever) turns to the left. Of course, there may be other controls instead, such as a joystick or other input device.

As we saw in Chapter 6, *Recognition*, a human hand can control a robotic hand when it uses a device such as the DataGlove or the Exos Dexterous Hand Master. But it may not only be a robotic hand; it could just as easily be a welding torch or gripper claw. The robot might also respond to voice commands from the operator, such as "Analyze this" or "Open the pod bay doors, Hal." As aural, audio, and haptic information passes back and forth between human and robot, the operator feels an amazing sense of "being someplace else."

This is, of course, a feeling similar to that of experiencing a synthetic environment, but in many ways even more convincing.

Perhaps the best example of why telepresence appears more convincing is the audio and visual display. A video feed from a camera is an exponentially better source than the crude computer graphics being generated in most virtual realities today. Similarly, the three-dimensional sound from positioning two microphones in a robot's head can be much more flexible and realistic than that processed by computer. Both of these may change at some point, but at this time telepresence *really* feels like being there.

The final attribute of a telerobotic system is mobility. The remote mechanism must be able to move within or around the task site. The first telerobotic systems developed during the 1940s weren't extremely mobile. They were primarily large arms that let scientists handle radioactive materials safely. Instead of a video display, the operator had to look through a thick glass partition to view the movement of the controlled robotic arm.

At that time teleoperated systems were controlled with mechanical linkages, such as rods, cables, or wires. Now systems might be controlled through a variety of sophisticated methods, such as electronic connections, radio and television links, and fiber-optic cables. A joystick is a popular method of controlling movement, but hand gestures or voice controls could potentially be better in certain situations.

Expanding the Senses

One of the most interesting elements of telerobotics is that it can be used to experience the world in ways that we don't usually experience it. For example, we can only see a small amount of the electromagnetic spectrum; we're limited to what's called the visible spectrum of light. We can't see infrared, ultraviolet, X-ray, or microwave radiation because the rods and cones in our retinas aren't sensitive to them.

However, we can create cameras that are sensitive to those forms of light and mount them on robots. For example, we can create a robot that can "see" infrared light and then creates a representation of it in our visible spectrum. We can then watch the colors and shapes that the robot is sensing. This might be useful in a number of areas, including robot night-patrol guards or planetary exploration.

Another way in which telerobotics can help to augment our senses is through size. A robot arm in a automobile plant doesn't have to be as large as the arm of the human operator controlling it. It could just as easily be enormous, able to pick up a truck or a steel beam. The hydraulic systems used in a forklift are the same way. A small movement by the operator's hand creates a large, forceful movement in the tool.

On the other hand, a robot could be extremely small, too. A robot shaped like a large spider could be placed into a system of empty water pipes and controlled through a wireless system. This robot could send stereoscopic video images and sounds to an operator wearing a head-mounted display who could control the robot's movements as it explores for cracks or holes in the pipes. This expands the spectrum of what we can see, hear, and manipulate.

✿ ✿ ✿

Applications of Telerobotics

In recent years, the number of applications that include telerobotic systems has grown rapidly. There are now dozens of examples of small, remotely controlled submersible observation vehicles that are fitted with cameras and some type of robotic arm. In fact, these sorts of systems have been responsible for identifying and exploring the remains of sunken ships like the Edmund Fitzgerald, the Titanic, and the Challenger Space Shuttle. Many of these are simple remote-control devices that give only a minimal sense of telepresence. Others use the technologies we've discussed throughout this book to create a fully immersed, three-dimensional sense of telepresence. In this section, we'll explore a few systems that are used primarily as research tools but may later find real-world application.

The Green Man

One of the most profound conceptual examples of a telerobotic system is simply called the Green Man. The Green Man was designed by David Smith and Frank Amrogida and built by Herbert Mummery, all researchers at the Naval Oceans Systems Center (NOSC) laboratory in Hawaii. It is a remote-controlled fully anthropomorphic (human-like) robot (see Figure 14-1). The human operator straps on a large, hinged mechanical exoskeleton equipped with mechanical tracking sensors and a custom CRT-based head-mounted display that shows the operator images fed from the two cameras that serve as the eyes of the robot.

Every movement of the human operator's head, neck, arms, and torso is measured by the exoskeleton framework and transmitted to the Green Man, which, in turn makes the same movements. At the same time, the system collects and displays binaural acoustic information from microphones on the sides of the Green Man's head.

FIGURE 14-1   The Green Man

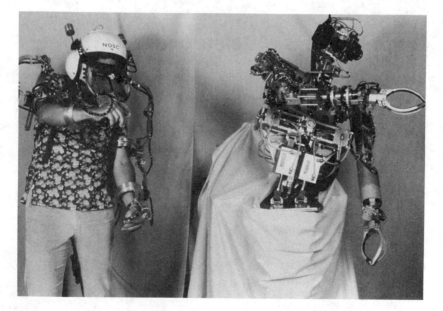

Note that the Green Man doesn't have legs and is intended at this stage to serve only as a laboratory research system. Nonetheless, this sort of anthropomorphic system is likely to be used in the future.

Teleoperated Jeep

The High-Mobility Multipurpose Wheeled Vehicle, also called the HMMWV or "Hum V," is the basis of another NOSC telerobotics project. Researcher Thomas Hughes and his colleagues have taken the standard HMMWV, the replacement for the classic US Army jeep, and fitted it with a pair of video cameras and microphones placed where the driver's eyes and ears would normally be (see Figure 14-2). A human operator can then see and hear as though he or she were actually in the vehicle by wearing a stereoscopic head-mounted display, similar to that used with the Green Man. The person can also control the jeep's movements (steering, acceleration, and so on) by sending signals to the jeep through a fiber-optic tether. While the tether is somewhat restricting, it is suitable for most basic research tasks.

FIGURE 14-2   The NOSC Teleoperated Jeep

The Airborne Remotely Operated Device

A remotely operated vehicle like the teleoperated jeep is a great idea for patrolling dangerous areas. But what about dangerous areas that can't be reached by a jeep? To address this issue, researchers at NOSC have created the Airborne Remotely Operated Device (AROD), a small, helicopter-like robot that can be controlled by a remote user in much the same way as the jeep. Although this system flies, it, too, is controlled by a tether (see Figure 14-3).

AROD stands about 2 feet tall and has two small cameras attached to its side. A small fan located within the main structure is capable of lifting the device into a hover. Steering is then accomplished by using control surfaces located below the fan housing. These control surfaces are similar to the aerilons found on fixed-wing aircraft, in that air from the fan moves over the control surface. When the surface's angle is altered, it alters the direction of the airflow, and the entire craft moves.

FIGURE 14-3   The NOSC Airborne Remotely Operated Device

VIRDEX

Perhaps some of the most innovative research in the area of tele-robotics and telepresence is being performed at the National Advanced Robotics Research Center located on the campus of the University of Salford in Manchester, United Kingdom. Code-named VIRDEX (Virtual Environment Remote Driving EXperiment), the project integrates various virtual reality and telepresence technologies with a mobile-robot platform. The researchers on the VIRDEX project are using a remote-controlled robot called the Cybermotion K2A (see Figure 14-4). Atop this system is a small high-speed pan-and-tilt platform that holds two cameras, two microphones for binaural sound input, and lamps to illuminate the area in front of the robot.

The researchers have used an innovative technology to construct an image of the area in hazy or otherwise obscured conditions. An infrared laser, mounted on the robot's head, produces a vertical stripe of infrared light that is reflected in front of the robot by a mir-

FIGURE 14-4   The Cybermotion K2A robot

ror that scans left and right. A small infrared-sensitive camera, off-set and inclined relative to the mirror, "watches" the vertical stripe move back and forth, scanning the scene.

Because the camera is offset, it can see distortions in the vertical line created by objects that the light hits. As this laser is panned back and forth across the area in front of the robot, image-processing software can interpret the camera's signals and construct a three-dimensional image of the scene. This information can be combined with a CAD model of the space to help determine the existence and location of any obstacles in the way of the robot and help the human operator to decide how best to proceed in moving the robot.

❀   ❀   ❀

Teleconferencing

The second application of telepresence that we'll discuss is teleconferencing. A teleconference is a combination of a videophone conversation (where two or more people both hear and see each other over a telephone line) and virtual reality. Perhaps an example describes it best. Imagine that you're the president of a large multinational company and you've scheduled a meeting with three of your vice presidents to discuss new company policy. However, these three people are located in Japan, France, and Mexico City. If you fly the vice presidents out to meet with you in San Francisco, two of them will have severe jet lag and all three will miss several days of work in transit. Instead, you decide to teleconference.

At a prescheduled time, each of you sits in a special teleconference cubicle and puts on a lightweight head-mounted display. You feel suddenly transported to a conference room, with a large darkwood table surrounded by four chairs in which you and the three other attendees sit. Although the people remain in their offices, each sees and hears the others as though they were in a common location. A computer generates a three-dimensional representation of each person that is passed through a network to the displays of the others. That is, you see everyone else, and they see you. When you raise your hand to get their attention, they see that. When you speak, they hear the voice coming from your direction (what appears to be your direction, from within the cyberspace). From within this space, you conduct your meeting with no jet lag and the minimum amount of effort.

We don't want to burst your bubble, but this scenario is completely fiction at this time. The idea is obviously a good one. However, turning the idea into a reality is not so easy. While most current virtual reality systems allow more than one individual to inhabit the same virtual environment at the same time, very few have successfully implemented these gatherings using telecommunication lines over great distances. Nonetheless, teleconferencing is getting a great deal of attention from various research groups, especially in Japan. But the details of the technology, the structure of a teleconferencing setup, and a means for conveying that much video information quickly between conference attendees are all major obstacles that must be overcome before the idea can truly become a reality.

Virtual reality teleconferencing has a great many potential benefits, though. Studies have shown that a great deal of person-to-person communication is actually not verbal. Instead, gestures, facial expressions, eye movement, and other nonverbal signals convey information relevant to the conversation at hand—all lost in a standard telephone conversation. In a videophone conference, you can see some nonverbal signals, but the conversation is typically only between two people.

Another benefit of virtual reality teleconferencing is the ability to quickly share documents among the conference attendees. For example, if you wanted to pass out a graph showing the growth of the company, you could simply command the computer to place the document on the virtual desk in front of each person. Even more, the graph could be an animated three-dimensional movie that changes and moves as you speak ("If we grow by 3 percent, this happens, but you can see how the graph changes if we grow by 4 percent"). Each of you could then fly into this graph or manipulate it to see it from a different angle.

Teleconferencing truly lives up to the phrase "the next best thing to being there."

✿ ✿ ✿

Projecting Presence

As we mentioned earlier, a virtual environment may be fully computer generated, a video image from a real source, or a composite of the two. By creating visual, aural, and tactile sensations, the virtual reality system is able to simulate a sense of immersion and real presence within a different world or space. Of course, the quality of telepresence can't be anywhere near as good as actually being present, but in many applications it is a far safer or more convenient mode of exploration and interaction.

In the next section, we'll look at where we expect all these applications to take us in the future and how they may affect our society. While reading, remember that many of the applications we've discussed have not yet even reached the demonstration stage but are generally thought to be likely to emerge in the next few years.

PART IV

Issues in Virtual Reality

SILICON MIRAGE

CHAPTER 15

Human Factors

✿   ✿   ✿

As we have shown throughout this book, virtual reality is an exceedingly powerful technology, which, despite its relative youth, is beginning to work its way into a wide variety of industries. However, like any new technology, virtual reality poses more questions than it answers. Two of the most pressing questions involve the effects of virtual reality on those who use it. What is the most effective way to implement virtual reality? And what are the health factors involved with the technology?

261

If the underlying goal of virtual reality is to make computers and other complex machinery easier to use, researchers must delve into the relationship between these systems and their human operators. How large must a field of view be? In what applications is virtual reality technology more of a hindrance than a help? What's the best way to design a virtual environment? What aspects of virtual reality might be considered unhealthy? Even the answers to these questions raise more questions. While we do not know all the answers to these questions, we can report on some preliminary findings by various researchers and describe some of our own experiences.

❋   ❋   ❋

Display Factors

As we discussed back in Chapter 3, *Seeing*, stereoscopic displays are useful for many applications. However, head-mounted, head-coupled, and other sorts of stereoscopic displays also offer some special challenges. In this section we'll look at four areas that virtual reality researchers are looking at regarding visual-display technology, as well as some solutions they've found. The four areas are virtual nausea, field of view, frame-refresh rate, and display resolution.

Virtual Nausea

Under ordinary circumstances, our sensory systems operate like a finely tuned piece of machinery. Even the seemingly simple task of walking upright and maintaining balance is accomplished through precise relationships among our various sensory mechanisms and muscles. So what happens if you alter, recombine, or remove these various cues?

If you've ever been in a boat on unstable water or sat in the back seat of an automobile you may know the feeling of motion sickness. One of the principle causes of this extreme discomfort is the conflicting sensory signals that you receive. Let's say you're inside a boat. As you move with the rocking boat, your visual cues tell you that you're stable. However, highly sensitive body mechanisms, like those in your inner ear, tell you otherwise. They *feel* that you're moving and pass this information on to your brain. The conflict of signals can result in anything from pallor and sweating to vomiting.

As virtual reality technologies have expanded in capabilities and quality, a unique form of motion sickness has emerged. This is referred to as visually induced motion sickness (VIMS). Almost exactly opposite in cause from normal motion sickness, VIMS occurs when there is a compelling sensation of self-motion without any corresponding visceral cues. For example, when people watch a movie filmed from a helicopter or airplane on a very large screen, they sometimes become disoriented because their vision is telling them that they should be moving, but their body isn't. They'll often sway their body in tandem with the movement on the screen.

In virtual reality applications, a similar thing happens. Immersed inside a three-dimensional environment based solely on visual, aural, and, possibly, haptic cues, a person can quickly get disoriented due to the lack of movement cues from within the body. This is a bigger problem in systems where the visual displays are better than average, because they are, in effect, fooling the eyes better. It is also an important issue in applications where the user or the environment moves a lot.

While researchers have known about the correlation between the conflicting cues and the occurrence of VIMS for some time, little research has been conducted to identify the specific factors that cause the nausea. Nonetheless, we do know that the actions and navigational capabilities of an individual within a virtual environment can play a part in their disorientation and discomfort. For example, the first time you use a particular system your movement will likely be less controlled and more erratic. This sort of movement, often jerky and disoriented, is likely to cause VIMS. Later, when you are familiar with the environment, your movements and your ability to navigate through the space are much more stable and controlled, causing less confusion.

Another method of combatting VIMS is including a "warming up" period in the virtual experience. Research shows that nausea tends to occur during a user's initial exposure to a particular simulation, especially when there are a lot of motion cues. For example, frequent start and stop motions and frequent changes in acceleration can cause sickness. However, if you minimize the initial level of activity in a virtual reality simulation, you are likely to adapt better and prevent VIMS. Gradually adapting by warming up to the virtual environment is obviously one key to reducing simulator sickness.

Field of View

The second area in visual-display design that we want to examine is optimal field of view. Just what constitutes the optimal field of view in a display device is difficult to nail down. What's optimal for one particular application is not necessarily optimal for another. As we mentioned in Chapter 3, *Seeing*, if someone is performing a task that requires his or her attention to be riveted in one particular area, then a wide field of view may be more of a problem than a solution, because there would be too many distractions. On the other hand, if the person needs peripheral vision or a sense of situational awareness, a narrow field of view could prove to be ineffective. In either case, though, the capability for stereoscopic display may still be quite useful.

Another issue involving field of view harks back to visually induced motion sickness. Researchers have found that a good way to avoid the vertigo and malaise associated with conflicts between visual and visceral cues is to limit the field of view to no more than 60 degrees horizontally. While this may be true, it's almost impossible to simulate the sensation of immersion within an environment when the field of view is this narrow. The catch-22 is frustrating and will have to be worked out by developers in the future.

Latency and Frame-Refresh Rate

The third issue regarding visual displays relates to the computer updating the image as you move through the virtual environment. In an ideal situation, when you turn your head while wearing a head-mounted or other display device, the images you see shouldn't appear jerky or seem to snap from one view into another. They should flow smoothly and change immediately as you move your head, thereby altering your field of view. However, this not being a perfect world, there are almost no virtual reality systems today that are this smooth.

As we noted back in Chapter 3, *Seeing*, there are two basic functions at work in creating a clean sense of movement in a virtual world: latency and frame-refresh rate. Latency is the measure of time between when a person moves and when the computer registers the movement. Frame-refresh rate is the number of frames that a computer can generate in a given amount of time (usually measured in number of frames per second). The key to success in displaying computer-generated animated images is low latency and high frame-refresh rate, concurrently.

Solving the latency problem is usually tackled by increasing the number of position-information samples generated each second. This relies on both a fast position sensor and an unhindered process flow from the position sensor to the computer. That is, if a signal from a position sensor must be processed or converted a number of times from one format to another, the latency will be high because the signal is slowed down.

Solving frame-refresh rate problems is also usually a hardware concern. The faster the computer, the more images can be generated and passed to the display device each second. The slower the computer, the more the images look as though they're racing to catch up with the moving scene; they almost never appear to be in synchrony with the user's motion. A minimum frame rate for intuitive, unhindered interaction in a virtual world is between fifteen and twenty frames per second. There are three basic factors in a virtual environment that relate to frame-refresh rates: polygons, display method, and display size.

Polygons. Each object in a virtual environment is made up of one or more polygons. A polygon is a two-dimensional segment inside a three-dimensional world that helps make up three-dimensional objects. For example, a cube is made up of six flat squares (sides); each of these squares is one polygon. A virtual object may be constructed from circles, triangles, rectangles, and any number of other polygons.

Polygons are a double-edged sword, though. The more polygons in an image, the better the image looks. But the more polygons, the longer it takes to create the image. That is, a crude sphere might be made up of under a hundred polygons, but a better sphere might have hundreds or thousands of polygons (see Figure 15-1). The crude sphere doesn't look great, but a computer can quickly make all the necessary calculations for how each of those polygons should look at any given moment. A refined sphere takes much longer to image because there are so many more polygons to calculate positions for.

To extend the example, if you were standing in a virtual environment, looking at a simple room made up of four walls, a ceiling, and a floor, the computer could probably generate the scene at or above real-time frame rates (twenty-two frames, or scene updates, per second), and it wouldn't be jerky. However, if you turn around in the virtual room and see a table, some chairs, a window with a scene outside, and another virtual person sitting sipping tea, the system's work load immediately rises, making for a much slower frame-refresh rate.

Display method. The second factor in frame-refresh rate is the quality of the images being generated. There are several methods of displaying three-dimensional images, and each has its particular

FIGURE 15-1   Virtual object made up of polygons

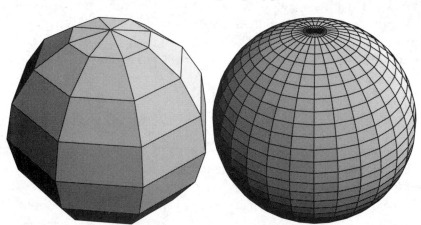

computational loads (see Figure 15-2). The most basic and fastest to manipulate are wire-frame images, which are transparent polygons. The computer only has to calculate positions for lines and objects. The next simplest is hidden-line wire-frame images, in which the polygons are opaque. That is, when you look at a cube from the front, you can't see the lines making up its back walls because they're hidden from view. Over the past twenty years, people have developed some fast algorithms for creating hidden-line wire-frame images. The computer can also make solid, or surfaced, images, by giving the polygons in hidden-line images a surface color or pattern.

However, the next step, shaded images, represents a major step in computational load. Shading happens when a light source is added to the environment. Areas that fall away from the light source are shadowed, and areas closer to the light source are highlighted. There are various forms of shading, each more realistic than the last. Phong and Gouraud shading are the most basic forms, but they still require significant calculation. Ray tracing and radiosity are high-end shading processes that create very realistic images, but can take hours to generate (one image we know of took over two hundred hours to create). When you're attempting to create twenty or thirty images every second, you start to wonder why people are even considering building ray-traced virtual realities.

Display size. The last factor in frame-refresh rate that we'll look at here is display size. We don't mean the actual size of the display device, but rather the number of pixels, or dots, that are in that display. Many computer monitors have display sizes of 640 pixels by 480 pix-

FIGURE 15-2   Display methods

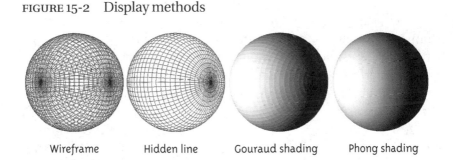

Wireframe   Hidden line   Gouraud shading   Phong shading

els. Others go much higher. Display size is also measured in scan lines, referring to the number of rows of pixels in the display.

Like the number of object polygons and the display method, a better-looking image takes longer to image. Because a computer must figure out exactly what to show in each and every pixel in the display, the higher the number of pixels, the slower the calculation of the full image. That is, it takes significantly longer to figure out how to show a 1,000-scan-line image than how to show a 300-scan-line image. But the 1,000-scan-line image looks significantly better (see "Display Resolution" below).

One method for handling computers' limited processing speeds is to have a dual-resolution display device. We talked about this back in Chapter 3, *Seeing*, when we talked about CAE's fiber-optic head-mounted display. This sort of display creates a high-resolution inset wherever the eye is looking. The high-resolution inset has more pixels to image and takes longer to generate, but the image is mostly low resolution for peripheral vision. This images much more quickly, saving processing time.

Display Resolution

You can get a sense for how bad the visual images are in a virtual reality system by looking at a typical eye examination. When you go to an optometrist for an examination, your ability to resolve images over a distance is measured using a Snelling chart. If you have "perfect" vision, they'll tell you your vision is 20/20. The easiest way to understand this number is that what you can see at 20 feet is the same as what an average person can see. On the other hand, if you have 20/100 vision, you must stand as close as 20 feet, to see what the average person can see at 100.

Technically, 20/20 vision means that you can visually resolve an object as small as 1 arc minute (one-sixtieth of a degree) in your field of view. If you were looking at a perfect display—one that created a perfectly photorealistic image—through 20/20 eyes, you would be able to see 60 pixels per degree (you could see 5,400 pixels over a span of 90 degrees).

A visual acuity of 20/200—where legally blind status begins—means that the smallest object you can visually resolve is 10 arc minutes (one-sixth of a degree). That means that someone with 20/200 vision looking at that perfect display would only see 6 pixels per degree (540 pixels over 90 degrees.)

Current LCD-based head-mounted displays have so few pixels to display that if you saw a virtual Snelling chart inside them, you would be tested as well beyond legally blind—you wouldn't even be able to recognize most of the lines. Obviously, generating the images is not the only problem. The display hardware itself must come a long way before we can show quality images, stepping out of blindness and into the light.

❁ ❁ ❁

Display Mismatch

What would happen if you heard a baby crying behind you, but when you turned to look, the baby wasn't where the sound was coming from? Or if you picked up a pencil but felt the sensation on the wrong fingers? First you'd probably think you were going crazy or had a neurological disorder; then you'd realize you were just in a poorly made virtual reality.

When various cues in a virtual environment don't match up, we say there's a display mismatch. Remember that when we talk about displays, we might mean that the computer is generating images, sound, or tactile/force feedback. We can "see" the displays with our eyes, ears, or fingers. There are two basic display mismatch concerns that we'll look at here: multiple sense and single sense. Either of them can be adjusted for in the hardware and software of a system.

Multiple senses. The examples above of seeing or feeling something different from what you expected are examples of multiple sensory display mismatch. That is, the elements in an environment are not matching properly. For example, if you turn your head 30 degrees, the virtual world should rotate 30 degrees as well. If this is the case, the virtual world is said to be orthoscopic. Unfortunately, most of the present-day commercial virtual reality systems leave something to be desired in this area. Often the anomaly is somewhat subtle and is caused by miscalibration of the equipment or software. Matching different elements of a virtual environment isn't really an overly difficult task, but it is a crucial one.

Another form of sensory display mismatch has less to do with the virtual environment than with the user's expectations. Imagine walking into a small room and putting on a head-mounted display and headphones. The virtual world you find yourself in is an architectural walk-through of a large concert hall. You listen to the violin playing onstage, but it sounds strangely tinny, as though you were in a small room. The problem is that you really *are* in a small room, and your brain isn't being fooled well enough. In the battle between what your brain expects and what it hears, expectation almost always wins.

This is another area where warming up to a virtual environment is beneficial. Also, simply being aware of the potential mismatch between your senses can help you talk yourself into believing the virtual world more completely.

Single senses. Another display mismatch concern is matching real life movements to movements in the virtual world. For example, if you take a step forward in the real world, you should move the same amount in the virtual one. If this doesn't occur, it's likely to be confusing. This is also the case with other visual cues such as perspective and size. If you move towards a large virtual building and the size of the building changes but the perspective doesn't, the sensory mismatch can cause disorientation.

❀   ❀   ❀

Observations from the Outside

While through much of this book we've focused on the details of virtual reality technology, we would like to share some observations that we've made from several hundred demonstrations given in laboratories, trade shows, and various other settings. Please understand that these aren't scientifically validated, peer-reviewed research results; simply general observations that we thought were interesting enough to add here.

How People Move

If there is anything more interesting than experiencing virtual reality for the first time, it's watching someone else make their first voyage into the new world. Even a basic demonstration using primitive graphics shown on a head-mounted display that can be explored with a DataGlove can generate a response like a child's first trip to Disneyland. Even after using a virtual reality system several times, people are astounded at the permutations of possibilities; all the different angles of perspective, variations on moving, experiments with the physics of virtual objects. In fact, we often surprise ourselves with our own reactions to these systems, even after using them for years.

Hands. One of the first things people do in exploring a virtual reality is to orient to their own virtual body. And because this virtual body usually consists of only a hand, people become fascinated with this virtual hand. A gloved hand is raised up in front of their face in order to see the representation of the virtual hand inside the display device. Moving a finger moves a finger in the virtual space. You make a fist and your virtual hand makes one, too. The simple fact that the computer can follow your body movements and recreate them graphically is so exciting to some people that this alone evokes a gasp or a giggle.

After people get used to their virtual body and are comfortably moving around the virtual space, they generally settle into a pattern of movement. For example, in demonstrations where someone is standing and the principle form of navigation through the virtual environment is a glovelike I/O device, many male users put their ungloved hand into their pants pocket. Women, on the other hand, tend to make the same hand gestures with their ungloved hand as the gloved hand. That is, if they point with their gloved hand, they'll point with their other one, too. We have no idea what these differences might imply, but they strike us as curious.

Exploration. It's also interesting to note that people have a tendency to let down their front while inside a fully-immersive virtual environment. For example, we've seen, on dozens of occasions, some of the best dressed and stuffiest corporate executives break societal restraint and actually get on their hands and knees to crawl around and explore the inside of a virtual environment. This is even more likely to happen if they're wearing audio display headphones and are more fully closed off from their surroundings.

Another common reaction to the new virtual world is walking into corners or positioning oneself next to large objects inside of the virtual environment. Looking up from these places so as to view the dramatic perspectives is particularly intriguing to people. Remember that because most systems today do not include any form of boundary detection, you can stick your head through objects. This provides a great deal of amusement and intrigue because these objects are usually hollow and give a fascinating perspective on the construction of the world. For example, in a demonstration called Virtual Seattle, people often flew over and then inside the virtual Space Needle. Popping their heads in and then out of the circular apex, they could explore the building's hollow core.

Grease and Other Sticky Items

As an onslaught of virtual reality systems is beginning to appear in the form of arcade games and home entertainment systems, we think it's appropriate to raise a couple of human factors issues that have been missed or outright avoided by most members of the press and industry participants.

In today's video arcades, games are relatively safe, from a health point of view. Other than hundreds of similarly grimy hands clutching joysticks and punching buttons on video games, there is little chance of communicable disease or infection. In the business place, keyboards, chairs, or telephones may be used by many people, but these are similarly innocuous. However, virtual reality equipment is generally designed to tightly enclose our senses: eyes, ears, hands.

This issue became crystal clear to us while standing in line at a computer trade show, waiting for a demonstration of a new virtual reality system. As we approached the front of the line, we noticed two people slightly ahead of us. The first was a stately looking gentleman in a fine suit. The second was a young man wearing blue jeans that covered only the essentials, what appeared to be a tie-dyed T-shirt (a closer look revealed the pattern to be stains of some sort), and hair with enough grease to repack the bearings of an automobile.

As the first man prepared to put on the head-mounted display, he pulled several long strands of hair from the helmet, noticing that other hairs had gotten lodged in the crevices and would probably have to be cut out later. After that demonstration, we watched as the greasy young man pulled the head-mounted display on. Everyone in line close enough to see him clearly had the same thought that we did. Who knew what his head would leave in the helmet, only to be rubbed into ours. Ten of us simply walked away.

Although we felt somewhat prudish after this experience, we felt justified soon afterwards when we encountered a piece of electronic mail describing a conversation between a video arcade owner and someone complaining about head lice. Need we say more?

Our concern is beyond lice or dirt in a head-mounted display. A gloved input device made of cloth may be able to transmit scabies. Other devices may transmit impetigo, a bacterial infection found most often in children. Note that each of these is relatively rare, and people shouldn't be afraid to use virtual reality equipment. But we mention them because sooner or later the industry will have to contend with making systems safe. Perhaps we will find inexpensive tissue caps or disposable latex gloves (like toilet seat covers in public bathrooms). Or perhaps an ultraviolet light source or disinfectant spray will be used to kill off potential bacteria or other life forms.

❋ ❋ ❋

Designing Virtual Environments

You may have noticed that up to this point we've successfully avoided much talk of the details of how virtual environments could or should be built. But, as Randall Walser of Autodesk recently noted, "Today the focus in virtual reality is on technology. Vital as technology is, however, it is not enough. Technology only makes new worlds possible. Building the worlds is a formidable challenge in its own right. Indeed, the art and craft of spacemaking is as essential to the VR industry as filmmaking is to the movie industry." Without films, Hollywood would only be some interesting photographic technology with the potential for great applications. In many ways, this is where virtual reality is now.

As we noted earlier in this chapter, virtual reality technology is in its infancy. Indeed, only recently could people even begin to start asking questions regarding the quality of virtual environment design. How could scientists ask "What's the best way to symbolize a virtual hand" if they couldn't create a good enough visual display to see it anyway? But now these questions are arising en masse and are beginning to demand answers.

Let's take a closer look at two design questions that virtual reality researchers are exploring—symbols and ambiguity—along with some possible answers.

Symbols

In any form of graphical user interface—whether it's a Macintosh or Microsoft Windows or a virtual reality—actions and computer commands are usually represented by some sort of picture. On the Macintosh, when you want to erase a file, you use the mouse to drag a document icon into a trash can icon. The computer handles the deletion behind the scenes.

The decisions about what icons and pictures to use are painstakingly made by software developers. It's up to these programmers to create a human interface that best allows users to manipulate the program or the computer. The more intuitive the interface, the easier it is to learn and use. For example, it's easy to learn and understand that an icon that looks like a folder means that there are files (or possibly more folders) "inside" that folder. On the other hand, to remove a disk from the Macintosh computer's disk drive you must use the mouse to drag the disk icon into the trash icon. "Trashing" the disk is very nonintuitive, as users generally think they're deleting the disk rather than simply instructing the computer to eject it.

With the advent of this new, three-dimensional interface, software developers are faced with a plethora of new decisions to make. How should a hand be represented in a virtual world? Must a virtual hand look different while grabbing and manipulating virtual objects than it does while moving or flying? Several virtual systems presently represent your hand as a free-floating armless hand in virtual space. You can reach out and grab an object by placing the hand inside the object and making a fist. When you release the fist, the computer recognizes that you have released the object. Then, while you make hand gestures signifying movement and navigation through the virtual world, the virtual hand is replaced with an arrow or airplane.

Many virtual reality systems let you do more than just navigate around the environment and move objects. If you're working with molecular modeling software, you may want to view the molecular structures in various ways. Early virtual reality systems would typically have required that you make a different hand gesture for each display method. For example, you might point with your index and pinkie finger to see a wire-frame model of the molecule and with just your pinkie to see a stick-and-ball model.

Scientists quickly discovered, however, that it's difficult to remember hand gestures because they're nonintuitive. Now some researchers are working with virtual menus and voice-recognition systems (see Chapter 6, *Recognition*). The menu-based system works with only two gesture commands: move (fly) and bring up the menu. When you make the bring up menu gesture, a virtual menu pops up in front of you. To select an item on the menu, simply point at it and make the menu gesture again. In the example above, If you wanted to switch to a new display method for molecular modeling, you could simply bring up the menu and select it. Scientists have found that this is significantly easier to work with, as long as the menu items can be seen (on some LCD-based head-mounted displays it's very difficult to read the menu).

As we saw in Chapter 6, *Recognition*, voice-recognition systems can also be used in virtual reality applications. A number of software developers have already released systems that incorporate voice-recognition capabilities with computer-aided design programs. In this sort of system, an architect could build a basic frame of a building using a CAD system, walk into it as a three-dimensional virtual environment, and then add a door by simply looking at a wall and saying "Door." Such a system could even include basic manipulation commands like "Open door" or "Add wall."

Ambiguity

An ideal photorealistic virtual world that looks just like our own is a fascinating goal to strive for, but it's not yet possible. As we described earlier, the more objects in a virtual environment, the more difficult it is to make the screen refresh fast enough.

For this and various other reasons, scientists are finding it imperative to explore the issue of ambiguity. How much do people really need to see or hear or feel before they understand what's being displayed? A brown cube that moves around on the virtual floor may be anything, but when you add a tail and a barking sound, it's easy to recognize it as a dog. Representing a person in hidden-line wire-frame form may be uninteresting and may leave out various physical features, but it may be perfectly adequate in relaying the important information in the virtual world. And using a lower-quality graphic image of a dog or a person could easily make the difference between whether a virtual image is updated fast enough to be convincing or not.

Artists have worked with the subtle world of ambiguity for thousands of years, understanding that it's not crucial to express everything in a painting or sculpture in order to express one's self. As Brenda Laurel noted, "Ambiguity and sensory incompleteness are key elements in the kind of deep participation we desire with a work of art." The filmmakers of tomorrow's virtual worlds must learn how to balance ambiguity and perfection in order to create virtual worlds that are effective in conveying ideas.

❂ ❂ ❂

User-Friendly Computers

Creating user-friendly computers through virtual reality interfaces is clearly a somewhat daunting task. However, it is just as clear how powerful and useful a virtual environment can be, if created well. Throughout this chapter, we've looked at only a few of the many difficulties involved with creating these worlds. Each application of the technology carries its own needs and challenges and must be approached with a clear head and a fresh eye. A public system may require a careful study of health risks. A system that includes very precise work (perhaps requiring a narrow field of view) with a lot of quickly moving objects may require hardware and software entirely different from anything we've even looked at in this book.

In the next chapter, we jump past many of the difficult questions regarding the creation of quality virtual environments and explore what social implications virtual reality may have when it enters widespread use.

SILICON MIRAGE

CHAPTER 16

Social Considerations

✿   ✿   ✿

Perhaps the most amazing thing about virtual reality, at least at this early stage of the technology, is not what it can do but rather how people perceive it. The spectrum of attitude surrounding the field is astounding: from brash excitement to outright condemnation, often with a moralistic tinge. In explaining virtual reality (answering the almost always asked question, "You're writing a book about *what?*"), we've had the chance to watch people's reactions. And while we haven't gone about this using the scientific method, we've noticed that the majority of people appear to react similarly.

The first stage almost always involves the raising of eyebrows and widening of eyes. Not infrequently the listener's first word is "Wow!" Then comes a stage of mild disbelief, and you can see their brows furrow as they attempt to figure out if we're being serious or not. And next, as we approach them with various applications of the technology (similar to those we've described in earlier chapters), they get excited, often offering their own ideas about future applications.

If we leave them at that, they'll usually sit and ponder, or perhaps just forget all about virtual reality until the next time they encounter the subject. But as soon as we bring up some of the potential social considerations, the final step settles in: anxiety. This anxiety stems from a number of sources, perhaps the most prominent being that no one really knows what will be done with this incredibly powerful technology.

In the 1970s and early 1980s there were groups of people who became somewhat hysterical about video game arcades. They were so troubled by what they considered a potential social disaster that some went so far as to picket and even bomb public video arcades. Similarly, today some people (including some prominent scientists) are deeply concerned about the future of virtual reality and its impact on society. In this chapter, we'll explore some of the scenarios and considerations likely to appear in the next five to ten years. However, our goal is not to cause fear or consternation in our readers. In fact, as much as possible, we want to dispel the troublesome myths about virtual reality that are already popping up. We feel strongly that because virtual reality technology will undoubtedly be put to both good and bad uses, it is only through education and responsible social concern that any positive action can be made.

We can't simply stop working on virtual reality technology any more than we can stop the advancement of medical science (in fact, as we've seen, each helps the other move forward). Nor can we create strongly regulated and yet stifling governing boards, as some people have suggested, determining whether each step of research is for the common good or not.

But we must, at least, ask some probing questions, carefully investigate the answers, and begin to develop a plan for this technology that takes social concerns into account. Fifty years ago, television was thrown into the world with no consideration of its potential social impact—which turned out to be considerable. Now organizations such as Computer Professionals for Social Responsibility and the Association for Computing Machinery are trying to facilitate the birth of this new technology by bringing together the wisdom that has come from years of media and computer studies and by helping to educate the public.

In this chapter, we look at potential social ramifications of virtual reality. These include virtual reality as a drug and as a role-playing facilitator. Obviously, we can't cover all the issues that society may have to deal with in the future; we don't know what surprises await us around the corner of time. Nonetheless, we think that focusing on at least some of these issues will help us understand where we might be headed.

Virtual Reality as a Drug

As we mentioned back in Chapter 1, *The Silicon Mirage*, the two topics in the field of virtual reality most asked and wondered about are sex and drugs. Can VR be used to simulate sex? Can it create altered states of consciousness or psychedelic experiences like those brought on by hallucinogens like LSD or psilocybin? Is VR "electronic LSD," made to blow our minds through high technology?

We hope this won't be unhappy news for too many of you, but the answer to these questions is a straightforward no.

We'll cover the hows and why nots of virtual sex in a later chapter (see "Teledildonics" in Chapter 17, *The Future of Virtual Reality*), but let's take a quick look at virtual reality as a drug. The idea is certainly an interesting one: if we can provide our sense organs with electronic stimuli, why shouldn't we be able to create any sensation we want. Make the walls breathe, create "tracers," make photographs talk. Wild psychedelic colors could swirl around in time with surreal three-dimensional sounds, and the entire scene could be interactive, so that you could reach out and grab a band of color, set it aflame, and make it sound like jingling bells.

It sounds psychedelic, it may even look psychedelic, but it really isn't. Nothing in your brain has changed. No chemicals have been altered. The sophisticated user of virtual reality (typically, anyone who has used a VR system more than once) knows that while there is a sense that you are "someplace else," there is no doubt that you can abort the scenario at any time by simply taking the virtual reality equipment off. Even in a scenario like the one described above, you'd remain fully conscious and would most likely say to yourself, "This is kind of cool, but it's getting tiresome."

Psychedelic virtual reality scenes, at best, will be like souped-up versions of the swirling colors on late-night 1970s television. If you haven't already imbibed something, it won't make much sense to you.

On the other hand, virtual reality does have the potential to become a drug of a different nature. It may come as no surprise to hear that the concern revolves around the ubiquitous television set and the zombielike effect it appears to have on people. The couch potato has become as much a part of our culture as the wide spectrum of sports and entertainments that appears on the television across from the couch. Certainly, watching television has far surpassed reading books, listening to the radio, or going to live performances. And the attitude of passively watching whatever is piped through the tube each evening is almost as ubiquitous as the television itself.

Virtual reality has the potential to become—at least in one of its forms—a form of entertainment even more captivating and alluring than the small electric portal in the living rooms of most of our homes. It is, by its very nature, a medium of communication even more powerful than television. If people already are trying to escape a dreary life through the brilliant colors of television, there's little doubt that these same people will jump at the chance for a home virtual reality system that completely replaces their surroundings with someone else's world.

Years ago in his *Farenheit 451*, Ray Bradbury depicted just this sort of system, in which people would sit in their living rooms all evening and interact with mindless soap operas, not caring that they didn't understand. Virtual reality technology could easily be used to create these sorts of passively viewed three-dimensional movies. There would be little interactivity—perhaps none at all—and the mass audiences could become the world's finest couch potatos, fully drugged by alternate realities, completely separated from their own.

On the other hand, virtual reality advocates argue with some merit that although many people use television as an escapist drug, many others are more interested in interactive media. They turn the channel when they want to watch something different, and they turn the television off when there's nothing good to watch. They also point to the appearance of community-access television stations and the popularity of home video-recording equipment, showing that people really do want to create and edit their own videos. The potential is certainly present for easy-access virtual reality to become a more effective and important tool for communication than the printing press, the telephone, television, or film. It will only require that people take virtual reality beyond passive entertainment and into exploratory and interactive experiences.

When It's as Good as Real

Throughout this book, we've tried to make it clear that present day virtual reality is a far cry from appearing realistic. Refresh rate is slow, displays are crude, and the number of objects present is always low. These days, most video games are of better quality because they are optimized to perform one task and that task alone. Nonetheless, there is every indication that this will change over the next ten years. And, at some point, virtual realities will become so good and so flexible that people may decide that they are preferable to the phenomenological world around us.

Or will they? We've already noted that we think that future scientists will have as much (or as little) luck as scientists today in creating realities that are as complex and deep as our own. Even if we create visual displays at the maxiumum resolution of our retinas (taking every rod and cone into account), the scenes and worlds that are displayed can't ultimately be as interesting as the world around us. In fact, as John Perry Barlow noted recently, "I think the effort to create convincing artificial realities will teach us the same humbling lesson about reality which artificial intelligence has taught us about intelligence...namely, that we don't know a damned thing about it."

An artist friend of ours recently noted that his work in creating extremely realistic synthetic images using computers had opened his eyes to the richness of the world around him. Now when he sees a dewdrop on a flower, he appreciates its subtle complexity so much more, knowing that he could never recreate it (see Figure 16-1).

We hope this reaction is mirrored by future users of high-fidelity virtual reality systems. The sensation of watching and manipulating a computer-generated image may be tantilizing, but we think they'll come out of the virtual world with a finer understanding of the world around them. There is another reason why we can rest assured that people won't spend days on end in virtual realities: there is no place to eat, and there certainly aren't any bathrooms!

Games People Play

There's no doubt in our minds that the most successful applications of virtual reality will be within the entertainment field. Currently, children and adults spend billions of dollars each year on video games and high-tech entertainments. These games span a wide spectrum of topics, styles, and locations. With parents doing

FIGURE 16-1   Greg Vander Houwen's *Paragon of Distraction*

the buying, it's no wonder that educational games for home computers are especially big sellers, though the kids themselves seem to prefer the violent, combat-style kick-boxing, sword-fighting, or monster-mashing games. It's fascinating to watch a child pick up one of these games: they're extremely focused on the task, mostly just pushing buttons, and can spend hours playing. Similarly, video arcades are popular hangout spots, where new computerized games are often kept busy for hours as patrons spend hundreds of dollars striving to master them.

Imagine, then, a not-so-distant scenario in which two kids are playing together in a virtual sandbox. Half in anger and half just in jest, one child picks up a virtual baseball bat and smashes it over the other's head. The environment reacts appropriately: the aggressive child sees his friend's head split open and blood pour out. Suddenly, the head joins together again and the child appears all right. The injured child never felt a thing (they weren't wearing force feedback devices on their heads!), and the hit becomes just part of the game. What, then, are the ramifications of this type of play?

Virtual reality games may not be much different than present-day video games except that the participants are fully immersed in the world and may not be physically anywhere near each other (fiber-optic communication across a city or a country is very fast). However, the potential lessons that children could learn from virtual reality may be significantly more powerful than those from two-dimensional games. Virtual reality games may teach children that it's okay to bash people over the head because they'll quickly get better. Or perhaps that shooting, stabbing, rape, or murder are just as reasonable. Studies seem to indicate that the more people are immersed in violent environments (television, neighborhoods, and so on), the more likely they are to react violently. On the other hand, a second possible reaction to these sorts of games is proposed by a vocal minority of people who say that the chance to play out fantasies in private actually relieves the violent tendencies that might otherwise come out in real life.

However, let's take a look at another scenario. Three children, each sitting in their own homes, are in a virtual dungeon, playing a game against computer-generated ogres and dragons. They may travel anywhere in the maze they want, but when they come upon an enemy they must fight it by answering a series of questions. Some questions try their math skills, others involve history, science, or a foreign language. The key to winning this game, the kids soon find out, is to stick together, make consensual decisions about where to travel, and solve the problems together. Only in this way can they succeed in battling the forces of the dungeon's dark magic.

These sorts of educational, nonviolent, problem-solving games can be as popular and interesting as violent and destructive ones, but they often take more imagination to create. Nonetheless, the rewards of designing and implementing these sorts of games are potentially great and possibly essential to our survival in the twenty-first century. The same issues crop up in evaluating present-day and future entertainments—violence vs. nonviolence, competition vs. cooperation—the difference being primarily in the order of magnitude. Obviously, it continues to be up to adults to make conscious decisions about what kinds of experiences best benefit children.

A Minimum of Risk

If you had felt that you had nothing to lose, wouldn't you have asked someone out on a date a lot earlier? Or tried a new game? Or explored a new city? Virtual reality offers a chance to do all these things (and more) in a safe environment.

For example, let's say that you have an important job interview. It's likely that in the future you will be able to practice various ways to conduct the interview in a virtual environment either with another person or "against" the computer. You sit in a virtual office across the desk from the virtual personnel director and start talking. As soon as you think you're acting like an idiot, you can say "Playback" and see a virtual video of yourself or say "Begin again" and start the interview over. The system might be programmable, so that you can warm up by talking to a jovial person first and then try again with someone who's having a really bad day. Role-playing has proven to be effective in teaching interpersonal skills to almost anyone and is now common in management and sales training seminars, as well as in psychotherapy sessions.

However, it's just as easy to use the computer to avoid risk altogether. In fact, it often seems that people easily fall into a low-level addiction to passive entertainment. An exciting television show, full of action and adventure, gives the illusion that there is really something happening in the viewer's life. The illusion says, "Don't worry, you're involved in this." In fact, the viewer has avoided the real world altogether.

Computer technology can enable or even encourage this minimum-risk activity, with a variety of results. Meeting new people from around the world is already easier due to electronic mail, and it's now not uncommon for people to become friends without ever seeing one another in person (we even know of a couple that met over computer lines and later, after meeting face-to-face, married). On the other hand, as one person commented in an online forum recently, "If I'm seventeen and not getting any, I might decide it's 'cause I'm ugly. So I present myself as Tom Sellick (or Madonna) to my VR buddies, and now I'm the life of the party. I ain't never going back."

Virtual reality technology will open doors to people who want to become involved. But those doors will also be open to those who want only to have the illusion of being involved.

❀   ❀   ❀

Virtual Reality Will Change Your Life

We've really only begun to scratch the surface of the ways in which virtual reality will affect our society. The issues and questions that arise seem to be unending, alongside the plethora of new applications of the technology in every phase of our lives. From increased access to information to new art forms, virtual reality will create opportunities that we have never thought of before. In this last section, we'll take a quick look at some of these potential applications, if only to prepare ourselves for the last chapter of the book, and, indeed, our own future.

Access

One of the most exciting aspects of computer technology has been its ability to bring people together and enable them to do things they couldn't have done otherwise. SeniorNet, a nonprofit group, has helped thousands of senior citizens network electronically, sharing messages and tasks and keeping their minds active. Desktop publishing brought the power of the press to school children, revolutionaries, and businesses everywhere. And now virtual reality is offering people with little access to information and computing power the potential for greater access.

Those who have physically limiting disabilities may find themselves able to travel farther and be more productive through the aid of virtual reality. For example, a person without the use of arms and legs may be able to travel through and manipulate a virtual environment, easily controlling and interacting with the virtual reality by mapping chin and eye movements to virtual hands or feet. Similarly, as we saw in Chapter 6, *Recognition,* an earlier chapter, technologies such as the Talking Glove make it easier for people who are deaf to communicate both in and out of artificial realities.

But the possibilities extend even farther. People are beginning to work at home, saving fuel and the environment by shuttling computer disks back and forth or linking their home computers to a main computer in the office. In the future, virtual reality may increase the number of jobs that can be performed at home, as well as augment what people can do from a remote location. Virtual teleconferencing systems will likely be used to reduce the amount of time and travel required to conduct business. In fact, several regional Bell operating companies (RBOCs) are already actively developing these sorts of systems.

Remember that a remote location isn't necessarily just across town. People can work together on projects while in different cities or from across the world. As we've seen throughout this book, virtual reality can remove language barriers and enable people around the world to access complicated information in a meaningful way. For example, a physician in Iceland who specializes in disorders of the hand could act as a consultant to a Korean hospital. Through fiber-optic links and virtual reality technology, the physician could study the hand of a patient in the Korean hospital. The doctor could then make recommendations through visual symbols such as pictures of medicines and physical therapies rather than through elaborate written prescriptions requiring translation. It is this type of work and communication that will truly tie people together and make the planet a global village.

Art

Virtual reality offers artists one of the most exciting opportunities in the history of art. Although people have painted and sculpted incredible masterpieces for the past ten thousand years, both painting and sculpture have strict limitations in what can be created and what must be left to the imagination. But now, where traditional art stops, high technology starts. Painting is generally a two-dimensional medium, where color and form mix together to create images. Landscapes, people, and abstract worlds are represented on a flat surface and then framed within a portal. Sculpture moves into the third, spatial dimension, but remains static, fixed in time. Or, if it does move, it is designed to move in certain ways.

In the past thirty years, artists have begun to work within the flexible, interactive worlds of video and computer graphics. Using electricity and computer technology, these pieces range from the photorealistic to the incredibly surreal. While some people maintain that true computer art only encompasses pieces that cannot be created using traditional, nonelectronic methods, others are perfectly happy to use the technology as a tool to create work similar to what they had done before.

But virtual reality opens a door to a medium so different that it defies any artistic pigeonhole. Unlike any other format, virtual art is three-dimensional, immersive, and interactive. You can step into a painting as though you were stepping through a looking glass and explore the artist's world. Moreover, as an "audience member," you may have the ability to actually take part in the piece, adjusting, erasing, adding where you want.

Creon Levit at NASA's Ames Research Center created a world called Tape World. Tape world is a mathematical place, generated randomly by algorithm, in which the viewer watches a scene consisting of slowly rotating mobiles of curlicues, cracks, and fractal dust. Each time someone enters the world, the computer generates a unique landscape. Beyond just watching and exploring this world, viewers can also modify it by specifying the width, curvature, torsion, length, and behavior of the objects.

One of the interesting aspects of interactive virtual art is that the artist rarely completes the piece. As Myron Kreuger wrote in *Artificial Reality II*, "Artificial realities also require the artist to accept reduced control, to think in terms of a structure of possibilities that leaves the final realization of the piece in the hands of each participant." This doesn't mean that artists can't successfully express themselves; only that using this medium requires a different mode of working.

Many entrepreneurs are starting to gamble that art will become easier to come by in the future. Just as we can create recordings of music and replay them anywhere we go on personal stereo systems, art may become "recordable" and therefore transportable. Bill Gates, founder of Microsoft Corporation, has started a new company called Interactive Home Systems that is purchasing licenses to digitally record artwork from all over the world. One of its first installations is Gates' home, where he can view high-resolution reproductions of a number of paintings at the flick of a switch.

In this way, we may be able to visit virtual art galleries, like the one created by Sense8 Corporation (see Color Plate 5), while sitting at home. In Sense8's gallery, a virtual room is filled with framed images, like an art gallery. The difference is that some of these images float in midair, some in the middle of the room, and all can act as portals that you can fly through into other virtual worlds. In a virtual gallery, we might see a piece like the one created by Fake Space Labs founder Mark Bolas. In an ironic twist on artist Piet Mondrian (who once said that a painter should never try to imitate the three-dimensional world on a two dimensional canvas), Bolas exploded Mondrian's "Composition with Line" into a three-dimensional virtual model called *Flatlands*. While looking at the piece from straight on, the world appears to be a neatly organized series of lines running both vertically and horizontially. But when you fly into the image, your perspective changes, and you can see that the world is really filled with a jumble of lines in three-dimensional space (see Figure 16-2).

Canada's Banff Center for the Arts is presently the leading organization exploring how virtual reality can be used within the arts. Working with a number of artists around North America, they are

FIGURE 16-2 *Flatlands*

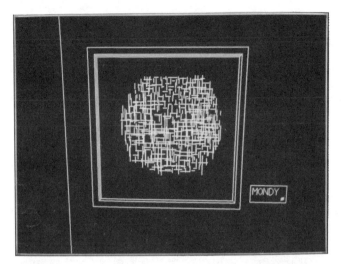

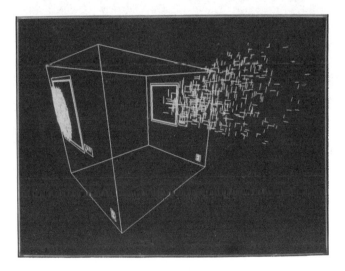

finding new ways of using voice recognition, video image processing, and interactive computer graphics to create worlds in which dancers interact with "intelligent and controllable" computer-generated objects, audiences view and interact with projected three-dimensional images, and everyone can brainstorm about where, exactly, the future of art is going.

Psychology

Psychology is clearly another area in which virtual reality can be used with significant results. Psychologists are just now beginning to look at ways in which virtual reality can aid in the treatment of phobias and other common mental illnesses. For example, if you're afraid of snakes, perhaps a first step might be to sit in a virtual room with a virtual snake 20 feet away. With a single gesture, you can make the snake go away.

Similarly, if you suffer from an extreme fear of heights, one form of treatment might be to create a model of a tall building where your therapist and you can put on head-mounted displays and walk together to the edge of the roof of the building. While you practice looking over, you can control the situation entirely, adjusting the height of the building, and so on. While this virtual excursion may, in fact, induce a fear response from the patient, this potential form of treatment has advantages over standard methods of treatment. Michigan-based Force Four Learning Systems is currently developing just these kinds of virtual reality systems for clinical psychologists, thereby widening the options for treatment and evaluation.

The role-playing discussed earlier in this chapter may evolve even further to the point where you can play and explore a number of different pychological roles in various situations. The activity may be playful, but the effects can be serious. Through learning to adapt quickly from role to role, you can actually become healthier, learning new interpersonal skills and seeing new ways to react to your environment. As Adam Blatner's theory of "multiple personality order" (a wordplay on *disorder*) explains, "The more you play multiple roles, the more you imply a metarole of manager or chooser."

Although some people have started to imply that virtual reality will blur the boundaries between reality and fantasy, causing some form of schizophrenia, we think this is a dangerous conclusion. While it's true that fantasy situations will be labeled a form of "reality," computer-generated environments will always be inferior in both quality and substance. We won't vouch for someone who is already prone to mental illness, but we think that virtual reality pushing people over the edge is the least worrisome of our future concerns.

The Military

Without question, the largest source of funding for basic research and development in virtual reality—and most other high technology, for that matter—is the US Department of Defense. The Defense Department funds the development of the fastest computers, the most advanced robotics, and the best communications technology. In fact, were it not for the Defense Department, virtual reality would probably not exist. Nonetheless, there are many researchers and scientists who feel strongly about not working for the military because they feel the technology will only be used for violent actions.

While there is little doubt that the military will use the technology in order to disable our country's perceived enemies (that is, after all, part of their job description), there is similarly little doubt that virtual reality technology will be used to help save lives. For example, virtual reality simulations of battles, terrorist attacks, or combat missions are sure to aid in fewer deadly mistakes being made and more of our troops returning home. And the same technology that creates telerobotic fighting machines supplies patroling guards in dangerous areas where people would otherwise be open to attack.

Law

The multitude of legal issues surrounding computer technology today fall into so many gray areas that lawyers and judges appear dumbfounded as to how to handle them. Is trespassing into someone's personal data account a form of breaking and entering? Is making an exact duplicate of data stealing it? What parts of computer software are copyrightable and what parts are, by necessity, public domain? These questions are being asked daily, around the world, in an effort to cope with the fastest-moving technology in the history of the world.

Virtual reality certainly won't help matters any. Although most of the legal questions will probably be easily handled using standard law practices, in a cyberspace containing potentially hundreds of thousands of people, a new form of law may have to be developed. People are already asking questions such as, "To what degree does a person in cyberspace legally constitute a person?" The questions nd odd at first, but we think that the future holds even stranger tidings. These major legal challenges may not happen in our lifetime, but they're sure to happen.

On the other hand, virtual reality has its hands full in the present, too. Copyright is a key issue in computer technology. And in the United States a copyright is based on personal expression. That is, pure data cannot be copyrighted, but an expression of that data can be. For example, the courts tend to agree that you can't copyright the information in the telephone book, but you can copyright how it's presented. It's still unclear if and how a virtual reality can be copyrighted when it's based solely on data. Perhaps the environment itself will be copyrighted, or the software to create the environment, or both. As we discussed earlier, one of the primary elements in virtual art is our ability to interact with it. Does an "audience member" have a part ownership in the copyright of that artwork when she or he walks away?

High-technology patents are discussed daily in the courts and newspapers, and virtual reality technology is no different. For example, VPL Research has been in the spotlight in the past few years, aggressively protecting its niche within the industry. VPL's patent on glovelike I/O devices and manual interaction with computer-generated imagery has been defended several times, much to the chagrin of other would-be developers. Owning a critical patent in a growing field is extremely beneficial, but can be a detriment to the technology as a whole. Which direction VPL's patent will take remains to be seen.

❁   ❁   ❁

Fears and Truths

As we said earlier, this chapter shows only the tip of the iceberg of social change that may occur because of virtual reality. The future is still mostly fuzzy, but one thing is already clear: how people use or abuse virtual reality technologies will be based on both how the technology is designed and what people want to get out of it. If a nation or a world of people is looking for a new escape, whether as an entertainment or as a drug, they'll find one here. If people want games or tools of destruction, they will find this, too, in virtual reality. And if the military is the primary developer of the technology, clearly it will be used for military applications.

On the other hand, if people want tools to access information, to empower themselves in an information-based world, or to entertain and educate themselves, the power will be there. Virtual reality is a double-edged sword that cuts where we swing it. It's only through heightening people's awareness of the potential effects of the technology we can help to control the blade. Virtual reality will have a major impact on our society, but it is up to us to decide what that impact will be.

SILICON MIRAGE

CHAPTER 17

The Future of Virtual Reality

✿   ✿   ✿

The tip of the iceberg. The first step on a long path. The infancy of the technology. There's almost no way to circumvent using a cliché to describe where we are right now in relation to the future of virtual reality. A century ago, Guglielmo Marconi, the developer of wireless telegraphy, couldn't even begin to understand how the transmission of radio signals would change the world. And even forty years ago if you had asked Alan Turing, one of the founding fathers of computer science, if computers could be used for creating three-dimensional worlds, he probably would have simply laughed and shaken his head.

So now we're in an interesting place. Virtual reality is a new technology, borne in a synthesis of many other fields, from robotics to chemistry, from computer science to the arts. And, like people at the birth of any new technology, we can glimpse through only the smallest crack in the wall to see how it will grow and evolve and what it will become.

In this chapter, we want to look as far as we can into the future of virtual reality, attempting to predict where this path will lead us and trying to explain why it won't take us elsewhere. So hold on to your hats for this last whirlwind tour.

❀   ❀   ❀

Future Hardware

We spent a good part of this book exploring the mechanics of virtual reality, how it works and why. Technology is the skeleton of virtual reality, and everything else relies on it to be strong enough and flexible enough to fit any situation. At the time of this writing, the hardware that researchers and developers are using is still immature. Computers are too slow, head-mounted displays are too clunky to wear, tactile feedback is crude at best. The technology can hardly be described as any better than "promising."

Industry pundits shuffle their feet when they hear this word, saying, "Well, this is where artificial intelligence was ten years ago: promising." Through the 1980s, computer scientists and media reporters made one claim after another about where artificial intelligence was going and how it easy is was all going to be. Computers would be modeled on how humans think, and our greatest experts, from physicians to auto mechanics, would be able to download their professional knowledge into a computer. But artificial intelligence stumbled when people finally realised that providing a computer with even basic commonsense knowledge is an extremely difficult undertaking.

But virtual reality is different than artificial intelligence, and although there are parallels, it can't be judged in the same way. Perhaps the most important difference between the two technologies is that the success of virtual reality is tied more closely to the evolution of hardware than to inventing new ways to program computers. Even if there were no major breakthroughs in software development but the hardware kept evolving as it has in the past, we would see important virtual reality applications appear. This is the most conservative approach, as hardware will inevitably become more powerful and less expensive in the years to come.

Let's look at some of the ways we expect the hardware to develop.

Speed

No matter how astounding a virtual environment is, watching it update at one frame every second or so is a deeply unsatisfying experience. Even the realisation that fifteen years ago none of this was possible can't stop you from feeling that if the computer was just a little faster it would all work stupendously.

Computer technology is based mostly on the central processing unit (CPU). This processor (often called the chip, although this is misleading as there are usually other chips in the computer) has gotten smaller and faster by an incredible amount over the past twenty years, making personal desktop computers now more powerful than large mainframe computers that would once fill a room. As researchers create new ways of building chips and sending binary information from one place to another, the chips (and therefore the computer programs run on the computers) get faster. As we write, there is no indication that this trend towards accelerated processing speed will slow down in the forseeable future.

This is nothing but good news for virtual reality. Creating visual, aural, and tactile displays for a virtual environment is extremely calculation intensive, involving millions of computer operations every second. This number crunching is so intense that some scientists joke about virtual reality applications "eating MIPS [millions of instructions per second] for breakfast."

Within the next five to ten years, computers will finally be fast enough to render somewhat realistic images in real time (fifteen to thirty frames every second). Of course, it's not just the CPU that will speed up this process. Specialized computer chips and add-in boards, like those found in video games, are already being designed to optimize certain calculations, such as three-dimensional graphic and aural rendering. Also, researchers are developing more efficient methods for programming computer software, including new algorithms for adding shading and texturing, calculating position in space, and compressing images so they can be sent across telephone lines quickly.

Equipment

One of the most common critiques of virtual reality is that the equipment is too large, too bulky, and incredibly inefficient. Even the people developing this technology admit that this is true, but technology rarely takes a quantum leap; rather it evolves slowly. Nonetheless, we think it's safe to say that, in the not-too-distant future, people will see the current batch of virtual reality peripherals— such as the head-mounted displays, cabled gloves, and so on—as outdated, clunky methods to display and manipulate virtual environments. The history of computer technology is one of miniaturization, and there is little evidence that this trend will stop here.

Because this technology blends together so many various fields, a breakthrough in metalurgy may pave the road to a breakthrough in creating tiny display systems. Or a new method of analyzing data may effect how we generate three-dimensional sound fields. The future is murky, partly because the technology of how to make lightweight, easy-to-use displays remains up in the air.

However, head-mounted displays are likely to become significantly smaller. A design based on wraparound sunglasses would be beneficial both from a size and weight standpoint and also because it may be see-through. Opaque displays, such as the EyePhones, are good for a number of applications, but a system that could be either opaque or transparent (allowing information to be overlaid on top of the world around us) would be significantly better.

As we noted in Chapter 4, *Hearing*, researchers have already reduced the need for headphones in creating three-dimensional sound. However, we don't expect that speaker-based sound will approach the kind of quality you can achieve through a headphone display.

Tactile and force feedback is clearly an area that warrants close attention in the years to come. This field, which has really only just begun, is growing rapidly, and for good reason. The abilty to feel virtual objects with our hands could be a major step forward in working with virtual realities. Nonetheless, we are aware that this technology is incredibly difficult, partly because we're still just beginning to understand why we feel things the way we do and partly because of the laws of nature.

For example, if you grab a brick in the real world, you feel the weight of the brick not only in your hand, but also throughout your entire arm and even in your back. Although restraining the hand or fingers is feasible, it would be tremendously difficult, if not outright impossible, to develop a system that simulates all the forces we encounter. What would the system look like? Perhaps the only way to create it would be to build a massive exoskeleton around a person that could move easily yet restrain movement when necessary.

Even then, it would be difficult to simulate the feeling of a cat squirming in your hands or someone touching your cheek. And there's almost no way to effectively restrain or manipulate your body when it comes in contact with a virtual object. You'll never lean against walls in a virtual world or slip on a virtual banana peel.

New Technologies

Research, like rust, never sleeps. Scientists are constantly developing new methods to make the interface between humans and computers less cumbersome and more intuitive, and each of these developments has a direct impact on the effectiveness of virtual reality. Let's look at several promising technologies that we expect to become standard elements in virtual reality systems of the future.

Direct neural input. The idea of a direct link between the brain and a computer has been talked about so much in articles and science fiction stories that we'd feel awkward leaving a discussion of it out of this book. Direct neural input is one of the most anxiety-producing concepts in high technology today. The idea is simple: bypass the body's sense organs and send information directly to the brain. There are some incredible applications of this: some blind people would be able to see, some hearing-impaired people could hear, and so on. There are also less noble potential applications, such as virtual orgasms produced by poking the right pleasure centers or virtual worlds in which prisoners could be kept mentally but not physically busy twenty-four hours a day.

However, this technology suffers the same malady as many talked-about technologies: the idea is simpler than the practice. The problem is that no one really knows how to create a system of this sort. First of all, science simply doesn't yet understand the brain and the nervous system well enough. After hundreds of years of pain-staking observation, doctors and scientists still know surprisingly little about how the brain works. Without knowing how the system works, we cannot hope to create effective neural inputs. Secondly, establishing direct neural input is basically an invasive procedure. That is, wires must be placed under the skin in various parts of the body, primarily the soft tissue of the brain in order to stimulate various nerve centers. Unless we want a number of wires sticking out from various areas of our heads at all times, we must look elsewhere for this sort of stimulation.

Still, direct neural input is a distinct possibility in the distant future (we don't expect to see any real progress on this within the next fifty years). People who are envisioning such a system are concerned that society may then have to figure out what to do with those who receive too much information too quickly or are subject to a computer bug that causes what they call "total neural meltdown." While the idea is scary, the realization of the practice awaits several major breakthroughs.

Retinal imaging. A technology that is more likely to appear within the foreseeable future is retinal imaging, the science of "painting" an image directly onto the retina of the eye. A computer steers a low-powered laser beam around the retina, activating rods and cones in order to display a virtual image. While this would certainly create an extremely high-resolution image, the problems are significant.

The first challenge is to create a laser system small enough and flexible enough to work in a personal virtual reality application. At this time, prototypes of a retinal-imaging system cover a tabletop. The second challenge is that of focusing the laser on the retina while still maintaining the user's ability to move around. All in all, we're still unsure about the practicality of this technology.

Another system, similar in nature to that of retinal imaging, could be based on a solid state imaging device recently developed by Texas Instruments. This small chip, called a deformable mirror display (DMD), contains thousands of small mirrors that each reflect light energy from a low-power laser into the eye. Such a device could be used to create high-resolution, low-cost display devices.

Image extraction. Imagine yourself working in an office of the future. You need to make some last minute changes to a financial report for your boss, but your virtual desk is a mess. There is a stack of graphical icons ten deep, each representing a project that you're working on, and you're not sure exactly where you placed this report. You put your light-weight head-mounted display on to see the workspace and then say into a small microphone, "Show me the Ranelli report." Immediately, two versions of the report pop to the top of the pile. One, you notice, is an old version that you forgot to erase from your computer's hard disk. To erase it, you simply grab it and place it in the virtual trash can to your right.

At this point, the chances that you are going to take the time to put on a glovelike input device are nill. Even a mouse or spaceball is still too cumbersome for grabbing and manipulating objects. Instead, what you really want is for the computer to be able to see where your hand and fingers are in space and to represent that in the virtual environment.

This technology, called image extraction, has been in development for over twenty years, but it's only now that researchers are gaining any headway. A simple scenario might be three video cameras pointed at you from various angles, feeding video information to a computer on your desk. This computer would act much like our visual cortex in processing the images to create a three-dimensional model of you sitting at your desk. When you raised a hand, the computer could "see" your hand raising. When you make a gesture of grabbing, the computer could understand the gesture. It is extracting your image from the pictures it sees.

The benefits of image extraction are mostly that of convenience. But convenience is a major factor in the advancement of technology. Personal stereos and fax machines are simply more convenient than large sound systems and the postal service, and yet they are now indispensible to many people. With an image-extraction system, you could potentially control a computer through gestures or movements without the encumbrance of wearing mechanical or optical sensors.

Teleconferencing applications (see Chapter 14, *Telepresence*) are another reason why people are so interested in image extraction. Five people from around the country could come together in a virtual conference room and carry out their business. As opposed to a telephone conversation, they could actually see each other's nonverbal communication in a three-dimensional setting, from how people are sitting to who's looking at whom. This aspect of image extraction technology in teleconferencing is of particular interest to some companies in Japan, because their business practices are often dependent on nonverbal communication, which cannot be transmitted via telephone or e-mail.

Magnetoencephlamography. The last form of computer input we'll look at here is magnetoencephlamography. This word is a mouthful until you break it down and see what it really means. The concept is that scientists will be able to measure the electromagnetic signals (*magneto*) coming out of your brain (*encephla*) and match them with a map of what previous brain scans revealed (*mography*). In other words, the computer will be able to "read" what's going on in your head.

Don't worry, no computer will be able to read everything you think. But early studies are already showing that we may be able to teach computers to recognize certain types of brain activity. The brain activity that goes into concentrating on a thought produces small magnetic currents that can be measured outside the head, using a technology similar to that used in making electroencephla-grams (EEGs). The theory is that particular thoughts create distinct brain patterns that a computer could be programmed to recognize, much like voice recognition (see Chapter 6, *Recognition*).

The potential applications for this technology are numerous. For example, a jet pilot could someday think "Bank to the left," and the aircraft's computer would understand and follow the command. Similarly, a quadraplegic may be able to control a wheelchair or a complex computer system by concentrating on certain thought commands. Anyone using this system in a virtual environment could look in a direction and think "Move there" and the computer could pick that up.

Needless to say, this technology, like any technology based on our biological nervous system, is extremely difficult to achieve. Measuring brain activity is the easy part. Understanding what it all means is going to take a considerable amount of time, alongside a couple of significant breakthroughs in the technology. Nonetheless, we expect to see electroencephlamography used in various com-puter systems, including virtual reality, in the next fifteen years.

❊   ❊   ❊

Teledildonics and Other Stories

Please don't get us wrong: we're strong believers in dreams and visions of the future. It's just that it's sometimes too easy to mistake fantasy for reality, and what we want is often seen over what we have. Many claims of paranormal events or psychic abilities are be-lieved wholeheartedly by those who want to believe but are later disproved by impartial observers applying scientific methodology. We can still believe that these sorts of extraordinary events occur—no one has proved that they don't—but until someone shows conclusively that they do, the belief remains a theory.

New technologies attract visionaries and dreamers like ice cream attracts the kid in all of us. There are so many flavors to choose from, and we're tempted to try them all. When alternating current electricity was first introduced, people went on a propaganda rampage for or against the technology. Some saw it as the end of the world. Stories tell of people demonstrating how dangerous alternating current was by attaching wires to a dog's ears and killing it with a jolt of electricity. Other people saw it as the beginning of a utopia, where all physical ailments and moral wrongs could be solved through using electricity.

We saw similar events take place around the first steps of artificial intelligence. In the late 1960s, stories were ubiquitous about computer intelligence and the problems it would cause. The classic example was the HAL 9000 computer in the movie *2001: A Space Odyssey*. It could read lips, it could understand voice controls, and it could make decisions. As you might remember, these decisions turned out to be disastrous for the crew of the spaceship. On the other hand, scientists all through the 1980s seemed sure that "any year now" we would find the key to creating computers that would either have their own intelligence or that we could "download our brains" into to make ourselves immortal and perfect.

None of these things has happened. But the stories and the visions keep people searching, one discovery blossoming into another, and the technology keeps progressing and evolving.

Virtual reality is certainly no different than its predecessors, and people from all over the world have raised discussions about the implications and future applications. Throughout this book, we've explored what we consider to be the most likely technologies and applications. Now let's look at a few of the *less* likely scenarios.

Teledildonics. As we noted at the beginning of this book, virtual sex is almost always one of the first ideas that people think about when considering virtual reality. The idea behind virtual sex—or teledildonics, as it's commonly (and humorously) called these days—is usually based on the notion that if we could only get a full-body virtual reality suit that would include coverage of our genitals and other erogenous zones, we could fool our bodies into thinking we were having sex. Our virtual partner might be someone at a remote location who was also wearing one of these suits or simply a computer-generated simulation. The idea goes further in that you could program the teledildonic system so that you saw your partner any way you wanted to see them. Or with a computer simulation, you could create any sort of partner you wanted, who would do anything you wanted them to.

Those with a particular moral bent generally wrinkle their noses at this concept and comment on how those computer types should get out more often. Other people have commented on the political issues surrounding virtual pornography, the social issues surrounding who would be sleeping with whom, and even the economic issues surrounding virtual prostitution using high-bandwidth telephone lines.

What few people have commented on is that teledildonics is just plain impossible on any grand scale. It will be relatively easy to create three-dimensional movies (or "voomies") that could be watched passively or possibly explored (level one and two virtual reality), but there will be no way to interact with the characters in the movies in any meaningful way. For example, how could you feel the weight of someone on you in a virtual environment? Or be held up from below by a virtual person? You can't be.

And even if you could somehow rig a system that would be limited but functional, it really wouldn't be worth it. The sanitary, custodial, and convenience of the system would make the enterprise somewhat less than titillating.

Intelligence augmentation. Another great myth that has popped up recently is that virtual reality will inherently make people smarter and more creative. As far as we can tell, this has its roots in one of two places. The first is the concept of intelligence augmentation, or IA (which is, of course, different than AI, or artificial intelligence). Computer scientists have been applying the phrase *intelligence augmentation* to computers and other tools for over thirty years. Doug Engelbart wrote in 1963, "By 'augmenting man's intellect' we mean increasing the capability of a man to approach a complex problem situation, gain comprehension to suit his particular needs, and to derive solutions to problems."

A computer is a tool that helps us augment our intelligence by increasing the amount of information we can take in and manipulate. Our brains, as we've seen throughout this book, are quite good at pattern recognition and other tasks, but are not optimized for storing, sorting , or making sequential calculations based on significant quantities of information. Computers, then, can aid us and augment our abilities. And virtual reality can help even more by making our interaction with computers easier and more intuitive.

Computers and virtual reality can also act as mind amplifiers insofar as they increase the amount of information that we can express or control. A single idea can now quickly be communicated around the world or expanded into a reality.

Just as owning a computer doesn't make you smarter, virtual reality can't make you smarter either. As John Eagan noted in a online virtual reality forum recently, "Virtual reality, or any computer, really, is a 'mind tool.' Does it make you smarter? Not inherently. I mean, a dolt who goes out and buys a computer isn't then a genius, he's a dolt with a computer! But any sort of tool can help your thinking and knowledge." You're no smarter after you purchase a book on quantum physics than before. But when you start reading the book, working with it, exploring its ideas, and then discussing it with others, you become more knowledgeable and possibly wiser. While virtual reality can't make you smarter in and of itself, it can act as a tool that you can use to help yourself learn, explore, and experiment, which—in the long run—can help your mind expand.

The second possible source for the myth that virtual reality will make you smarter is that magazines like *Mondo 2000* write fantastical articles about virtual reality and place them next to articles and advertisements for "smart drugs." These smart drugs are supposed to make you smarter, more creative, or able to retain more memory simply by taking them. While we love this magazine and have great fun reading it, we think you'd be nuts to believe everything that's in it. (Half the fun of the magazine is trying to find out which parts to believe.)

❂   ❂   ❂

Into the Mirage

Each month, for over 20 years, Dr. Strange has saved the world from the bad guys while sitting in his Greenwich Village apartment. This Marvell Comic superhero shops in the neighborhood stores, does his laundry, and pays his rent. But when he goes home, he lights incense, recites incantations, and does battle with the forces of evil in the psychic underworld. His job, as it were, is to use his tools to manipulate the unseen from the comfort of his living room.

Dr. Strange may not be such a strange character in a few years, when people routinely don lightweight wearable technology to do their jobs in cyberspace. In fact, we've already begun joking about virtual reality being "astral projection for the rest of us." The trillions of bits of data crossing and recrossing the globe each day will carry more than just images, voices, and information. It will carry intention, manipulation, and presence. And each of us will tap into that river of data to build virtual realities.

The road to that day is a long one. It includes massive growth in the technologies of communication, visual and tactile displays, and processing capabilities. It also depends on software developments that can effectively empower people to build, experience, and manipulate realities. Certainly, the road will be paved with ineffectual and primitive devices and methods that will be quickly replaced with better ideas, fancier designs, and more powerful technologies.

Just who will develop these technologies and how they will be used remains to be seen. Judging by the recent history of technological development, the American companies who conceive of and build the technology may, in the end, become software developers for Japanese machines. And if trends continue, we may see the telephone and communications companies holding the reins to the incredible amounts of information that could be passed from one place to another: the three-dimensional movies that we could explore from our homes, the teleconferencing between cities, the access to understandable and intuitive visual models of current commodities markets around the world.

Certainly, in the next ten years the incredible excitement and novelty of this new technology will pass, and we will begin to acknowledge virtual reality as an integral part of how we do business, how we communicate, and how we understand the massive amounts of information that surround us. We have little doubt that the journey will be a fascinating one, twisting and turning in ways perhaps only science fiction writers and other visionaries have forseen. The dream of building worlds from information—worlds that embody processes or designs or abstract ideas, worlds built from silicon and electricity—is finally possible. Now only our imaginations can hold us back.

Index

⚙   ⚙   ⚙

About the Authors

Steven Aukstakalnis is founder and vice president of Matrix Technical Services, a consulting service based in Southfield, Michigan that focuses on the use of head-mounted display technologies for design prototyping. Educated in physics and computer science, he is a former member of the professional research staff at the Washington Technology Center at the University of Washington.

A recognized authority on the topic of virtual reality, he frequently lectures at such organizations as the Smithsonian Institution, Purdue University, the Center for Creative Studies, the Cranbrook Center for the Fine Arts, and a host of other schools and companies across North America. He is a member of the editorial advisory board for *CADalyst* magazine. His writings appear regularly in such publications as *Cadence, CADalyst,* and *Design Net.*

His first book, *Virtual Reality: The Next Revolution in Computer/ Human Interface,* served as a principal background information source for hearings held by the Senate Subcomittee on Science, Technology, and Space, in 1991.

He is also technical editor of *VR Monitor.* Published bimonthly with a subscription rate of $59.00 per year, the publication is the foremost information source available on this industry. For a free sample issue, contact Matrix Information Services at (313) 559-1526 or via electronic mail at 70117.2546@compuserve.com

David Blatner is an award-winning author known for his easy-to-read writing style and his definitive coverage of computer technology. He has spoken on the subject of electronic publishing at conferences around the United States and Japan.

SILICON MIRAGE
The Art and Science of Virtual Reality

"Reading this book is a delight for me because it fills a surprisingl long-standing gap in the literature of virtual reality. For the enormous amount of interest and activity that virtual reality has inspired in the last few years, it is absolutely remarkable that I ha had no book to recommend to people who come to me with the simple question, 'What can I read to understand what this is all about?' I feel that now there is such a book, and you are holding in your hands."

—Jaron Lanier, founder and chief scientist, VPL Research, Inc.

"Anyone who is interested in virtual reality should have this boo

—Creon Levit, research scientist, NASA Ames Research Center

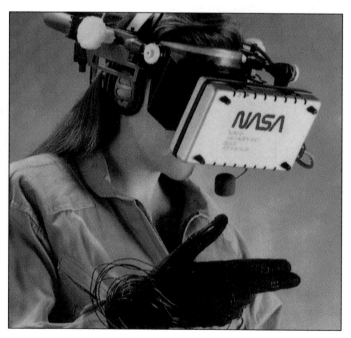

You've read the media hype about goggle that display virtual worlds and the "smart" gloves that let you control them. Now find out the truth about this new technology.

- **The Senses.** How virtual reality devic fool our eyes, our ears, and our body's sense of movement.
- **The Tools.** How virtual reality will cha the way we work and the way we play, fro architecture to surgery to entirely new forr of entertainment.
- **What It All Means.** The impact of th new technology on society, the arts, the military, and even on how we think about our own bodies and minds.

Whether you're looking for an introduction to the field or a comprehensive overview, you'll find it in *Silicon Mirage*.

ISBN 0-938151-82-7

90000>

9 780938 151821

USA $15.00
Canada $20.00

Peachpit Press, Inc.
2414 Sixth Street
Berkeley, CA 94710
800 283-9444
510/548-4393
fax: 510/548-5991

185
280
294
297

212
220